# PROGRAMS, LEADERS, CONSULTANTS and Other Resources in GIFTED AND TALENTED EDUCATION

# PROGRAMS, LEADERS, CONSULTANTS and Other Resources in GIFTED AND TALENTED EDUCATION

*By*

**FRANCES A. KARNES, Ph.D.**

*Department of Special Education*
*University of Southern Mississippi*
*Hattiesburg, Mississippi*

*and*

**HERSCHEL Q. PEDDICORD, JR., Ed.D.**

*Department of Curriculum and Instruction*
*University of Southern Mississippi*
*Hattiesburg, Mississippi*

**CHARLES C THOMAS • PUBLISHER**
*Springfield • Illinois • U.S.A.*

Published and Distributed Throughout the World by
CHARLES C THOMAS • PUBLISHER
Bannerstone House
301-327 East Lawrence Avenue, Springfield, Illinois, U.S.A.

© 1980, by CHARLES C THOMAS • PUBLISHER
ISBN 0-398-04099-0
Library of Congress Catalog Card Number: 80 16413

With THOMAS BOOKS careful attention is given to all details of
manufacturing and design. It is the Publisher's desire to present books that are
satisfactory as to their physical qualities and artistic possibilities and
appropriate for their particular use. THOMAS BOOKS will be true to those
laws of quality that assure a good name and good will.

Library of Congress Cataloging in Publication Data

Karnes, Frances.
   Gifted and talented education.

   Bibliography: p.
   Includes index.
   1. Gifted children—Education—United States.
I. Peddicord, Herschel Q., joint author.   II. Title.
LC3993.9.K37          371.95'0973          80-16413
ISBN 0-398-04099-0

Printed in the United States of America
OK-1

# PREFACE

The 1970s will be known as the decade in which the American public recognized the need for specialized education for the gifted and the talented, our nation's most valuable human resource. This recognition has been reflected in the increase in federal and state funding during the past several years. The gifted and talented were included in Title III (presently Title IV) of the Elementary and Secondary Education Act in 1971. Many innovative and replicable projects have been developed through this provision. Additionally, the Office of Gifted and Talented has funded many state programs, model projects, and leadership training projects, including university training programs.

Congress has increased appropriations for gifted education from \$2.56 million in 1975, to \$6.28 million in 1979. More substantial funding has been evidenced by that allocated by the states and local communities. Reimbursement for teacher salaries, materials, and general program development has increased in the past five years. The number of state consultants has doubled during the same period of time.

Although money and subsequently programs for the gifted are increasing, school board members, administrators, and others involved in program development for the gifted and the talented are confronted with a paucity of publications devoted to program design and implementation. Although there are several excellent publications on gifted education which contain selected chapters on programming, there is no composite and comprehensive overview of programs that could be replicated.

To initiate, develop, and evaluate programs, the assistance of national leaders, state consultants for gifted education, and other resource persons from individual states is often necessary. A compendium of these resource persons, not previously available in one publication, is included in this volume.

The book is designed to meet the needs of the following groups:

    1. Superintendents, school board members, administrators, central staff personnel, principals, guidance counselors,

department chairpersons, curriculum specialists, and
other interested persons who have the responsibility for
establishing and conducting programs for the gifted and
the talented

2. Teachers of the gifted and talented, both within the
regular classroom or in specialized programs, who are
seeking alternatives and innovative ways to serve the
gifted and talented

3. Faculty involved in teacher education who have the
responsibility for training administrators, teachers, and
others in innovative programming for the gifted and
talented

4. State consultants of gifted education and related areas
and other resource personnel who need to have knowledge
of the major programs available across the United States
for the gifted and talented

5. Parents and other interested citizens who desire to give
support in designing and implementing appropriate
programs for the future leaders of our nation.

Introductions to and descriptions of programs focusing on
preschool, elementary, elementary/secondary, secondary, and the
performing arts, both public and private, are presented in Section
I. Programs for gifted handicapped and culturally diverse gifted
are included. General information on the program, student
selection procedures, curriculum, and evaluation are described
for individual programs.

National leaders, who have distinguished themselves in every
aspect of gifted education, are cited in Section II. Their many
accomplishments are summarized and their current positions are
given.

State consultants provide a wide range of services in the
development of programs for the gifted. Section III contains an
overview of their many responsibilities and accomplishments.

Within each state, there are individuals, representing every
facet of education as well as other areas, who have knowledge and
experience in gifted education. Section IV contains a listing by
states of these persons and their areas of special interest.

A wide range of other resources exists in gifted education.
Information on funding sources, organizations, publications,

alternative schools and programs, and teacher training institutions is provided in Section V.

Certain limitations of this book should be noted. The number of outstanding programs described was limited by space and the selection process itself. Also, the selection process may have limited the number of national leaders presented, although several individuals nominated chose not to be included because of professional and/or personal reasons. The omission of a state consultant for the gifted and the talented for several states is due to a number of factors, including a change in personnel. Perhaps there are many more resource persons at the local level than were identified and listed. Any omissions of programs or persons was not intentional.

All indications are that the growing interest in the gifted and the talented will result in increased efforts to develop stimulating programs and activities appropriate for the group of high ability young people so critically important to the strength and the development of our society. It is hoped that this publication by highlighting outstanding programs, leaders, and other human and material resources, will add appreciably to the total effort to enhance the quality of education for the most gifted and talented in the future.

# ACKNOWLEDGMENTS

The authors gratefully acknowledge the contributions of the many individuals, groups, and agencies which made this publication possible. Our gratitude is expressed to the state consultants in the area of gifted education who assisted in the identification of outstanding leaders and exemplary programs in the area of gifted education at the local, state, and national levels and who provided personal and professional information for their biographical entries.

To those individuals identified as knowledgeable in the field of the education of the gifted and the talented, we express our appreciation for their assistance in identifying and selecting those leaders who have achieved national and international recognition and who are included in our book. To these leaders, we express appreciation for the personal and professional information provided for their biographical entires.

As rather special people who afforded us not only encouragement but also expert assistance are two groups deserving of special mention: those individuals who provided descriptions of the programs included in the book and the resource persons listed for each of the states who provided personal and/or professional information.

To personnel in the Office of Gifted and Talented, Council for Exceptional Children, the Association for the Gifted, and the National Association for Gifted Children, we express our appreciation.

To our students, past and present, and our professional colleagues we owe an expression of thanks for their many suggestions and their support. We express gratitude to administrators at the University of Southern Mississippi who provided encouragement and support: Dr. Aubrey K. Lucas, President; Dr. Charles W. Moorman, Vice President for Academic Affairs; Dr. Bobby D. Anderson, Dean, College of Education and Psychology; Dr. William V. Plue, Chairman, Department of Special Education; and Dr. Milton B. Baxter, Chairman, Department of Curriculum and Instruction.

Dr. Philip C. Kolin and Mrs. Norma Pearce deserve a special word of thanks for their able editorial assistance, and we thank Mrs. Gladys Kavanaugh for her expert preparation of the final manuscript. To the several secretaries who deciphered the early drafts, we also owe special thanks.

Finally, the patience, tolerance, and support of our immediate families during the long period of data collection and manuscript preparation we gratefully acknowledge.

F.A.K.
H.Q.P.

# CONTENTS

xi

# PROGRAMS, LEADERS, CONSULTANTS and Other Resources in GIFTED AND TALENTED EDUCATION

# SECTION I.
# PROGRAMS FOR THE GIFTED
# AND THE TALENTED

The search for outstanding programs in gifted and talented education was undertaken through correspondence with national leaders and state consultants. In addition, a thorough review of the literature was undertaken. Although many programs were identified as being exemplary, only twenty-four were selected for review in this publication because of their special characteristics in terms of the population served, philosophy, goals, screening and identification, programming, and evaluation. These programs should not be considered a random sample of the programs offered nationwide for the gifted and the talented. Admittedly, preschool programs and programs offered by private institutions are underrepresented.

Space limitations precluded the review of all programs identified as outstanding and worthy of replication. Identification of other outstanding programs in states not represented could be accomplished through inquiries directed to appropriate state consultants.

The directors of the twenty-four programs selected for presentation cooperated by supplying program descriptions which are presented under the sections designated preschool, elementary, elementary/secondary, secondary, and the performing arts. These programs represent both enrichment and acceleration models, with more emphasis on the enrichment concept. Many of these programs are located in large urban areas, however, certain components of these programs may easily be adapted for rural school district implementation.

A wide geographic distribution is apparent with programs located in the North, South, East, and West regions of the United

States. Both public and private schools are represented, with a high percentage of programs based in the public schools and supported with public funds.

One program began as a class for the gifted in 1921 and several programs were established as early as 1940; however, the majority of the programs were initiated in the 1960s. It is interesting to note that the programs focusing on early childhood, gifted/handicapped, and gifted/culturally diverse were undertaken primarily in the 1970s and are relatively new developments in gifted education. In most instances, elementary programming was initiated prior to the establishment of secondary programs.

While there are common elements to be found in the descriptions of programs ranging from preschool to college level, the programs vary widely in terms of dates established, sources of funding, populations served, program philosophies, goals and objectives, identification and screening procedures, content emphases, grouping and scheduling practices, and program evaluation. A strong case can be made for variety in the schools of a democratic nation, especially in programs developed in response to the needs of the gifted and talented.

## PART A
## PRESCHOOL PROGRAMS

All three of the preschool programs described in this section were initiated between 1974 and 1976. Each enrolls children ranging in age from three to five. Two of the programs serve an urban population, and the third is based in a rural environment. Two of the programs, including the one in a rural setting, cater especially to highly talented and gifted children who possess one or more handicapping conditions. Emphasis, however, is on the gifts and talents, not the handicaps. Early identification with emphasis on parental observations and individualized testing characterizes the screening and selection methods and procedures.

The philosophic considerations, goals, and objectives expressed in the descriptions of programs for the very young gifted and talented tend to reflect a child development concern with emphasis afforded intellectual and social development as well as psychomotor development. In the interest of optimum development commensurate with the individual child's potential, importance is attached to environmental enrichment and to school, home, and community involvement. Individualized instruction, small group activities, self-pacing, and the student's involvement in formulating goals and planning for their achievement are perceived as major educational strategies important to the child's growth and development.

Content and activity areas thought to facilitate growth and goal achievement include language arts, social studies, math, science, and the fine and performing arts. Emphasis is placed on activities designed to promote the development of communication skills, social sensitivity, creative thinking, and problem solving facility. Counseling and speech therapy are presented as support services for the gifted/handicapped.

Funding for all three of the programs described came in part from the Office of Gifted and Talented, Bureau for the Education of the Handicapped, U.S. Office of Education. Local funds and in some cases tuition paid by parents are involved. Foundation funding provides some of the support for one of the programs.

Tests for measuring achievement of preschool children, especially in the realm of concept, attitude, and social development, are not as numerous and reliable as are the ones designed to measure the achievement of older students. Therefore, pretesting and posttesting are somewhat limited as a means of gathering data for evaluating progress made in the three programs described. While some performance and achievement testing is undertaken, teacher observations, anecdotal records and progress charts, along with parent observations and assessments, form the major basis for evaluation of pupil progress.

**CHILD DEVELOPMENT PRESCHOOL**
Child Development Research Group NI-20
University of Washington
Seattle, Washington 98195

*Reported by:*
Wendy Conklin Roedell

*Administrative Responsibility:*
Halbert Robinson

*For Further Information, Contact:*
Halbert Robinson, Wendy Roedell, or Nancy Jackson
Child Development Research Group NI-20
University of Washington
Seattle, Washington 98195

### Overview of Program

Funded by a grant from the Spencer Foundation, the core project on gifted children began in 1974 as a pilot study to demonstrate that there were many intellectually advanced young children in the Seattle area. The Child Development Preschool, established in the fall of 1976 as a model program through funding from the U.S. Office of Education, grew out of the core project.

In addition to the Child Development Preschool, two other educational programs are associated with the project. The Individual Progress Program, a kindergarten through twelfth grade program developed by the Seattle Public School District in collaboration with the Child Development Research Group, serves children with advanced intellectual skills from the first through sixth grades. This program will be expanded several grades each year until all grades are served. The Early Entrance Program provides entrance to the University of Washington for qualified students who are thirteen years old or younger. Taken together, the three educational programs will soon offer a comprehensive accelerated educational option extending from preschool through college for extraordinarily advanced students in the Seattle area.

The Child Development Research Group sponsors a comprehensive set of research and service projects related to the identification and nurturance of intellectual and academic precocity in children. The core project is a longitudinal study of the development of children nominated by their parents before the age of five as having advanced intellectual or academic skills. Of particular interest to this study is a group of children who have demonstrated extraordinarily advanced intellectual abilities. On standardized tests, their performance has been four standard deviations above the mean or more, or at the level of average children at least twice their chronological age. The preschool serves a total of thirty-six children.

All children in the preschool program have demonstrated advanced intellectual skills in some area, and all are part of a long-term study of children with unusually advanced intellectual abilities. The average Stanford-Binet IQ of the group is 144; IQs range from moderately above average to beyond the scale limit. A few of the children are reading fluently, some are just beginning to read simple texts, while others are still learning their basic letter sounds. On the *Peabody Individual Achievement Test,* the children as a group have scored at about an advanced kindergarten level. Some individuals, however, have scored as high as the sixth grade level in reading, and the second grade level in mathematics.

Also associated with the project is a diagnostic and counseling service, which provides families of children with advanced intellectual abilities a detailed assessment of their intelligence and academic skills as well as counseling regarding their educational placement and personal/social development.

The educational philosophy of the project is based on the idea of providing the optimal match of educational curricula with the competence levels of the learner and allowing the learner to move through the curricula at his or her own rate. In educational practice, this means that programs are individualized to meet the differing needs of the students and that children with advanced intellectual and academic skills are presented with learning material usually taught to older children. The academic programs are enriched as well as accelerated, and students are encouraged to make creative use of their superior abilities.

## Selection of Students

Identification methods vary depending on which educational program is involved. The skills necessary for entrance in the Child Development Preschool program are identified in preschool-aged children using a combination of information from parents and from the child's performance on a battery of standardized tests. Parent information is obtained on a questionnaire which asks detailed questions about each child's current activities and interests. The test battery includes the short form of the *Stanford-Binet Intelligence Scale*; the Block Design, Mazes, and Arithmetic subtests of the *Wechsler Preschool and Primary Scale of Intelligence*; the Numerical Memory subtest from the *McCarthy Scales of Children's Abilities*; and an informal test of reading skill. The identification system is based on the premise that it is best to search for each child's best possible performance in each skill area. Information is collected from different sources about different types of tasks in order to provide children with many opportunities to display their most advanced skills. Some children qualify for the program by demonstrating generally advanced intellectual ability. Others qualify on the basis of unusually advanced skills in specific areas, such as reading, memory, or spatial reasoning.

Final decisions on enrollment reflect the school's need to preserve a balance of ages and sexes in the program, to serve children from diverse ethnic backgrounds, and to enroll a group of children whose superior intellectual talents lie in a variety of domains.

A child must be at least two years of age and toilet trained to be considered for the program.

## The Program

The Child Development Preschool is part of the long-term study of the development of children with unusually advanced intellectual abilities. The individualized program is designed to foster optimum development of each child's unique capacities.

A variety of learning experiences is offered in a balanced mixture of teacher- and child-structured situations. The program includes individualized instruction in language arts, science, mathematics, and social studies. Art, music, and drama are also integral parts of the curriculum. Daily outdoor activities allow children to develop self-confidence and coordination in active play. Considerable emphasis is placed on helping children acquire the social sensitivity and interpersonal skills which will allow them to participate comfortably in different social situations.

Since the preschool is part of a research project, children occasionally leave the classroom to participate in individual test sessions. Research activities are designed to be enjoyable experiences for children and are limited so as not to interfere with the classroom program. Parents may decline to have their children participate in any particular activity.

The development of social skills is emphasized in every aspect of the program. Children are guided in becoming independent, in learning to be assertive, in increasing their social sensitivity, in developing new friendship-making skills, and in improving their social and problem-solving skills. Some of these skills are taught through small group lessons using puppets and stories. In addition, teachers are aware of the fact that children's behavior which is immediately followed by adult attention tends to increase, while behavior which receives no attention tends to decrease in frequency. Teachers focus their attention, therefore, on children's appropriate behavior and ignore inappropriate behavior whenever possible.

Operating costs of the Child Development Preschool are provided by parent fees. During the 1978-79 school year, supplemental funding was provided by the U.S. Office of Education and the Spencer Foundation. The Child Development Research Group's projects have been funded by grants from the Ford, Medina, and Spencer Foundations and from the U.S. Office of Education.

### Evaluation of Program

Evaluations of all programs include teacher reports, standardized tests, and observational measures. Evaluation of the preschool component indicates gains in achievement, increased social skills, and parent satisfaction. Evaluation of other programs is still in progress.

Assorted papers have been prepared by project staff members describing various aspects of our work.

## A MODEL PROGRAM FOR RETRIEVAL AND ACCELERATION OF PROMISING YOUNG HANDICAPPED AND TALENTED (RAPYHT)

Institute for Child Behavior and Development
University of Illinois at Urbana-Champaign
Urbana, Illinois 61801

*Reported by:*
Merle B. Karnes, Director

*Administrative Responsibility:*
Merle B. Karnes, Director

*For Further Information, Contact:*
Merle B. Karnes, Director
Institute for Child Behavior and Development
University of Illinois at Urbana-Champaign
Urbana, Illinois 61801

### Overview of Program

In the fall of 1975, the Institute for Child Behavior and Development at the University of Illinois received a grant from the Bureau of Education for the Handicapped to develop and demonstrate a model program known as Retrieval and Acceleration of Promising Young Handicapped and Talented (RAPYHT). Handicapped children from three to five years of age who demonstrate exceptional talents are included in the project, which has completed its fourth year of operation. The past three years were given to development and demonstration, with the past year serving as the first year of a three-year cycle charged with demonstrating the model at the University of Illinois and assisting other sites in adopting or adapting the model.

One of the primary goals of RAPYHT has been to develop and demonstrate two approaches for educating young talented handicapped children who are enrolled in programs that also serve gifted children with no handicaps, average children with no handicaps, and multihandicapped children who are of higher but not of gifted ability. Since the target subjects are relatively few, it was considered important to program for the handicapped children with gifts and talents in a mainstream setting. Each of the demonstration classes represent opposite ends of a continuum relative to the role of the teacher.

Gifted and talented in this program include children who appear to be potentially or functionally talented in intellectual and creative abilities. The handicapped children included in the program are those whose full development is impaired through sensory, social-emotional, and/or learning deficits.

The overriding goal of the project has been to identify and appropriately program for young handicapped gifted and talented preschool children. This segment of the population has been markedly neglected and/or underserved. Customarily, the focus of instruction has been on the child's handicap(s) with his gifts and talents ignored.

## Selection of Students

The identification of preschool talented and handicapped children begins when children are screened for placement in a preschool special education program and continues throughout the intervention period. This ongoing process is essential because the talents of the handicapped child may not be initially recognized; however, after several weeks or months, previously hidden talents may emerge, especially if they are nourished. Thus, RAPYHT staff members rely on identification procedures that are part of initial screening and diagnosis as well as procedures continued when children are enrolled in the program.

RAPYHT is an integral part of a larger program involving a joint agreement between the University of Illinois and fifteen school districts in the county. The larger program, the Joint Early Education of the Preschool Handicapped (JEEPH), locates children to be screened in the fifteen school districts through a variety of techniques, including lists from local school principals, announcements, flyers sent home with children in school, and a telephone census. The children, ages three through five, who are located in the fifteen school districts are then screened by the Comprehensive Identification Process (CIP) to determine if there are developmental delays. The primary purpose of this screening is to select children who are thought to be handicapped, however, information obtained from parents or through observation of the child during screening which suggests potential talent is recorded. All children selected are referred for detailed study by a team consisting of a psychologist, a speech clinician, and a social worker who assess each child's performance on a battery of standardized instruments. The information obtained by the team is presented at a staff meeting where a child's talent, either potential or functional, is determined. Such children, with the consent of their parents, are placed directly in the program.

Some childrens' talents are identified in the program stage through the use of *Talent Checklists* developed through the RAPYHT program to help teachers rate children in six areas of talent. Children who receive high rankings in at least one talent area receive a follow-up.

## The Program

The federal government funded this program during the first three years. Currently, the demonstration classes are funded locally and are part of a larger preschool program coordinated by the Institute for Child Behavior and Development. The replication staff provide technical assistance to sites replicating the RAPYHT approach. The costs of the technical assistance are covered by an outreach grant from the Bureau for the Education of the Handicapped.

The demonstration and service activities are based on the implementation of two different approaches for meeting the needs of handicapped gifted and talented children. The Structure of the Intellect (SOI) approach assumes that many children will require careful structuring of the environment so that the knowledge, attitudes, and skills that the children need to develop are specifically provided. Such an approach seems to be particularly appropriate for the more severely handicapped child and for those children with learning disabilities and/or social-emotional problems interfering with a child's perception of reality. The open education approach, being more covertly structured, seems to pose problems for children who need the clearer overt structure of the SOI approach. On the other hand, the open education approach appears to be more appropriate for children who are able to structure their own functioning, if they are given help with more covert structure.

In the SOI classroom, the teacher observes the child as he participates in a planned game to determine how he is progressing. In the open classroom, teachers observe and record skills while the child is spontaneously involved in child-initiated activity. If the teacher needs certain information to assess progress, she may need to provide the child with an activity to assess progress. In the SOI classroom, the teacher precisely plans daily experiences, whereas in the open classroom, the teacher helps children understand their environment and how they feel. Encouragement, feedback, guidance, information, and clarification are all responsibilities of the teacher. In the open classroom, the child begins interactions and in the SOI classroom the teacher usually initiates interactions. A specific time schedule is followed in the SOI classroom. The schedules in the open classroom are flexible blocks of time. A highly specific schedule used in the SOI classroom structures the day's activities into blocks of time.

The teacher of the SOI approach conducts structured lessons in small groups for several periods during the day, making sure that children work well together and will enhance each other's development. Children in the open classroom form their own groups.

## Evaluation of the Program

The general steps for setting objectives, charting progress, and evaluating accomplishments in both SOI and open classrooms are summarized as follows:

1. The child is diagnosed by the team and placed in either the open or the SOI classroom and the child's talents and deficits are defined and general goals are written.

2. A systematic observation, assessment, and programming procedure developed at the University of Illinois determines the child's functioning in six developmental areas: language, math, gross motor, fine motor, social, and self-help. Lags and acceleration in development are determined. During this diagnostic period, trial teaching activities are presented. Near the end of the period,

*Talent Checklists* are administered to help determine if previously unrecognized talents surface.

3. At the end of the diagnostic period, individual education plans are prepared for each child to set goals and objectives for each area of talent and handicap for a semester. Classroom assessments are supplemented with information from the diagnostic team and the child's parents. SOI objectives are based on periods of one to seven days and are often formulated through referral to the SOI model. In the open classroom, objectives are longer, up to a month in length.

4. The individual education plans in the SOI classroom are implemented through weekly lesson plans for groups of children engaged at the same time in similar activities. Expectations differ, but the lesson plans are directly related to the objectives in the individual education plans. Activities to measure the attainment of these objectives are included in the plans. If an activity eliminates or minimizes a handicap as well as fosters a talent, these objectives appear on the worksheet. For example, "The child will hold a pencil in an appropriate grasp (fine motor handicap) and draw three different symbols (divergent thinking talent)." In the open classroom, however, teachers make plans involving children and interacting with them. Criteria for attainment are based on the observation of naturally occurring behaviors directly related to written objectives.

5. In the SOI classroom, weekly charts based on the number of objectives attained compared to the number set during the time period are prepared to show each child's progress. Each child has at least three charts, for each area of talent, area of deficit, and other developmental areas. In the open classroom, each child's progress is charted monthly. Charts are similar to those for children in the SOI classroom; however, fewer numbers are entered because the objectives cover longer periods of time.

6. Finally, a battery of standardized tests is administered on a pre and post basis and provides information on the progress of each child in important areas of development.

Other instruments are used when, due to handicapping conditions, one or more of the standardized instruments do not provide a valid measure of a child's abilities.

Parent needs are assessed through structured interviews. The project relies heavily on the opinions, feelings, and input of the parents in determining progress. Forms are developed to help sites adopting the approach to assess their progress in the various components of the model. Activities of replication specialists are evaluated by site staff using a form developed for that purpose.

Through the outreach project, RAPYHT staff members work with state consultants in the gifted and in the handicapped to identify a site in their state and to train the staff at that site to implement the model. Strict criteria are used in the selection of sites to safeguard against spending time and federal money on sites that do not have a real commitment. Essentially, the outreach project works with five new states each year. The second-year technical assistance is reduced to a site, but supportive services by mail and telephone are provided along with a limited number of site visits. During 1978-1979, the states of Minnesota, Michigan, Connecticut, Wisconsin, and Illinois are developing and demonstrating the RAPYHT approach in their states. Next year, the approach will be replicated in Iowa, Florida, and New York.

**A RURAL PRESCHOOL GIFTED AND GIFTED/HANDICAPPED PROJECT**
Panhandle Child Development Association
418 Coeur d'Alene Avenue
Coeur d'Alene, Idaho 83814

*Reported by:*
Gail Hanninen, Director

*Administrative Responsibility:*
Gail Hanninen, Project Director

*For Further Information, Contact:*
Gail Hanninen, Director
Panhandle Child Development Association
418 Coeur d'Alene Avenue
Coeur d'Alene, Idaho 83814

## Overview of Program

The Rural Preschool Gifted and Gifted/Handicapped Model Project was established in 1976 to provide services to thirty-six youngsters ages three through five who resided in a rural county of northern Idaho.

The philosophy of the program is based upon the needs of the total child. Thus, a child's psychomotor development is perceived to be as important as his intellectual development, and, subsequently, should be reflected in the project curriculum. A second element of the philosophy is that of developing a learning environment which nurtures enriched learning experiences. This means that a child is encouraged to identify areas of specific interest and to start developing skills which will help him or her toward becoming an independent learner. A third component of the philosophy is that of striving to employ strategies which nurture higher levels of thinking. Emphasis is placed on the use of quality questions, problem solving activities, and an integration of the community as a part of the learning environment.

The major objectives of the project are:
  1.  To develop a rural model to serve gifted and talented and

gifted and talented handicapped preschoolers, age three to five years, and their parents

2. To develop curriculum for preschool gifted and talented
3. To provide follow-up in the continuity of placement of gifted and talented preschoolers into the first grade
4. To expand services in the five northern counties to existing preschools for the handicapped students to enhance the inclusion of gifted and talented handicapped in such classrooms

The projected outcomes of the project are:

1. Developing two classrooms with a maximum of eighteen gifted and talented students in each room
2. Developing curriculum strategies for use with preschool gifted and talented students
3. Providing consultative services to rural area preschool programs for handicapped children as they relate to the gifted and talented handicapped child
4. Involving parents in the classroom
5. Disseminating information regarding the activities and results of the project through the means of media, site visitations, and conferences
6. Providing continuity in a child's educational experience by working with the public school districts
7. Involving federal, state, and private agencies in the delivery of services to the preschool gifted and talented and the gifted and talented handicapped students.

## Selection of Students

Students are referred to the program by several sources, including parents, public school psychologists, Head Start personnel, child development centers, and itinerate staff for the school for the deaf and blind. Priority is given to providing services to the gifted/handicapped child. All other referrals are screened on a first-serve basis. The master teachers for the project are the individuals who manage the screening process, thus establishing a high efficiency and low cost screening procedure.

Screening procedures include: (1) administration of the *Peabody Picture Vocabulary Test, Columbia Mental Maturity Scale* and/or a draw-a-person test and (2) completion of a parent involvement form. A student may qualify for entrance into the program by scoring one and one-half standard deviations above the mean on either of the instruments administered. If the parent, however, believes that the test results are not indicative of the child's ability and are inconsistent with the responses recorded on the parent interview form, the child may be admitted into the program for a period of observation. During that time, further testing occurs, and a final decision is made with the parent on the basis of additional test results and the child's participation in class work.

## The Program

The model project is exemplified by the activities of two classrooms located in Coeur d'Alene and Post Falls, which together serve a maximum of thirty-six children, three to five years old, during three two and one-half hour sessions weekly. An enriched learning experience occurs through the development of (1) communication skills, (2) social skills, (3) curiosity and problem-solving skills, (4) self-awareness skills, and (5) pre-academic skills. The above are accomplished through individualized and group program planning.

The project develops curriculum materials and teaching approaches which can challenge the preschool gifted and talented child. Bloom's taxonomy is used to identify and design teaching strategies to meet the individual's needs.

Parents are involved in the project by transporting their children to and from the classroom, participating in classroom activities on a scheduled basis, serving as mentors in the classroom, providing snacks for the children, participating in parent meetings, initiating fund-raising efforts, participating on the advisory board, participating in parent education sessions, and conferring with the classroom teachers on both an informal and formal basis.

Supplementary services to the children reflect one form of community involvement and include health education and speech therapy. Also, the use of the community as an experimental classroom is a valuable part of the program, and examples include field trips to a local supermarket and fire station.

Additional support has been gained through borrowing many items which are necessary for classroom operation.

Success is dependent upon the integral involvement of parents and the federal, state, and private agencies currently serving children. The project is funded through parent donations, tuition, and federal funding.

## Evaluation of Program

Internal evaluation has been the only form that has been used to date and takes three forms. First, a time sample is used to ascertain the distribution of time being spent in each curriculum area. Programmatic changes have been made on the basis of that evaluation, and a follow-up evaluation will be made at the end of the school year. Second, staff evaluation has included two processes: classroom observation of the teacher and a self-evaluation by the teacher. All results are discussed with the respective staff member involved and appropriate objectives are developed. Third, pretest and posttest data, including behavioral observation and standardized measures, are utilized.

## PART B
## ELEMENTARY PROGRAMS

Of the five elementary school programs described in this section, one was initiated in 1962, one in 1969, one in 1973, and two in 1974. Four of the five programs admit children of kindergarten age. Pupils who make satisfactory progress may continue in the programs until they complete elementary school, and in one of the programs students may continue through grade nine.

Nominations for admission to programs may be made by parents, teachers, principals, or other professionals. In general, criteria for admission include high scores on individual intelligence tests as well as exceptionally high scores on standardized achievement instruments. In one of the programs, special provisions are made for admission of culturally and economically deprived children who score high in aptitude, but who may yield achievement scores somewhat depressed. From program to program, minimum admission requirements vary. In one case, admission is limited to the upper 4 percent of the school population. In another, a score of 125 serves as the minimum IQ, whereas in yet another program, an IQ of 140 is required for admission.

Statements of philosophy, goals, and objectives stress the diversity and wide range of interests characteristic of the gifted and their need for differentiated educational experiences. Companionship of intellectual peers, opportunities for creative experiences, development of research and exploration competencies, stimulation of intellectual curiosity, and critical thinking at sophisticated levels are among the goals and objectives thought to be especially important to the education and growth of the gifted and talented.

While basic academic studies receive emphasis in elementary programs, students are afforded opportunities to choose projects which involve them in the identification and definition of problems, formulation of hypotheses, planning strategies, seeking out, collecting, and analyzing relevant data, and drawing conclusions and inferences—in a word, research. Small class size of between twelve and sixteen students, individualized instruction, seminars, student participation in goal-setting, three-and four-hour blocks of time, and extensive utilization of resource personnel and other community resources are employed to provide optimum opportunity for learning.

Federal, state, and local tax monies, private grants, and substantial tuition in the case of private schools, constitute the sources of funding.

Teachers, students, parents, principals, and directors participate in the assessment and evaluation of student progress. Pretests and posttests, both academic achievement tests and attitude scales, and administered. In addition, logs and anecdotal records are kept by teachers and in some cases by students.

**ASTOR PROGRAM FOR GIFTED CHILDREN**
New York City Public Schools (local Districts)

*Reported by:*
Virginia Z. Ehrlich, Director

*Administrative Responsibility:*
Virginia Z. Ehrlich, Director

*For Further Information, Contact:*
Virginia Z. Ehrlich, Director
Box 126, Teachers College
Columbia University
525 West 120 Street
New York, New York 10027

## Overview of Program

The grant for the Astor Program included a planning period which began in September 1973 with actual classes beginning in February 1974. The program functioned initially in two school districts under private funding which continued through June 1977. The program has been extended to include eight of the thirty-two school districts of New York City and is supported with public funds as part of the regular school budget, thus attaining a major goal of the program. Through June 1980, the director will continue to service the program by training all teachers working with Astor classes as well as others who were involved in teaching the gifted. The director also provided follow-up and guidance services to all pupils admitted during the period of private funding as they progressed through the upper grades.

The target population of the program was the intellectually gifted child, beginning at age four, represented by the top one percent of the pupil population. In practice, this meant that almost all pupils served had IQs of approximately 140 and above, although no specific IQ was set as a base limit. The program was intended to reach those very young children who are not normally served by the schools.

The two major goals of the Astor Program are:

1. To promote continuing research, experimentation, and education of the gifted in the New York City public schools at all levels

2. To implement a "host school" concept for gifted children on two levels: (a) children aged four and above who exhibit unusual evidence of academic ability and (b) students in regular grades who have exceptional ability and cannot be accommodated by their local schools

The first goal of the Astor Program is not as well known as the early childhood classes have become, yet it was the more significant of the two goals. It impacted on the entire school system and literally reversed the negative trend of education for the gifted in the city. Activities planned under the first goal included:

1. Availability of the director as a consultant on a full-time basis to all branches of the city system on subjects related to the gifted

2. Funding for dissemination of information and educational materials

3. Conducting citywide conferences on the gifted where personnel could become acquainted with local, state, and national endeavors in gifted education

4. Continued participation by the director in conferences held by national, state, and regional organizations focusing on the gifted.

The term "Astor Program for Gifted Children" has become associated primarily with one aspect of our second goal: the establishment of classes for the intellectually gifted, beginning at age four. The activities planned under this category were broad:

1. To establish procedures for early identification of the gifted

2. To establish "host" classes in central locations for children in the top one percent of the intellectual ability

3. To develop classroom management procedures that would be consistent with the nature and needs of the pupils

    4. To develop a differentiated curriculum that would reflect what is known about the learning needs of the gifted

    5. To plan in a manner that would insure the ultimate institutionalization of the program, independent of private funding.

The philosophy of the Astor Program holds that gifted children need:

    1. To be in an understanding, accepting school environment with teachers and administrators empathetic to their special needs

    2. To enjoy the companionship of peers of comparable abilities

    3. To discover early the joys of learning

    4. To be allowed to develop socially and emotionally at a pace consistent with their ages

    5. To acquire a sense of social and civic responsibility early in their school experiences

    6. To be exposed to a differentiated and enriched curriculum suited to their ability levels and their special needs

    7. To learn to think and reason precisely and logically

    8. To develop basic skills needed in reading, mathematics, science, social living, and other curriculum areas as early as possible and to the greatest extent possible

    9. To learn to accept responsibility for their own behavior and for the consequences of their acts

    10. To be allowed to enjoy their childhood while realizing their intellectual potential.

## Selection of Students

Criteria for selecting children for the Astor Program were flexible and multiple. Many factors had to be considered in making final selections. Some of these were related to administrative considerations required by the nature of the program. The most important of these follow, but not in order of importance.

1. Students were selected by borough, school ·district, and local school. All children had to live within the borough. A certain proportion of places were reserved for children residing in the "host" district and for those attending the "host" school.
2. Students selected were between four years and five years and seven months of age as of the first of September of the school year.
3. An attempt was made to have both sexes represented on an approximately equal basis.
4. Where no local bus service was available, the ability of parents to arrange transportation for the child was considered. Funds were given to those on welfare or receiving public assistance to meet this cost.

Screening and identification criteria for pupil selection included:

1. Recommendations by professional persons, for example, teachers, psychologists, principals, case workers, nursery school directors, pediatricians, and so forth
2. Telephone and personal interviews with parents and child
3. Emotional and social maturity of the child
4. Readiness for school experience, both cognitive and affective
5. Intellectual ability as evidenced in biographical data
6. Intellectual ability as evidenced by individual psychological examination, including administration of the Stanford-Binet
7. Pupil products and performances, for example, reading, drawing, and so forth
8. Parent nomination, based on the screening interview
9. Previous school history of the child, if any
10. Date of application.

Since there were very few openings and funds were limited, only those children for whom there was justifiable supporting data were given psychological testing. Parents could submit results of psychological testing by accredited testing agencies or certified psychologists. Data from the *Stanford-Binet Intelligence Scale,* along with the examiner's report were required. Parents were informed that they could authorize agencies or psychologists to send this information directly to the program director.

When it was determined that a child met most of the criteria, his or her name was included in a pool of those eligible. All applicants were then ranked according to their IQs, and usually those with the highest scores were accepted. Since enrollments were limited and the program was privately funded, even though administered through the public school system, it was possible to use these procedures to save time and money. It was found that classes were composed of children with IQs of over 140, ranging through the ceiling of the *Stanford-Binet Intelligence Scale.*

## The Program

The Astor Program was a full-time program, which followed either the current practices in the public school system or extended the time. The prekindergarten-kindergarten classes met for three-, four-, or five-hour sessions, and eventually settled for the most practical, a four-hour day. All classes above the kindergarten level met for the full school day.

The grade ranges began at the prekindergarten level and extended through the grades as pupils progressed from year to year. For the period of the private funding, the classes extended through the third grade. Under public funding, the schools have extended the program through the upper grades and intend to further expand the program into the junior high schools.

During the period of private funding, pupils met as an organized class for the entire day. Within the class, the pupils worked individually or in small groups. Each class had two regular teachers for approximately thirty pupils. Resource teachers in special subjects were made available in music, art, and foreign language. Under public funding, most of the classes through grade four have one regular teacher and a paraprofessional, frequently a college graduate with teaching preparation.

It was the goal of the Astor Program to match a curriculum

to the characteristics of the pupil population. This meant, first, consideration of the nature of the gifted learner and, second, an awareness of the many approaches possible. The goal was to use any techniques that met learner needs, modifying, adapting, creating, if necessary, those approaches that the pupil population dictated.

With the child as the focal point, the following curriculum questions were asked: Who am I? Where am I? What am I? Why am I? In response to these questions, the following curriculum topics were selected:

1. *The Child in His Time Space.* This topic explores the child's identity in relation to himself, to his family, peers, coworkers, immediate social contacts, and also in relation to those who have lived before him and will come after him. It is a view of man in his social, sociological, and historical space.

2. *The Child in His Geographical Space.* This topic explores the child's geographical location in terms of his classroom, school, home, neighborhood, city, state, nation, and the universe.

3. *The Child in His Environmental Space.* This topic explores the natural environment of plants and animals and the child's interdependence with all living things.

4. *The Child in His Physical Space.* This topic explores the interdependence of the child and the physical constants of his universe: chemical relationships, physical laws, mathematical equations, and so forth.

These four topics formed the basic themes around which basic skills were developed and gave rise to the special interest topics at the core of an integrated curriculum.

The philosophy of the Astor Program is that intellectually gifted children need to learn early the process of learning and to initiate their own learning experiences. To accomplish these ends, skills are developed which will have lasting usefulness with emphasis on critical thinking skills, the ability to analyze, evaluate, and synthesize.

All classes were equipped with the regular materials provided for their grade level as a basic requirement. These were supplemented by the private funding with a variety of enrichment materials and resources. These included:

1. A classroom library of selected books, in fiction and nonfiction, and at various levels of difficulty
2. Reference materials, including maps, globes, atlases, encyclopedias, dictionaries, and magazines at various levels of difficulty
3. Tape recorders, primer typewriters, phonographs, classical and popular records, and cassette viewers
4. Art supplies, including a variety of media and art reproductions
5. Musical instruments, including a piano in all kindergartens
6. Mathematics games and puzzles, unifix cubes, tangrams, geoboard, chess and checker sets, balances and scales, weights, attribute blocks, parquetry blocks, cuisenaire rods, graph paper, metric rules, and containers
7. Science equipment, including models of animal and human bodies, prisms, magnifying glasses, convex and concave lenses, magnets, telegraph sets, microscopes, seeds, solar system models, pulleys and inclines, science kits and series, and live animals and plants
8. Materials as required in conjunction with carrying out the goals of the curriculum and in pursuing the many special interest topics studied by the classes.

The program was completely funded, including teacher salaries and fringe benefits, by the private grant through June 1977. After that date, the program was supported by tax levy or public funds, supplemented by occasional small grants from state and federal funds. All teacher training was supported by foundation monies through 1979.

## Evaluation of Program

The Astor Program was designed as a longitudinal research study with evaluation focused on the following aspects of the program:

1. Consistency of IQ over time
2. Pupil achievement growth in mathematics, reading, and vocabulary

3. Pupil attitudes toward various aspects of school
4. Reactions of parents, teachers, principals, and district superintendents
5. Classroom observations of pupils and teachers
6. Follow-up of pupils

All pupils were tested at the beginning of the program with an individual IQ test (usually the *Stanford-Binet Intelligence Scale*), a figure drawing test, and a reading test (*Wide Range Achievement Test*). These tests were administered again at the end of the first, second, and third years of the program, depending on pupil admission dates. All pupils were also given achievement tests (*Metropolitan Achievement Tests*) in mathematics, reading, and vocabulary at the end of the first, second, and third years of the program, depending on their dates of admission. All were given a simple test of attitude toward various aspects of school at the end of the first year and subsequent years of attendance.

All parents completed a background data questionnaire at the beginning of the program, when their children were interviewed for admission. Parents, principals, and teachers completed reaction questionnaires at the end of each school year. All classes and teachers were observed several times a year informally and once a year formally, using classroom observation schedules in the latter instance.

**CREATIVE LEARNING IN A UNIQUE ENVIRONMENT (CLUE)**
Memphis City Schools
2597 Avery Avenue
Memphis, Tennessee 38112

*Reported by:*
Jo Patterson, Coordinator

*Administrative Responsibility:*
Jo Patterson, Coordinator

*For Further Information, Contact:*
Jo Patterson, Coordinator
Memphis City Schools
2597 Avery Avenue
Memphis, Tennessee 38112

## Overview of Program

The Creative Learning in a Unique Environment (CLUE) program represents an effort on the part of the Memphis City Schools to provide an educational program to meet the needs of academically talented and gifted students in elementary and junior high schools. CLUE was begun in October 1969 as a federally funded Title III Elementary and Secondary Education Act program for academically gifted and talented students in grades four through six. At the conclusion of the three-year federal funding period, the city and state assumed fiscal responsibility for the program, which currently operates on primary, intermediate, and junior high school levels. The program serves approximately twenty-four hundred students in kindergarten through the ninth grade.

The CLUE program is designed to provide differentiated educational experiences to meet the needs of gifted students not generally met in the regular classroom. The program attempts to involve the students both as a group and as individuals in learning experiences that will result in self-actualization and effective participation in society.

The primary objectives of the program are to aid students in acquiring cognitive skills that will allow for the maximum development of higher levels of thought; to aid students in developing an understanding of group processes and the dynamics of group interaction; and to aid students in developing techniques that will increase their ability to do independent research.

## Selection of Students

There are primary and intermediate/junior high selection procedures. Outstanding reading ability is the only criterion for the selection of CLUE students at the primary level. Recommendations may be made by parents, teachers, or principals. The students recommended are administered an informal reading test by primary teachers in the CLUE program in the spring of each year. Both the word recognition and comprehension levels are considered. Students entering the first grade must have a reading and comprehension level at a third-grade level or better to be included in the program. Second grade students must be reading at the fifth-grade level or higher.

In considering intermediate and junior high school students who have been recommended by teachers, parents, and/or principals, the identification committee considers a combination of the following criteria: group IQ scores, achievement scores on reading, and teacher evaluations. The identification committee is composed of three individuals who are either school psychologists, guidance counselors, parents, or staff members of CLUE. Students having IQ scores as low as 120 must be reading two and one-half to three years above placement. When there is a question about a student's qualifications, the committee may request that an individual IQ test be administered. Along with achievement and IQ scores from the past two years, the classroom teacher's assessment of qualities related to characteristics of the gifted and the teacher's comments are taken into account.

## The Program

The content emphasis and instructional strategies employed in the CLUE program are designed to involve the students as active participants in their own learning and to aid them in the development of processes and skills that can be used in their lifelong pursuit of knowledge. These activities are also designed to allow for the maximum development of the academically talented child's thinking, learning, and creative abilities. To achieve this end, the activities involve students in experiences such as: interpreting data, summarizing information, stimulating the imagination, decision making, problem solving, making discoveries, formulating hypotheses, analyzing propaganda techniques, and developing logical thinking.

The primary and intermediate divisions of CLUE operate on a semi-separation basis. Each week identified students attend two half-day sessions at a centrally located school which serves several neighboring schools. Transportation to and from the designated school is provided by the parents. Classes are scheduled for alternate morning and afternoon sessions so that students do not miss a particular subject more than once a week. Students spend the remainder of the school week in their regularly assigned classrooms. The composition of the CLUE classes includes both multi-grade and grade-level grouping. On the primary level, an effort is made to limit the classes to twelve students and each teacher has approximately forty-eight students. Intermediate classes average sixteen students, with each teacher serving about sixty-five students.

On the junior high school level, identified students attend the CLUE class one period each day in the student's home school. Composition of the class is on grade level only and is generally limited to twenty students. The program is subject-oriented and is the basic English course, which is not accelerated but incorporates the same philosophy and objectives as the elementary program.

A variety of publications containing brain teasers, values clarification, group dynamics, and creative activities are useful aids for the teacher who must write and develop the differentiated curriculum for gifted students. Several college dictionaries, a thesaurus, almanac, and the *Guinness Book of World Records* are important reference books in the CLUE classroom. The school housing the CLUE program usually supplies encyclopedias, and the students have access to the school library. Limited use has been made of prepared kits and materials because teacher-prepared activities are more successful. However, students do engage in games such as "Propaganda" and several games of strategy which are provided for each room.

The CLUE program makes extensive use of the media to allow students to express their creative abilities and/or to share results of their independent study. Specific audiovisual equipment made available for these purposes includes the tape recorder, videotape recorder, Ektagraphic Visualmaker®, super 8 mm movie camera, slide projector, and 8 mm projector. Overhead projectors, microscopes, opaque projectors, record players, and other equipment are available at the school where the program is housed.

A regular classroom is satisfactory, but because students from neighboring schools are served at a center school, it was found convenient to select a classroom located near one of the entrances. The use of round tables and plastic chairs in the classroom is recommended because traditional classroom desks restrict the mobility that is desired and essential in the seminar setting. However, this is not to suggest that the program cannot be successful in a traditional classroom setting.

The CLUE program is funded through state and local funds. Approximately one hundred dollars is allotted to every teacher annually to purchase consumable materials.

## Evaluation of Program

Program evaluation is a continuous process using both formal and informal assessments involving teachers, students, and parents. Student self-evaluation as well as peer evaluation is ongoing. Students are trained in the process of critiquing so that they are better able to evaluate both written and oral activities engaged in by individuals and groups. In addition to written self-evaluations, students also participate in the mid-year and annual written evaluation of the program. The mid-year program evaluation also involves parents. The data collected reinforce or suggest changes needed in the program.

**THE LIGHTHOUSE PROGRAM**
Jefferson Lighthouse School
Racine Unified School District
1722 West Sixth Street
Racine, Wisconsin 53404

*Reported by:*
Barbara LeRose, Director

*Administrative Responsibility:*
Linda King, Coordinator

*For Further Information, Contact:*
Barbara LeRose, Director
2326 Mohr Avenue
Racine, Wisconsin 53405

## Overview of Program

The Lighthouse Program is a model for educating gifted children. It was developed during a four-year Elementary and Secondary Act, Title III project in the Racine Unified School District, Racine, Wisconsin.

Funded in January of 1973, An Early Program for Gifted Children, or project Engine, had two major goals: (1) to identify gifted youngsters at the entry point of their schooling and (2) to provide comprehensive, specialized programming designed to allow the fullest realization of their early potential. The major findings of the Title III experimental study provided the framework for the present Lighthouse Program which served 360 children in kindergarten through the fourth grade during the 1978-79 school year. An additional grade will be added each year until a comprehensive program through the twelfth grade is accomplished.

Based on a philosophy which views gifted education as a total system, the Lighthouse Program has a broad goal to achieve a continuous, comprehensive plan which will include valid identification procedures, appropriately differentiated instruction, teacher training, developmental guidance, and ongoing formative as well as summative evaluation.

## Selection of Students

Personnel of the Title III gifted project, working in coopera-
tion with the Racine Unified School District Research and
Development Department, have developed a promising screening
procedure for identifying the very young gifted child. Individually testing all entering kindergarteners, the personnel of the
project seek to identify those developmental variables which
children bring to school and which predict both high intellectual
achievement and high creative productivity and problem-solving
capacities.

Validity studies involving both the Title III gifted sample and a
district random sample of kindergarten through second grade
students indicated that of a total of thirty criterion measures
predicted by both the screening battery and an individually
administered intelligence test, twenty-nine showed prediction
levels for the battery which are as high as or higher than the
intelligence test.

Using the preschool screening battery, consisting of eleven
individually administered instruments which cover a wide range
of intellectual abilities and developmental skills, program personnel select approximately the top-scoring 4 percent of the
population for gifted programming.

In addition, further provisions are made for the identification
of children who are economically deprived or referred to or
nominated for the gifted program at points later than school
entry. Reports and copies of the individual identification instruments utilized are available upon request.

## The Program

In the design of the Lighthouse Program, creativity is the
objective and the major content emphasis is the thinking process.
The *Curriculum for Thinking* was developed by the project staff
and is used as soon as the children enter the program at the
kindergarten level. The thinking curriculum is based on the same
developmental theory that provides the basis for the entire design.

Instruction begins with individual units of thinking. Both
divergent and convergent thinking terms are taught to students,

and then applied thoroughly through all content strands. Once students have enough applied knowledge of individual thinking units, they begin the study of thinking classes.

The first thinking classification model the children are introduced to is Bloom's taxonomy of objectives for the cognitive domain. At this point, they are able to begin producing their own curricula, using the thinking process framework provided. Thinking units and classes serve as the prerequisite to real integration of content through process. This integration allows students to move to general systems, where they can see new world views and make new connections.

The general organizational plan of the program resembles a nongraded open classroom structure. The children are grouped into units. The kindergarten through second grade units are called "clusters." In each cluster, there are approximately 120 students, four teachers, and an aide. Our older students are grouped into units of similar size, called seminars, and have similar staffs.

Instructional time blocks have been reorganized to permit integration of curriculum, and content subjects are divided into three areas of study: (1) basic studies which include thinking, reading, language, and mathematics; (2) environmental studies which include science, social studies, health, guidance, and foreign language minicourses; and (3) art studies which include music, art, physical education, creative drama, and others.

The classroom facility has also been designed around the three blocks of studies. Teachers have combined their materials and established classroom space as centers related to the specific studies involved in by the group.

The program is presently located in the Jefferson Lighthouse School in Racine, Wisconsin, and is serving approximately 625 students. The student population consists of approximately 360 identified gifted children and an additional 260 nonidentified students who are enrolled in gifted programming. This grouping mixture presents the challenge of developing curriculum that is appropriate for both gifted and nongifted children. The *Curriculum for Thinking*, as explained earlier, has afforded us that vehicle.

The gifted program is funded by the Racine Unified School

District at the same per pupil cost as regular district programming, with the exception of additional funding for a project coordinator and four classroom aides. In addition, a Title IV-C gifted project, beginning in July of 1977, has as its purpose the development of the *Curriculum for Thinking*, based upon developmental stage theories and reflecting a general systems approach to the development of gifted education.

## Evaluation of Program

Evaluation of the Lighthouse design is a joint function of the project director, the project coordinator, and personnel of the Research and Development Department of the school district. Evaluation is concerned with the answers the program provides to two key questions—what is going to be taught and how are we teaching it? As a working model of teaching and learning processes, the Lighthouse thinking curriculum lends itself to evaluation on several levels and includes the following components: (1) process monitoring—documenting the activities undertaken to achieve the program goals (answering the question: Is the treatment in fact being applied?) and the impact of instructional activities on the children; (2) academic progress; (3) student attitude; (4) parent involvement and attitude; (5) curriculum development; (6) identification validation; and (7) research and development.

In the evaluation design of the Title III and IV-C gifted project, two schools of current thought about evaluation were considered: (1) instruments should be "project-fair" and clearly measure project-specific objectives and (2) since projects happen in a system, system-oriented, standardized measurements should also be taken. Thus, since 1973, large amounts of data have been accumulated, particularly on the group of children identified in the spring of 1973. Most easily acquired was the information related to standardized measurements. Much more problematical was the lack of validated instrumentation for measuring growth in higher-level cognitive abilities and creative problem-finding.

Research and evaluation in the Lighthouse Program is ongoing and longitudinal. It will help reveal in time, it is believed, those variables that contribute to success in teaching higher level thinking to gifted students and to the establishment of an experience-validated core of tool subjects which will be stable through constantly changing content—literally the basic skills for gifted.

A list of specific tests and instruments used for research and evaluation in the Lighthouse Program is available upon request.

**PROJECT REACH**
Sunnyside School
2070 County Road H
St. Paul, Minnesota 55112

*Reported by:*
Joyce E. Juntune

*Administrative Responsibility:*
Joyce E. Juntune

*For Further Information, Contact:*
Joyce E. Juntune
Sunnyside School
2070 County Road H
St. Paul, Minnesota 55112

## Overview of Program

When the faculty of the Pike Lake School reviewed many of the research findings in gifted education, they decided to concentrate on a program for developing each teacher's creative potential. If the research findings were valid, such a program should result in creative growth on the part of the students. Thus, Project REACH with an emphasis on teacher training was begun on July 1, 1974, under a Title IV-C grant of the Elementary and Secondary Education Act.

Project REACH is based on several cognitive models and teaching strategies: the Multiple Talents of Calvin Taylor; the Structure of the Intellect by J. P. Guilford, as interpreted by Mary Meeker; the Four Factors of Creative Thinking from E. Paul Torrance; the Five Steps of Creative Problem Solving from Sidney Parnes; the Eighteen Teaching Strategies of Frank Williams; the Theory of Creativity by John Gowan; the Imagery Strategies of Joe Khatena; and the Transformation Theory of George Land.

The projet is centered in New Brighton, Minnesota, a suburb of the Minneapolis/St. Paul metropolitan area. The community is served by the Mounds View School District, which is comprised of ten elementary schools, three middle schools, and two high schools. The project has served designated elementary schools with enrollments of five hundred to seven hundred students.

The project goal was a modification in classroom instruction that would result in 75 percent of the students improving their creative thinking abilities as measured by the *Torrance Tests of Creative Thinking* and *Multiple Talents Test* at the .05 level of significance.

## Selection of Students

A high percentage of the families of the Mounds View School District are middle class, Caucasian, professional families with children in school. As a group, the pupils served score above national norms on the *Iowa Tests of Basic Skills,* and many are individuals of high academic potential. The REACH program is designed to serve all students in the project schools who can and are enhancing their creative thinking abilities, regardless of academic achievement.

Within each school, the students are grouped according to their academic performance level for each subject. Teacher recommendations and student performance on the *Iowa Tests of Basic Skills* and district-developed competency tests are used in assigning students to instructional groups. Within these groups, teachers use the project activity evaluation guidelines and observation to determine which students need further challenge or work in the various thinking processes emphasized in Project REACH. These students then work in small groups or at specially designed learning centers. Students who exhibit high ability and self-motivation are directed into individual investigations and small group projects.

## The Program

Project REACH was a teacher development program, based on the theories and research of several educators and psychologists. By combining the ideas of these various researchers, a more complete and precise picture of the self-actualization of creative potential for individual students was achieved. From this theoretical core branched the various teaching strategies that could be applied in the classroom, experiences that could be encouraged by the parents and community, and thinking processes that could be used by the students in or out of school.

The core of the project was a systematic, in-depth, research-based teacher development program. It was decided that teacher development could best be accomplished by providing them with as much exposure as possible to the work of the authorities in the field of creative thinking by asking some of these authorities to hold workshop training sessions with the faculty and large and small group meetings where there was time for interaction and sharing. Graduate level courses were conducted on various theoretical aspects of thinking and teachers were provided with access to books written by the authorities in the field.

The strength of this in-service model lies in the meshing of many complementary theories into one framework for thinking plus the ongoing in-service training that still exists through additional graduate courses and regularly scheduled update sessions.

As the theories were studied and understood, the teachers and members of the project staff worked to mesh the many complementary theories into a framework for thinking.

Teaching strategies were developed to help teachers use the traditional curriculum content in encouraging creative thinking. These strategies were an outcome of the research study and were grouped into the following categories: productive thinking, forecasting, communication, decision making, planning/implementation, and creative problem solving skills.

Each thinking lesson was built on a specific curriculum concept. The teacher meshed the thinking process being emphasized and the curriculum concept into one lesson.

Successful classroom activities were recorded and compiled into curriculum guides for the areas of reading, math, science, social studies, and language arts.

The next area of concentration was home involvement. Activities were planned for the parents, to expose them to the project thinking processes and encourage them to reinforce the use of these processes at home.

For three years, twenty-five teachers served on curriculum writing teams. Several of these teachers were on more than one writing team. Prior to the writing projects, teachers were trained in recognizing necessary elements of a successful lesson.

The project is also collecting a set of videotapes showing classroom teachers using the Project REACH processes. They are presently being edited. It is hoped that they will be used by schools that cannot observe a classroom demonstration.

The project was and is funded through a combination of Title III and Title IV-C grants under the Elementary and Secondary Education Act and local district monies.

## Evaluation of Program

The evaluation design for Project REACH has two major components related to the success of teacher in-service on student performance.

1. The comparison of Pike Lake students who have had a program for development of creative thinking strategies, and students in a comparison school not having the specific development program. The *Torrance Tests of Creative Thinking* (TTCT) were used to measure that status present in the samples and the differences between the two groups were analyzed. During the third year, the *Multiple Talents Tests* (MTT) were also given to a sample of students in grades three, four, five, and six at the comparison school.

2. The longitudinal analysis of the performance of Pike Lake student groups on the MTT was the second effort.

The REACH program for developing creative thinking behaviors in students resulted in statistically reliable increases in creative thinking performance by the project students on the TTCT and MTT instruments.

The project students performed increasingly better throughout the duration of the project when compared to their own pretest performance and when compared to students from a similar comparison school not having a program.

Subjective evaluation of the program was based on teacher logs that were maintained on each project school teacher. They contained involvement expectations (as indicated on a teacher participating checklist), classroom observation reports, a record of lesson ideas contributed in each of the project areas, a record of project activities in various curriculum areas, and a summary of each teacher's participation in a variety of extra class activities.

During the third year of the program, approximately one hundred students who were experiencing learning difficulties were tested with Meeker's *Learning Abilities Test* to determine their strengths and weaknesses on visual imagery and to develop individual thinking profiles. Several students who were weak in visual imagery were given weekly tutoring. Observations were recorded for each tutoring session, including the degree of difficulty the student experienced while completing the activity.

**SEATTLE COUNTRY DAY SCHOOL**
2610 Nob Hill Avenue North
Seattle, Washington 98109

*Reported by:*
Lucile Beckman

*Administrative Responsibility:*
Lucile Beckman

*For Further Information, Contact:*
Lucile Beckman
Seattle Country Day School
2610 Nob Hill Avenue North
Seattle, Washington 98109

## Overview of Program

The Seattle Country Day School was established in 1962 as a nonprofit, coeducational, state approved, elementary school dedicated to providing special educational opportunities for young gifted children. The program serves approximately one hundred and seventy to one hundred and eighty children, ages four through thirteen in kindergarten through eighth grade. Since 1975, the school has reassessed its philosophy and has added a strong research component.

The basic objective of the program is to develop intellectual curiosity, creativity, and capacity for critical thinking. The vehicle is to place students in small classes with their mental peers and give them skilled, imaginative, and highly educated teachers.

Class size is limited to no more than sixteen students. The students go to different classrooms and teachers for each subject. Within the classroom, students may be divided into smaller cluster groups. The flexibility thus provided, combined with continuous monitoring of each student's pace of learning, assures placement in those groups best suited to the student's level in each subject. This grouping arrangement provides for the most favorable social setting for each student.

In 1975, it was noted that all gifted children did not respond with equal interest to inquiry learning. Investigation indicated that the intellectually gifted could be divided into two principal categories: those that preferred speed, the rapid information processors (verbal) and those who preferred complexity, the creative problem solvers (spatial). Differentiated programming was achieved by placing verbal learners in analytical, sequential curriculum and spatial learners in open-ended inquiry curriculum. Over the last four years, the staff has researched reliable methods to identify a child's principal mode of information processing, whether it be verbal or spatial. The staff has developed spatial curriculum designed to replace traditional core curriculum. The arts have been employed to develop new spatial core curriculum designed to further the student's creative problem-solving potential. The result is a program that more ably serves the gifted. Additionally, the research generated from the program serves the total educational community by assisting in the recognition of children's individual differences and learning styles. There are few institutions in the United States that are developing spatial curriculum.

## Selection of Students

The students are selected from among many candidates applying for the available vacancies. The following criteria are considered in the selection process:

1. A minimum IQ of 125 on the *Wechsler Intelligence Scale for Children-Revised* or the *Wechsler Preschool and Primary Scale of Intelligence* is necessary for entrance. In addition, a minimum of 13 on the Block Design subtests of these scales is required. Consideration is given to the balance of the performance and verbal scores on the scales. The mean IQ at the school is 140; therefore, children with IQs of 125 are not candidates unless they have other strong recommendations.

2. Achievement test scores are considered if the child has been in school. High scores in conceptual subtests and low scores in skill subtests are indications of underachievement. The school does not serve the underachieving student.

3. Good or excellent social and emotional adjustment

is required. This is assessed through interviews with the parents and child, the psychologist's recommendations, and recommendations from personnel of the child's previous school.
4. Consideration is given to minorities, siblings, sex, ability, and socioeconomic background. The school endeavors to maintain a balance in all these areas, using a scholarship program to insure attendance for low socioeconomic students.

### The Program

Seattle Country Day School is a full-time program for gifted children. Many children attend year after year; therefore, the school has the responsibility of the child's total in-school development. The school is divided into two instructional units. One is a lower school, consisting of five units of sixteen children each, and one unit of sixteen kindergarten students; and the other is a middle school, consisting of five units of sixteen children each. All children have a basic core program consisting of language arts, mathematics, science, social studies, physical education, art, and music. The core program is in the morning and an enrichment program is conducted in the afternoon. A wide variety of electives is offered, including such subjects as physiology, gothic cathedrals (their architecture and history), rocketry, debate, bridge, chess, math, art, drama, music, poetry, photography, foreign languages, archeology, typing, and so forth. One of the features of the school is a midweek ski program. Extensive use is made of field trips, visiting lecturers, and performers. Funding for the school consists of private tuitions, grants, and donations.

### Evaluation of Program

Evaluation is best accomplished by follow-up of the school's graduates. Experience indicates that the students maintain the same success after they leave the school that they obtained while attending the school. The responses from students completing the program indicate an approximate 98 percent success rate. The older a child is when he or she leaves the program, the more likely he or she is to maintain the success pattern.

The school provides parents with a written evaluation of the child's progress in January and June. Parent conferences are held in the spring. Additionally, either the parents or the school may request conferences, if desired. Achievement tests are administered each spring and scores are given to the parents.

## PART C
## ELEMENTARY/SECONDARY PROGRAMS

Four of the eight programs described in this section were initiated between 1941 and 1961, three in the late 1960s, and one in 1974. A review of dates of initiation in relation to the age and grade range of gifted youth served tends to indicate that, with the passage of time and with the acquisition of experience with programs for the gifted, communities move to provide continuity of services for the most able young people from their preschool years through completion of the secondary school. This continuity is essential to steady growth and development at an optimum rate in order to prepare the gifted and talented to take full advantage of the opportunities afforded them by institutions of higher learning.

Gifted students may be admitted to four of the eight programs described while in kindergarten or in grade one and continue until completion of high school. In three programs, admission is deferred until children reach grade four, and in one case, grade five. One of the programs in a very large city school system serves in excess of eighteen thousand gifted students in kindergarten through the twelfth grade. Another program is national in scope in the sense that more than six hundred schools participate, and approximately thirty thousand students in grades four through twelve are served.

While there is some variation in minimum admission requirements, outstanding performance as attested to by both local scholastic records and scores on standardized achievement tests, along with high expectations as expressed by high scores on aptitude tests, are required. Scoring high enough to register an IQ of 130 or higher on an individual intelligence test and placing among the upper 3 percent of one's peers on achievement tests are the basic requirements for admission. Measures of social and emotional development are also taken into account. Self, peer, teacher, parent, and administrator nominations are considered.

Recognition of the strategic importance of the individual in a democracy and special concern about the realization of the high potential of the gifted and talented and their preparation for effective participation as contributing members of society dominate expressions of philosophy, goals, and objectives of the elementary/secondary programs. Creative expression, development of problem solving skills, research insights and competencies, aesthetic sensitivity, and self-direction become the educational goals as teachers and students plan instructional activities, select and execute individual special projects and research endeavors, and engage in group experiences.

The evaluation of student performance involves rigorous pretesting and posttesting, informal self and peer assessment, teacher ratings, and observations made by parents, administrators, and consultants.

**CALASANCTIUS SCHOOL FOR THE
ACADEMICALLY TALENTED**
Calasanctius School
167 Windsor Avenue
Buffalo, New York 14209

*Reported by:*
Laura Perot, Secretary, and
Rev. Bela Krigler, former Headmaster

*Administrative Responsibility:*
Rev. Peter B. Huiner, Headmaster

*For Further Information, Contact:*
Rev. Peter B. Huiner, Headmaster
Calasanctius School
167 Windsor Avenue
Buffalo, New York 14209

### Overview of Program

Started as a preparatory school for boys in 1957 by Father Stephen Gerencser, the nonresidential school, now coeducational, is designed for the academically talented. In general, chidren must show a 130 IQ on the *Wechsler Intelligence Scale for Children-Revised* to be admitted. Although there are a number of faculty of the Piarist Order, it is not a Roman Catholic school. Students do take religion courses, but these are developed on various denominational lines.

The initial concept in planning the program was a five- or six-year sequence for students who had finished the fourth or fifth grade. As time passed, parents requested a lower school that would accommodate children through the fourth grade. Currently, there are approximately 90 students in the lower school, aged five to ten; 90 in the middle school, aged ten through thirteen; and 80 in the upper school. There are a total of 260 students, twenty-four full-time faculty members, and between fifteen to twenty part-time faculty, and forty proctors.

The stated principles of the school include the following:

1. To have convictions based upon solid knowledge and

insight, without intolerance and fanaticism
2. To aspire to be responsible men and women in an age of creeping infantilism
3. To have our internal sources and deep enthusiasm shine through, even in the dark nights of struggle and crises which we may experience in our life.

The purpose of the program has been to encourage brighter-than-average children's natural love of knowledge and inquisitiveness. The program tries to transform the children from spectators into active participants. The teaching evolves around the children's participation in the learning process, through exposing them to a variety of experiences in diverse environmental settings. To achieve this goal, various learning situations are planned and field trips are provided for the children. The learning process is individualized through small groups to involve all children in interaction among themselves and with the teacher. The diverse socioeconomic and ethnic backgrounds of the children through the common aspect of above average intellectual ability create a challenging and interesting learning environment.

## Selection of Students

In order to be enrolled in Calasanctius, the student must score 130 or above on the *Wechsler Intelligence Scale for Children-Revised,* which is administered by a school psychologist. In the Buffalo area every year, there are about two hundred students from each age who meet the IQ qualification of 130. The Wechsler scale has proved to be an excellent tool for insight into mental functioning. To determine visual creativity and some aspects of perceptual ability, the *Wartegg Picture Completion Test* and a modified draw-a-person test are administered. To this is added a standardized short reading test plus a discussion of topics related to a given text. For those who are able (usually by age seven), a written story of approximately two hundred words entitled "My Ideal" is requested. Immediately after the testing, the results are discussed with the parents and they are informed whether the child is capable of facing the challenge of the program. If the child is of the age to benefit, he is included in the discussion. In borderline cases, the parents are informed why it would be better for the child to attend a different school. In a few instances, children are accepted on a trial basis, for example, when the child shows a high level of motivation. In some of these cases, the motivational forces are so strong that the difficulties that might have arisen due to the lower measured mental functioning are overcome. Proper placement is especially important in such cases. Each year, four to five emotionally disturbed but highly talented children are admitted.

## The Program

At Calasanctius, all students are exposed to a great variety of learning experiences in clearly circumscribed fields early in their schooling. In the first three years of the school, all courses are required with the only choices being in foreign languages and some areas of creative arts.

The six-year program of the upper two schools is a carefully developed schema in which inside and outside class activities are balanced. The school recognizes that the program is heavily intellectual and is trying to counterbalance this emphasis with required electives in the arts in each of the six years as well as required music and studio art in the first two years. Mathematics is used as the link between the humanities and sciences. The six-year sequence in the history of civilization is interdisciplinary in nature and is directed toward understanding, rather than judging, the various forms of human civilizations. There is a strong English language and literature sequence and also a foreign language program. In the last four years, there is a series of integrating courses labeled "Phenomenon of Man." These include all the social sciences as well as philosophy and religion courses.

Also important to the Calasanctius program are the Field Study Trip Program and the Seminar Program. The objectives of the former are to coordinate and integrate school learning experiences with real life experiences. These trips may last two to three weeks.

The Seminar Program is an independent research and study program, under the guidance of a proctor. Students are expected to do serious research in the field of their choice, under the guidance of a professional in that particular field who is interested in sharing his knowledge or talent. For each of three consecutive years, students are expected to present a serious paper based upon research (laboratory work and other sources) or creative artwork. The presentation is made in front of a committee of experts. The student is expected to defend his findings in a serious, traumatic, but in all cases a maturing confrontation.

Practically no tax funds are presently available for the education of the gifted in independent schools. Thus, the school relies on three resources: tuition and fees, donations, and contributed services. Many interested people and local foundations have become involved in the school. Donations to the development fund have been in excess of $500,000. To this are added the donations received through a variety of fund-raising activities.

### Evaluation of Program

At the Calasanctius School, high academic achievement is a requirement to remain in school and to graduate. The quality of programming is evaluated in terms of student academic attainment as measured by standardized tests of academic achievement and scholastic aptitude. In the lower grades, students are required to score at or above the eighty-fifth percentile on standardized measures to remain in the program. In the upper school, students are required to take the *Scholastic Aptitude Test* annually and are expected to achieve a sixty-point gain on the combined score each year. As one of several academic requirements for graduation, the student must take five *Advanced Placement Examinations* and receive advanced placement for three of them.

Information obtained from follow-up studies of graduates provides an additional data base for program evaluation. The high quality of the program of studies is further evidenced through these studies by the number of graduates (approximately 96 percent) who attend college, the number of graduates who are admitted to the college or university of their choice, and the number of graduates (approximately 72 percent) who attend graduate school.

**CHICAGO PROGRAM FOR THE GIFTED**
Chicago Public Schools
Room 1114
228 North LaSalle Street
Chicago, Illinois 60601

*Reported by:*
Richard W. Ronvik, Director

*Administrative Responsibility:*
Richard W. Ronvik, Director

*For Further Information, Contact:*
Richard W. Ronvik, Director
Chicago Program for the Gifted
Room 1114
228 North LaSalle Street
Chicago, Illinois 60601

## Overview of Program

The Chicago Gifted Program was established in the late 1960s to provide special programs and services for gifted and talented students in the Chicago public schools. Gifted children are defined as those whose mental ability is accelerated to the degree that special educational services are necessary for them.

Approximately eighteen thousand children in the Chicago public schools participate in a variety of gifted programs which provide differentiated curricula, instructional strategies which accommodate the learning styles of gifted students, and special environments conducive to learning.

The underlying philosophy of Chicago's gifted program is to serve gifted students through special programs. It is the intention of the Gifted Program Office of the Chicago public schools to assist school personnel in the establishment and development of programs specifically designed for gifted students. Basic considerations for developing a program include recognition of the need to provide educational opportunities suitable to individual characteristics and a willingness to introduce new elements into the school curriculum and instructional procedures.

## Selection of Students

The responsibility for identifying and selecting students for participation in programs for gifted children remains at the local school level. The criteria for selection involve various methods, depending upon individual programs and administrative philosophy, but generally includes aptitude scores, achievement scores, class rank, and teacher or counselor recommendation.

The specific methods of selection and identification of gifted students for the various gifted programs are noted in the proposals for each individual program. For some of the citywide gifted programs, special selection criteria are established which are based upon direct performance, such as auditions or regional recognition received. All local program proposals include multiple criteria for identification as required by state guidelines.

A summary of the specific requirements for selecting students for a gifted program is as follows:

1. Identification criteria for the selection of children for gifted programs must be established before the children are selected.
2. A minimum of three factors must be involved in such identification.
3. A part of the criteria used should be based on objective data.
4. Where nationally standardized tests are used as a part of the criteria, specific qualifying scores must be indicated.
5. If teacher recommendation or administrative nomination is used as a part of the criteria for selection, a checklist of observable student behaviors should be included.
6. The criteria for selection should have a direct relationship to the type of program being provided.
7. The criteria for selection should be applied equally to every child in the target population.
8. Students who have been classified in the special education categories of emotionally disturbed, socially maladjusted, early remediation approach, learning disability, speech

impaired, visually impaired, hearing impaired, and physically handicapped should not be precluded from consideration for gifted program selection procedures.

9. Student participation should be voluntary and requires parental consent.

## The Program

The program format varies for each of the programs and services offered. The majority of the programs are partial pull-out arrangements. A description of three program types follows.

LOCAL GIFTED PROGRAMS. The majority of Chicago's 397 gifted programs are local in nature and were developed by individual schools to provide a different type of educational program for a specific type of gifted child. Since there are more than 200 schools with gifted programs, the curricular content and grade levels included vary from school to school. The programs range from strictly academic, including Advanced Placement classes to multitalented programs that involve larger numbers of students. Opportunities are available for gifted students in such topics as the study of man, aerospace technology, earth science, and humanities. Students may also perform various roles in theatrical, dance, or musical productions.

Gifted programs developed by individual schools meet at least 150 minutes a week in a regular classroom with classes ranging from small groups to normal size classes.

DISTRICT CENTERS. In addition to local school programs for the gifted, another organizational structure to meet the needs of highly gifted students is the district center. There are currently fourteen district centers in Chicago offering specialized programs for the gifted students in their respective districts.

District centers have the advantage of having a wider population from which to screen, identify, and select gifted students. Personnel at the centers can more readily plan a program that is both accelerated and in-depth for the very able student. The centers draw a limited number of students from schools in the district, usually bringing them into the program one full day or two half-days per week. Two of the centers enroll students on a full-time basis.

ALL-CITY PROGRAMS. All-city gifted programs are administered by the central gifted office and are conducted in local schools throughout the city or in facilities outside school buildings. Chicago museum programs represent one of the most unique offerings for gifted children in the nation. All Chicago public high school students identified as gifted by local school criteria are eligible for consideration in these programs. Final selection is made on the basis of applications, recommendations, interviews, and auditions. All-city programs include making use of Chicago's museums, planetarium, zoos, and other educational facilities.

Services for gifted children in the Chicago public schools are funded by the Gifted Unit, Illinois Office of Education, under Article 14A of the School Code of Illinois. In the Chicago public schools, the gifted program is administered through the Department of Government Funded Programs, Bureau of Special Programs. Hence, funding is basically from the state and is authorized by a section of the school code. The state budget for gifted education is appropriated annually by the state legislature.

## Evaluation of Program

Evaluation is accomplished by outside agencies when required by the state and by annual on-site visits by state evaluation teams.

Also, each program director completes a year-end final report which is based on objectives and activities and the degree to which these were accomplished. The individual reports are summarized in a final report to the state.

A series of comprehensive evaluation visits are made to various programs throughout the year by gifted program specialists from the central office of the Chicago Board of Education. Each of these visits is followed by a recommendation report of the program with a follow-up schedule of assistance from program personnel in three decentralized gifted program offices.

A fiscal evaluation of every program is accomplished annually by a team of auditors from the Chicago school system's Department of Government Funded Programs.

**THE CULLOWHEE EXPERIENCE: A SUMMER PROGRAM FOR GIFTED STUDENTS**
Western Carolina University
216 Killian Building
Cullowhee, North Carolina 28723

*Reported by:*
J. Milford Clark

*Administrative Responsibility:*
J. Milford Clark

*For Further Information, Contact:*
J. Milford Clark
Western Carolina University
216 Killian Building
Cullowhee, North Carolina 28723

## Overview of Program

"The Cullowhee Experience" is a summer enrichment program for academically gifted students in grades five through ten. The program was established in 1958 and has operated annually since that time. Students come from several states with North Carolina, South Carolina, Georgia, and Florida being most represented.

The program emphasizes enrichment experiences different from those in which students are involved during the regular school year. The program provides a broad, flexible structure, allowing the student to pursue areas of personal interest at his or her own level of ability. Students are encouraged to operate on higher levels of cognition, such as those classified by Benjamin Bloom.

## Selection of Students

Students who attend the program must be nominated by their schools. Students are generally required to have an IQ of 130 or higher on either the *Wechsler Intelligence Scale for Children-Revised* or the *Stanford-Binet Intelligence Scale*. The student's achievement test scores must be two grades above grade placement. Personal data, such as interests, accomplishments, health, etc., are also considered. Members of a selection panel review all nominations and then select students based primarily on the above criteria.

## The Program

Students are grouped according to the grade level which they have just completed during the regular school year. The content for each grade is organized around a broad theme rather than a specific subject area. Students are involved in independent research, group discussions, group presentations, simulations, and field trips. Resource personnel are regularly invited to the classroom. Students have access to all university resources.

The program has an afternoon recreational component. All students participate in a variety of cultural arts and physical recreational activities. Students live in university dormitories supervised by counselors and a housemother. Classes are conducted in the university laboratory school adjacent to the campus. Academic teachers are public school teachers who have experience in teaching gifted students.

The program is completely supported by student tuition and fees.

## Evaluation of Program

A nonstandardized questionnaire is administered to parents, teachers, and counselors to ascertain strengths and weaknesses of the program and to elicit suggestions for improvement. Evaluation is the responsibility of the director of the program and is undertaken on an annual basis.

**FUTURE PROBLEM SOLVING PROGRAM**
Programs on Gifted and Talented Education
Department of Educational Psychology
University of Georgia
Athens, Georgia 30602

*Reported by:*
E. Paul Torrance

*Administrative Responsibility:*
Anne B. Crabbe

*For Further Information, Contact:*
Anne B. Crabbe
Gifted and Talented Programs
Nebraska Department of Education
P.O. Box 94987
Lincoln, Nebraska 68509

## Overview of Program

The Future Problem Solving Program was initiated in 1974-75. During the first year, it involved only seven senior high schools in northeast Georgia. During 1975-76, the program became statewide and involved about thirty schools. In 1976-77, the program became nationwide and involved approximately one hundred and fifty schools and about three thousand gifted and talented students. In 1977-78, over three hundred schools and six thousand students in twenty-six states participated. For 1978-79, the best estimate was that over six hundred schools and thirty thousand students in forty-three states were involved. In addition, there is active involvement in Guam, the Marshall Islands, and South Africa.

In general, the population served consists of students in identified gifted programs in grades four through twelve. However, these essentials are not monitored rigorously. Some teachers have made successful modifications for children as young as kindergarten. In a few instances, the program has been tried with classes including a wide range of abilities.

It is believed that a considerable part of differentiated curricula for gifted students should be devoted to helping them enlarge, enrich, and make their images of the future more accurate. It is also important that gifted children become proficient in the use of a disciplined, deliberate process of creative problem solving, as they will need to solve future problems.

The broad objectives of the program are to:

1. Develop high level skills in a deliberate, disciplined approach to creative problem solving
2. Develop high level skills in teamwork and interdependence
3. Develop high level skills in interdisciplinary thinking
4. Develop research skills for studying the future.

### Selection of Students

Students are selected by the participating schools and/or school systems, using whatever criteria they normally employed in identifying gifted and talented students. The *Handbook for Training Future Problem Solving Teams* (Torrance, Torrance, and Williams, 1977) gives suggestions for selecting students, but there is no insistence that these suggestions be followed.

### The Program

The specific content will continue to vary from year to year, depending upon the interests of the participants and the emergence of future problems. In 1978-79, much of the content of the program was based upon the results of a survey of the interests and preferences of students involved. The following description of the 1977-78 program will illustrate different aspects of the program, scheduling, and so forth.

In September, the *Handbook* was mailed to participating teachers. This *Handbook* described the objectives of the program, gave suggestions for training teams in each of the stages of the creative problem solving process, provided practice problems for each stage of the process and for the entire process, and listed additional resources for the study of the future and for teaching skills in creative problem solving.

In October, teachers were asked to administer a brief pretest to help evaluate the program. For one random sample of schools, this consisted of a survey of attitudes about the future, an abbreviated self-directed study readiness scale, and a brainstorming instrument based on a future problem. For a second random sample of schools, the pretest consisted of a scenario writing exercise.

In November, the first practice problem was mailed to participating teams. The problem was concerned with problems growing out of predictions concerning future shortages of safe drinking water. Practice was given only in obtaining and analyzing information about the problem, defining the problem, and brainstorming alternative solutions. Teachers selected the three best team solutions and mailed them to the University of Georgia for evaluation and feedback. Each team was sent an evaluation of its performance and suggestions for improvement. Top ranking teams in each division: junior, grades four through six; intermediate, grades seven through nine; and senior, grades ten through twelve, were sent certificates of excellence.

In January, the second practice problem was sent and concerned problems of developing a will to end hunger. This time, teams were asked to carry the problem solving process through the development of appropriate criteria and the application of criteria to evaluate alternatives and to make a decision about the best solution. In February, the third problem was distributed and was concerned with the problems of the increasing heterogeneity and diversity in society and in educating people to understand the point of view of a person from a different culture. On the basis of performance on this problem, teams for the annual Future Problem Solving Bowl competition were selected.

In March, participating schools were invited to involve all students in a scenario writing contest. Students were asked to use their solutions in the third practice problem as the basis for their scenarios concerning the future of our increasingly heterogeneous society. This practice involved teams in all phases of the creative problem solving process, including solution selling and planning for implementation.

Ten teams in each of the three divisions were invited to the University of Georgia for the team competition. In addition, all participating schools were invited to send individual competitors. Teams from the following states were invited: Georgia, Florida, Mississippi, New York, New Jersey, Pennsylvania, Michigan, Colorado, Kansas, California, and Washington. Awards were made for team problem solving, individual problem solving, scenario writing, and solution selling. The audience served as judges.

The major source of funds has been the royalties from the books and tests of the originator of the program. In 1979-80, the national bowl was funded through the joint efforts of the University of Nebraska, the Nebraska Association for Gifted Children, and the Nebraska State Department of Education. The statewide and system-wide programs have also had various local supporters. Generally, parents, sponsors, and local school boards have provided transportation to the bowls. Efforts are now being made to establish a permanent home for the program through the University of Nebraska Foundation.

## Evaluation of Program

Since the program has always operated on limited funds, it has not been possible to have an external evaluation of the program. Evaluations by teachers and sponsors participating in the program have been used. During the past three years, pretesting and posttesting, teacher evaluation, and student evaluation have been employed. Large quantities of evaluation data have been accumulated, but lack of resources has limited the analysis of these data.

**MENTALLY GIFTED MINOR PROGRAM**
Garden Grove Unified School District
10331 Stanford Avenue
Garden Grove, California 92640

*Reported by:*
Judith J. Roseberry

*Administrative Responsibility:*
Judith J. Roseberry

*For Further Information, Contact:*
Judith J. Roseberry
Garden Grove Unified School District
10331 Stanford Avenue
Garden Grove, California 92640

## Overview of Program

The Mentally Gifted Minors Program of the Garden Grove Unified School District was established in 1961. The program is designed to accomplish the following objectives: gifted students will excel in academic achievement; learn a degree of self-directedness appropriate to their maturity level; learn to take responsibility for their own conduct and obligations; learn to seek opportunities for creative expression; increase their aesthetic awareness; improve their ability to think critically; learn tolerance of divergent views; seek alternative solutions to problems prior to action; grow in their commitment to democratic ideals, philosophy, and process; gain career aspirations commensurate with their abilities; develop broadened positive interest; and be more motivated to attend school.

To accomplish these objectives, a qualitatively differentiated program is offered to approximately fifteen hundred students in grades one through twelve. Both the elementary and secondary gifted classes are based on the premise that the development of the unique abilities of the gifted can best be served by association with other gifted students; by diversification and expansion of the curriculum; by teachers whose interest, personality, and skills are suited to education of the gifted; and by appropriate and special materials and techniques for advanced study.

At the elementary level, there are six primary classes and sixteen upper grade classes. These are full-time special day classes. Children go through a district testing and screening process each year in an effort to identify all gifted pupils. The primary classes have been established for those gifted pupils whose needs manifest themselves in the early grades. Parents of these youngsters attend an orientation meeting and have the option of placing their child in the special classes.

The elementary program of special classes is qualitatively different in the following ways: the basic skills essential for acquiring advanced level knowledge are introduced to the students earlier; basic state required curriculum content is accelerated; and the approach to the basic content is upgraded so that differentiated enrichment units may be introduced. There is greater emphasis on higher levels of cognition; specially designed enrichment units become the major curriculum emphasis; provisions are made for the self-selection of some topics by students, based on their specific and sometimes unusual interests.

The secondary program consists of special classes, seminars, advanced topics, honors sections, and advanced placement within each secondary school. Special classes are designed to further develop the gifted students' high aptitude for reasoning and conceptualization, to stimulate inquiring minds to pursue intensive investigation and problem solving activities, to allow for the development of the great variety of individual interests, to permit students to develop and use their own initiative, and to develop awareness of the interrelatedness of all subject matter.

Staff development is provided at all levels so that teachers of the gifted can expand and broaden the student's learning experience. Staff development provides the basis for developing suitable organizational patterns to implement the qualitatively different curriculum—nongraded, individualized, interdisciplinary, team-teaching approaches—at both the elementary and secondary levels.

The heart of the program is, of course, the students. The administration, teachers, and psychologists work closely together to provide optimum placement, guidance, and instruction to the gifted child.

## Selection of Students

All students in the district have an equal opportunity for screening for the program. Various screening devices are used. Nominations come from parents, teachers, administrators, and other school personnel. Screening instruments vary and change as more reliable methods are determined.

Each elementary student is tested by a school psychologist using the *Stanford-Binet Intelligence Scale*, the *Weschler Intelligence Scale for Children-Revised*, or the *Leiter International Performance Scale*. This process is prescribed by state guidelines. Secondary youngsters are identified on the basis of scores on group tests in subject matter areas. The state of California requires that the student score 132 on an individually administered intelligence test. In addition, a case study is developed on each child, including as much data as possible. When all documentation is assembled, a committee reviews the case and recommends for or against placement.

The guidelines allow committees to include a small percentage of students who do not achieve the required test scores but give every evidence that they would benefit from the program through successful experience. Great care must be taken any time a child's educational program is changed.

A program for culturally different students also exists in Garden Grove. It is recognized that some students are able to demonstrate gifted ability and still be unable to qualify on the basis of test scores because of cultural factors.

## The Program

The program is full time for elementary students and consists of basic skills development with enrichment to provide the experiences necessary for the gifted student.

Instructional content of the program includes research skills, debate, public speaking, ancient Greece and Greek mythology (fourth grade), Italian and the European Renaissance (fifth grade), and Elizabethan England and Shakespeare (sixth grade). Science units include great people of science, archaeology, paleontology, and oceanography.

Teaching strategies employed include: individualized instruction, team teaching, nongraded classrooms, inquiry method, direct teaching, instructional aides, community mentors, peer counseling, and others.

Secondary students participate in the gifted program from one to three hours each day. Elementary students are scheduled for all-day programs.

Total funding is from the state of California, based on the number of students identified and participating each year.

## Evaluation of Program

The evaluation design of the Mentally Gifted Minors Program of the Garden Grove Unified School District was implemented in April 1976 and is outlined as follows:

1. The eighteen students now in grade one will be tested in April each year for three years starting April 1976 with the *Comprehensive Tests of Basic Skills* (CTBS)—Form S, Level B. In grade two, the test will be CTBS—Form S, Level C. In grade three, the test will be CTBS—Form S, Level 1.

2. Each year fifty students from each class in grades five, six, seven, and eight will be chosen at random for testing with the appropriate level of the CTBS—Form S. Those students in grades six and eight will not take separate tests, but will be tested with their grade level as part of the district's testing program.

3. Fifty eleventh grade students from a single high school will be tested with the CTBS—Form S, Level 4, each year in April. The full battery test will be used for this group.

4. Fifty ninth grade students, chosen at random, will take the *Watson-Glaser Critical Thinking Appraisal* each year for three years starting in April 1976.

Additional information for program evaluation is collected annually from questionnaires directed to students, teachers, and parents and from anecdotal records of atypical activities maintained by teachers in the gifted program.

**PINE VIEW PROGRAM FOR GIFTED**
Sarasota County
2525 Tami Sola
Sarasota, Florida 33577

*Reported by:*
John D. Woolever, Principal

*Administrative Responsibility:*
John D. Woolever, Principal

*For Further Information, Contact:*
John D. Woolever, Principal
Pine View Program for Gifted
2525 Tami Sola
Sarasota, Florida 33577

## Overview of Program

The Pine View program was begun in July 1958 under Title III of the Elementary and Secondary Education Act of 1965. After the termination of federal support, the program continued under state and local funding, as prescribed by law in Florida.

The program serves any qualified student resident of Sarasota County in grades four through twelve, in a departmentalized program on a daily schedule which parallels other district schools' programs. In addition to meeting admission requirements, students in the program are expected to maintain higher than average skills in required studies as well as in elective and enrichment courses, based on state and district approved guidelines.

The philosophy of the Pine View program is that typically gifted children have certain needs and abilities which may vary in depth, latitude, and intensity. The goal of the program is to meet these needs through a special flexible curriculum which fosters individual creativity and greater rates of development and fluidity in the instructional program. The development of special interests is provided through an environment and instructional schedule which permits the student to explore, experiment, and move beyond the routine curricular offerings of the typical classroom. Personal development focuses on self-direction, independence, self-concept and motivation with greater responsibility, performance, and obligations expected of each student enrolled.

Program goals are aided by flexibility of scheduling of program offerings and instructional personnel, the physical structure of the classrooms, and opportunities to move beyond curricular and physical boundaries of traditional pre-college instruction.

## Selection of Students

Students are selected from all schools in the district. The screening procedure starts with referrals from teachers, parents, interested students, and identification through data processing. Scores from district tests are analyzed annually, and student data are studied at the school level using grades, standardized tests, evaluation checklists, recommendations, group IQ scores, achievement tests, and the *Slosson Intelligence Test*. After local school personnel have examined these data, the information is forwarded to the program's staff. After initial favorable screening, and depending upon the age of the child, *The Quick Test*, the *Academic Promise Tests*, the *Survey of Study Habits and Attitudes*, and a standardized mathematics and reading test are administered. Children in the upper 5 percent are administered the *Wechsler Intelligence Scales for Children-Revised*, the *Wide Range Achievement Test*, the *Children's Personality Questionnaire*, and any other psychological test of the psychologist's choice. Occasionally, the *Stanford-Binet Intelligence Scale* is given when necessary. Data are then given to a staffing committee of no less than five persons who individually and collectively make written evaluations to justify their recommendations for the child's admission. Usually a member of the staff and/or the principal will interview the parents and child prior to admission.

Data are also collected from the parents and child pertaining to student characteristics, student needs, special program requests, and objectives. When indicated, other appropriate tests are also administered if there is some indication of a learning disability, so the child when enrolled may be admitted to the specific learning disability program.

Since enrollment in the program is on a voluntary basis if the child qualifies, the student must maintain a degree of performance which is examined every grading period by a special staff committee. Should the child not maintain a suitable academic performance, he or she may be redirected to the district school with an option to return to the program later. Retesting with the same assessment instruments would not have to be undertaken.

## The Program

The facilities include a collection of twenty-five separate, moveable buildings, each serving as a classroom and located on five wooded acres adjoining the campuses of an elementary, junior high, and senior high school. The program is administered as a school unit, but the children are scheduled into classes at the other school sites also. This facility serves as a broad campus program, utilizing the least restrictive environment, which permits students to have a wide choice of courses, to participate in a greater variety of activities, to cross grade levels, and to avail themselves of services of several schools which might emhasize certain fields and areas of concentration.

The Pine View program emphasizes acceleration as well as enrichment, making no specific distinction, based on its goals and philosophy of attempting to meet the needs of the child in his total environment, exclusive of time and space constraints. The program is an accountability one where the children are enrolled in classes and/or courses required by the state, the local school system, and choices that are exclusively those of the Pine View staff. There is no exclusive set of teaching strategies, since both individual teachers as well as each department are involved in establishing and/or modifying its offerings and approaches. The keystone is flexibility and adapting to need as identified by the child as well as the community.

Class grouping is basically by grade; however, children are scheduled into classes based on mastery, performance, and interest, which results in many ungraded sections. The master schedule takes into consideration a range of nine grades, four through twelve, as well as the schedule of the adjoining schools in which some children may be enrolled for one period or more. Some courses are scheduled for varying lengths of time, different days of the week, or even on alternate days and alternate weeks. Some classes are by appointment. All children are individually scheduled annually with input from children, teachers, and parents. A three-year plan beginning in the seventh grade is proposed for each student to enable the staff to project some anticipated requests. The plan may be modified by the parents at any time.

Equipment is typical of any school, with the exception that elementary and junior high school students may be taking classes in which equipment is also used by upperclassmen. An example would be in a science class where sixth graders use a laboratory in which advanced chemistry, radiation, and so forth, are also taught. Sophisticated equipment is also available to students as required by their science instructor or individualized project. This is also true in art studio, media, and other areas.

Besides a strong emphasis on broadening, acceleration, mini-courses, and special clubs, noncredit classes specially designed by teachers or requested by students, are offered from eight to eighteen weeks. A subject of interest may begin with some students wishing to enrich themselves in a particular area and may conclude as a course or an academically oriented club extended into after-school sessions. In addition to teachers in specialized subjects, volunteers and guests from the community are used throughout the year. Advanced placement, performance contracting, professional experience off campus, and independent study combinations are also offered, depending upon the grade level and proficiency of the students requesting individualized programming.

Funding is provided through the usual state sources and on a comparable basis with other programs, since the program is managed and operated as a typical school but with some variations that are inherent in an exceptional child program. Parents and the community in general contribute much to supplement resources, from money for expendables and special instructional equipment to construction of some of the buildings.

## Evaluation of Programs

Evaluation is undertaken by individuals appointed by the Florida State Department of Education, Exceptional Child Division. The evaluation is entitled an Educational Program Audit, which consists of an inspection and evaluation of all data to see that the program conforms to both state and local guidelines, the details of which could change annually. The expectations to be met are standardized by the state and are made available every fall, and the audits are made on a ten-day notification. Although a regular pattern of audit dates by month or year is not in existence, in the past ten years Pine View has been audited seven times on a random selection basis. Items for evaluation include student selection and identification procedures, conformance with state laws and local guidelines, adult and child input regarding needs, programming, academic performance, and others.

**ROEPER CITY AND COUNTRY SCHOOL**
2190 North Woodward Avenue
Bloomfield Hills, Michigan 48013

*Reported by:*
Ruthan Brodsky

*Administrative Responsibility:*
Annemarie Roeper and Philip Parsons

*For Further Information, Contact:*
Ruthan Brodsky
Roeper City and Country School
2190 North Woodward Avenue
Bloomfield Hills, Michigan 48013

## Overview of Program

Roeper School was founded in 1941 as a nursery and lower elementary school. In 1956, the school was accredited as an independent school for gifted children as it expanded into a school program for nursery through eighth grade. In 1965, the school again expanded to include a high school, and in 1969, the first twelfth grade class graduated.

Roeper School draws students from over forty communities in the Detroit metropolitan area. The students represent a variety of ethnic, racial, religious, and economic backgrounds. Over 10 percent of the students receive scholarship aid in varying amounts to enable them to attend the school.

The educational program for gifted students at Roeper School is an environment and a model to experience the events that take place in a person's life. It is impossible to separate how this school may prepare a student for his future from the objectives of the school's philosophy. Roeper School embraces a holistic approach to human development. Every facet of the school is interwoven in this philosophy, which is concerned with the impact of life on gifted students and the impact they will make on our society.

The school's concept of the belief in basic human rights for all persons is the focal point for equipping its students for their futures. To work toward the consummation of this belief, Roeper School offers its students an educational milieu with far more than academic efficiency as the primary goal. Holistic education is essential.

Human awareness and the role of the individual in society are of equal importance. Society is built around the quality of human relations. In this school, an attempt is made to mirror society by recognizing and dealing with the vibrant web of human relations that both entangles and improves human enterprises. Gifted children are acutely aware, and at a very early age, of their environment, of hidden curricula, of morals, ethics, and injustices. Therefore, in addition to providing direction for learning to use the intellect and acquire skills, Roeper School endeavors to prepare its students for life by giving them a place to observe and an opportunity to practice being rational, humane, and creative individuals. Students are also given an awareness of social needs which involve the values by which society lives.

This philosophy requires the following commitments for the adult, both parent and teacher.
1.  Making equal human rights for all people a priority
2.  A complete commitment to justice rather than power
3.  A willingness to allow the child to participate in the shaping of his own destiny and to consciously prepare him for it
4.  To prepare this future generation to deal with the unknown
5.  To view the needs of each child independently.

Implementing these goals, the Roeper School teaches the child about controls and interpersonal interaction. This includes the concept that trust motivates a child to learn and to direct himself.

## Selection of Students

Students approved for admission must have outstanding intellectual and creative ability and the capacity to function at a level commensurate with the school population so that they can become a contributing member in a group of children of similar abilities. All children applying must take a diagnostic test either at the school or through other arrangements. A generally acceptable IQ level is 130.

All school records are screened, and an interview with the parents and child by the admissions director is also held. Elementary age applicants spend part of a day in a classroom situation with the teacher and additional faculty to observe. Faculty and administrators then evaluate the student. Upper elementary, junior high, and high school students are also given placement tests. Placement is based on academic levels and social and emotional development.

## The Program

The Roeper School is divided into a Lower School and an Upper School. In the Lower School, students are grouped according to age in stages as follows:

STAGE II. In this stage, children ranging in age from three to seven are housed in the domes. Enrolled are approximately one hundred and ten children in six groups, served by six homeroom teachers, assistant teachers, and special teachers.

STAGE III. In this stage, children ranging in age from seven to nine are housed in a small building by themselves. Enrolled are approximately eighty children, served by four homeroom teachers, assistant teachers, and part-time special teachers.

STAGE IV. In this stage, children ranging in age from nine through twelve are housed in three separate buildings. Enrolled are approximately one hundred and twenty students in five classrooms, served by five homeroom teachers and special teachers.

Some principles of operation are similar in all areas of the Lower School. Others, of course, change according to the different development levels of the children. Specific goals are set for each individual, based on a particular child's characteristics, needs, and interests. General goals are developed for all, based on the philosophy of the school and the reality of the world. The philosophy encompasses not only the structure of the classroom, but also the administrative structure. The school is operated on democratic principles.

A unique feature in the Lower School is the network of special classes. Most of these classes, with expert instructors teaching each subject area, are available for all students, beginning at age three. These classes include physical education, music, library, science, art, French, photography, and drama. This program of special instruction has been found to be very important to gifted children, for it gives them greater opportunity for individual choice. In addition, as the child grows and matures, he is given more freedom in choosing those special classes outside the homeroom. At the same time, the child is asked to accept an increasing degree of responsibility to these special classes in terms of a commitment of attendance and course length.

The Upper School enrolls students thirteen years of age and older. The program of studies is composed of courses in math, science, social studies, English, physical education, foreign language, and fine arts. Any of these can be adapted, modified, or waived in terms of the specific need of the student at any given point in time. The goal is to provide a challenging, meaningful, individual learning experience, based on each student's abilities, needs, and interests. The classes are varied in size from six to twenty-four students, and a class period lasts from forty minutes to two hours. For example, on a daily basis, teaching foreign languages is more effective in shorter periods of time, whereas art and laboratory sciences need a longer class period. Each student has his or her own daily schedule with time for study in the library, for socializing in the student lounge, for conversations with teachers, or for independent study in the art room, science lab, or specific classes. Since students have a choice of classes they take within the program of courses offered, they are expected to be in attendance in those classes. They are also expected to be on campus from 9:00 A.M. to 3:15 P.M. every day and may leave only if participating in a work-study program and/or with special permission from their counselor.

The students in the Upper School are expected to support the whole community in a variety of ways. A wide choice of community services offers an area of interest for everyone to volunteer. A student-staff court was also established to see that students are held responsible for their behavior and to assist in community concerns. Other than this elected group, there is no student government in the traditional sense for the whole community deals with its own governing in assemblies, committees, or whatever is appropriate to the problem at hand.

Roeper School is an independent school. Its finances are based on tuition, fees, and contributions.

## Evaluation of Program

Every faculty member, student, and parent is involved in the evaluation of the students and the program on a continuing basis. Because the program is individualized, each student is evaluated on a regular basis by the teacher or counselor, and other teachers on a regular basis. Written reports on the student's progress are required twice a year in addition to parent conferences. All students participate in their own evaluation. Letter grades are not used for evaluation until a student reaches the ninth grade.

Within the framework of the specific and general goals of the three stages of the Lower School, each teacher establishes her own classroom environment, including choice of texts and materials. Programs are evaluated on a continuing basis within each stage by the teachers and administrators. This is considered staff development and is an integral part of the education program. All faculty members, including special teachers, administrators, and parents have input regarding all programs.

The Upper School faculty is divided into traditional departments. Programs are developed and evaluated within these departments, together with administrators on a continuing basis. Teachers at this level also select their choice of materials and texts. At the end of each year, Upper School students also evaluate their teachers.

Because the program at Roeper School is individualized both for the student and teacher, new programs and courses may be introduced with great flexibility.

Formal evaluation of teachers is also undertaken. New teachers are evaluated by their peers and the administration after their first year. Subsequently, faculty are evaluated at any time by any other faculty member, administrator, or parent.

## TALCOTT MOUNTAIN SCIENCE CENTER PROGRAMS FOR THE GIFTED
Talcott Mountain Science Center
Montevideo Road
Avon, Connecticut 06001

*Reported by:*
Donald P. LaSalle, Director

*Administrative Responsibility:*
Donald P. LaSalle, Director

*For Further Information, Contact:*
Donald P. LaSalle, Director
Talcott Mountain Science Center
Montevideo Road
Avon, Connecticut 06001

### Overview of Program

Talcott Mountain Science Center programs for the gifted were begun in 1969. For the most part, the programs serve Connecticut students in grades four through twelve; however, a few programs have reached students from a much broader geographical area.

The programs are divided into three categories: both Saturday and summer independent study programs and regular school day enrichment activities for students already enrolled in their school system's programs for the gifted.

The philosophy of all three programs is similar—namely, that science investigation is an ideal process in which to engage gifted young minds. By observing nature, formulating questions, seeking answers, and developing natural principles which lead to new observations, the students are participating in an exciting spiral of growth. Given the tools of scientific investigation to extend their senses and a highly trained, enthusiastic staff, each student can become a whirlwind in this learning spiral.

### Selection of Students

Students are nominated for the Talcott Mountain Science

Center programs by teachers and administrators from the students' schools. A broad spectrum of criteria is examined, ranging from IQ scores, standardized achievement scores and school grades, to the Renzulli-Hartmann behavioral characteristics form, teacher recommendations, and self-nomination. The objective is to identify those students who are capable, creative, analytical, and able to work independently. A student is expected to score in the upper 3 percent in both objective and subjective measures, although no single score on the nomination form guarantees a student admittance.

## The Program

The programs follow closely the stages of Renzulli's Triad Model. Following brief exploratory activities or overviews to each of Talcott Mountain's specialties (astronomy, chronobiology, computer sciences, alternate energy sources, ecology, geology, meteorology, radio/electronics), each student selects a subject or topic of interest. Skills are taught to allow each student to succeed at the tasks he or she has selected, and the student undertakes an independent study project for the semester or a longer period for older students.

Students in grades four through six, who are in the weekday in-school programs, are more involved in teacher directed and in-depth explorations into topics selected by students and/or staff.

Typical student-teacher ratios are less than ten to one. Each student is responsible to a particular staff member, who supervises and advises the student in his or her work. For much of the time, each student is absorbed in individual project work. At other times, groups of five to one hundred students may be grouped in order to instruct the students on technique, to present latest research findings, and so forth.

Fundamental to a successful science program is adequate equipment. Talcott Mountain Science Center students utilize seven computer terminals connected to three different processors, fifteen telescopes in the six-inch to twelve and one-half inch range, a complete weather station, geology and ecology field equipment, medical instruments, electronic test and construction equipment, and extensive new laboratory space. Students are encouraged to use this equipment and are instructed in its proper use. Resource persons and equipment from nearby universities and colleges, hospitals, and research laboratories are utilized.

The programs are supported financially by the communities sending students to the Center's programs. Since the programs are approved by the Connecticut Department of Education, two-thirds of the tuition costs are reimbursed to the town by the state of Connecticut. This incentive has contributed to the success of the program.

## Evaluation of Program

The programs are evaluated by students and, in the weekday courses, by the students and their teachers in the gifted program. Components evaluated include attitudes of students toward the program and toward science, skills and subject matter acquisition, relevance of acquired skill and knowledge to other studies, and instructor teaching techniques.

In addition, each student is evaluated each semester by his or her advisor on a variety of items related to both cognitive and affective development.

**PART D**
**SECONDARY PROGRAMS**

The six secondary programs described in this section maintain to some degree the type of continuity of educational opportunity which characterizes the combined elementary/secondary programs described in the previous section. Many of the students accepted for admission in these secondary programs are from feeder schools which conduct programs for the gifted and the talented from the kindergarten through the eighth grade, but which may or may not provide services for highly promising youth through high school.

Three of the six secondary programs described are conducted in well-known specialized, full-time, self-contained secondary schools established by individual school districts in 1952, 1957, and 1965, respectively. In two other programs, gifted students from throughout the state area are brought together in a single location for intensive study during the summer to constitute what is known as the Governor's School in one state and the Governor's Honors Program in another state. These two state-wide summer programs were initiated in 1963 and 1964. The sixth program, starting in 1971, is developing as a consortium involving a major university which provides leadership for research, curricular developments, and assists with a comprehensive, statewide search in six eastern and southeastern states which are currently providing weekend and summer programs for approximately seven thousand mathematically precocious secondary school students. The consortium is in the process of adding science and language arts as major areas of study.

Criteria for selection and admission to these six programs are consistent with the rigorous requirements for admission to the other programs described in this section. High prior achievement commensurate with high scores on standardized aptitude tests, nomination by responsible lay and professional personnel, and the applicants' own expressions of goals and aspirations influence acceptance into a given program.

The three full-time schools offer comprehensive college preparatory programs with heavy emphasis on problem-solving and research skills, while at the same time providing a wide range of opportunities for participation in the performing and other creative arts. Many students earn college credits in cooperating institutions of higher learning by the time they complete high school graduation requirements. The two statewide programs conducted full time during the summer and the university-sponsored program conducted on weekends and during the summer are designed to augment, extent, and enrich the programs students pursue in their regular secondary schools.

Funding for these six programs comes in the main from local and state tax sources, with some support from private foundations. The allocation of state and local monies to specialized programs for the gifted and talented seems to suggest a growing recognition of the importance of enhancing educational opportunities for this exceptional group of young people.

Evaluation of student and staff performance in these programs seems to be as rigorous and demanding as the study and activity components in the curriculum. Standardized and nonstandardized tests are administered regularly. Teacher and student assessments are also considered in the evaluation process.

**BENJAMIN FRANKLIN SENIOR HIGH SCHOOL**
719 South Carrollton Avenue
New Orleans, Louisiana 70118

*Reported by:*
Mildred Guichard, Counselor

*Administrative Responsibility:*
Carolyn F. Schofield, Principal

*For Further Information, Contact:*
Carolyn F. Schofield, Principal
Benjamin Franklin Senior High School
719 South Carrollton Avenue
New Orleans, Louisiana 70118

## Overview of Program

Benjamin Franklin Senior High School is administered by the Orleans Parish School Board. The school began operation in 1957 with only a tenth grade. In subsequent years, ninth, eleventh, and twelfth grades were added; and in 1960, the first class graduated. Franklin brings together students from the entire city area who, working together, develop the social maturity so necessary in today's highly mobile society.

Since Franklin's minimum admission requirement is an IQ of 120, all instruction is geared to the level of the superior student. Arrangements have been made to allow some of our most outstanding students to attend college concurrently. Approximately fifty talented students are enrolled in the New Orleans Center for Creative Arts, attending Franklin for four class periods a day and the New Orleans Center for Creative Arts for three or four class periods for specialized and intensified training in the arts. Students are also given the opportunity to participate in Franklin's Executive Intern program.

The general objectives of the Benjamin Franklin Senior High School are as follows:

1. To develop those work-study skills and habits in the subject matter areas necessary for high level success in college

2. To develop the ability to do critical thinking in mathematical, scientific, and social situations and in the language arts
3. To develop an appreciation of the contributions of both the humanities and sciences to the welfare of man
4. To develop intellectual curiosity in the humanities and in the sciences
5. To develop initiative and originality in the humanities and the sciences
6. To develop an awareness of the individual's capacities and an awareness of the enjoyment that can be derived from the exercise of these capacities
7. To develop a feeling of responsibility to the family, the school, and the community in which the individual may find himself

### Selection of Students

The admission requirements at Franklin require a minimum IQ of 120. Students may be admitted at the ninth, tenth, and eleventh grades. For grades nine and ten, a composite score at or above the seventh-fifth percentile on the *SRA High School Placement Test* is required. For the eleventh grade, a composite score at or above the ninety-fifth percentile on the *Iowa Tests of Educational Development* is required.

To continue in the school, a student must maintain a satisfactory grade average the previous year as follows:

1. Ninth Grade—C average for eighth grade English, mathematics, and social studies
2. Tenth Grade—an overall B average for all ninth grade subjects except physical education with no failing grade in any subject
3. Eleventh Grade—an overall B average for all tenth grade subjects except physical education with no failing grade in any subject

### The Program

As a school for students of superior intellectual capacity, less time is needed for routine drill; therefore, greater emphasis can be placed upon problem solving, creative activities, exploration, and upon experiences which involve difficult and abstract thinking.

To permit greater flexibility in programming, Franklin operates on a seven-period day. All classes meet fifty minutes a day, five days a week, thirty-six weeks a year. The seven period school day permits students who so desire to complete requirements for graduation in three years.

Students who desire to enroll as part-time college students may do so with the approval of the principal. College credit earned may be used as high school or college credit.

The school participates in an active program of interscholastic sports, including football, basketball, baseball, track, golf, and swimming for boys and basketball, softball, track, and swimming for girls. Students have an opportunity to participate in a variety of other extracurricular activities.

There are a number of program options available at Franklin. These include the following:

COLLEGE PREPARATORY. The college preparatory program consists basically of academic subjects designed to give the student a foundation to enable him to cope with the demands of college work. In choosing electives, the student is encouraged to choose those most closely related to his or her chosen academic course of study.

NEW ORLEANS CENTER FOR CREATIVE ARTS. Participation in the New Orleans Center for Creative Arts (NOCCA) allows Franklin students to include drama, dance, visual arts, instrumental or vocal music in their high school studies. Sophomores, juniors, and seniors from any Orleans Parish high school are able to attend their home school half a day and to receive credit for participating in one of NOCCA's programs.

EXECUTIVE INTERN. Students are given a chance to gain experience as in intern at the executive and management levels in various disciplines. They also participate in the decision making processes. Work assignments vary from working in the zoo to working in museums, in city government, in large hospitals, with private physicians, in research labs, and in local industry. This program lasts one semester, during which time students report to school only once weekly for general directions to meet with the director of the Executive Intern program. They do not carry a regular class load. Most take no subjects during the semester they intern. However, the student is still required to complete all of Franklin's requirements in order to receive a Benjamin Franklin High School diploma. The intern receives no monetary remuneration when involved in the program.

As a part of the Orleans Parish public school system, the superior college preparatory education at Franklin is available to qualified students at no cost to the student's family.

### Evaluation of Program

Program evaluation at Benjamin Franklin High School is accomplished both formally and informally. At the end of every fourth year, questionnaires are mailed to all graduates eliciting personal, educational, and career information. Informal evaluation of program effectiveness is accomplished at the end of each year through student evaluation of courses. Another index of program effectiveness is the published Senior Class Study compiled by seniors during the last two weeks of school. This study lists the names of seniors, the colleges or universities they have chosen to attend, scholarships they have been awarded, and their majors.

**GEORGIA GOVERNOR'S HONORS PROGRAM**
Georgia State Department of Education
Room 220
156 Trinity Avenue
Atlanta, Georgia 30303

*Reported by:*
Jean Fant, Director

*Administrative Responsibility:*
Jean Fant, Director

*For Further Information, Contact:*
Jean Fant, Director
Room 220
156 Trinity Avenue
Atlanta, Georgia 30303

## Overview of Program

Section 51 of the Minimum Foundation Program for Education Law authorized the State Board of Education to inaugurate a summer honors program for students in Georgia who have manifested exceptional abilities, unique potentials, or who have made exceptional academic achievement. On February 26, 1964, the State Board of Education approved a proposal for Georgia's first summer honors program to be known as the Governor's Honors Program.

This instructional program is designed to provide gifted tenth and eleventh grade students enrolled in Georgia's public and private secondary schools challenging and enriching educational opportunities not usually available during the regular school year. The program is also designed to assist students in recognizing their potential. The staff attempts to develop and demonstrate differentiated instructional techniques which, in addition to recognizing academic excellence, stimulate and challenge the abilities of gifted students. Opportunties for laymen, teachers, counselors, and administrators to observe the program are provided.

## Selection of Students

Students are nominated in an area of instruction by a classroom teacher. Each public school system and each private school in the state of Georgia is assigned a nomination quota based on average daily attendance. These locally selected nominees are sent to the statewide screening interviews. A transcript of grades, a nominating form from student and teacher, and a local school compilation of records and endorsements are sent to the state to substantiate the nominations. Interviews are scheduled at a central location in the state, and teams of teachers from high schools and colleges meet with each nominee. A number of finalists are selected from the highest ranked students in each discipline. A composite score of the written evidence and the student's performance at the interview are used to rank nominees. The number selected in each subject matter area is determined by the ratio of applicants in that area to the total number of applications received. In all, six hundred students attend the Governor's Honors Program.

## The Program

The program is administered in the Office of Instructional Services through the Division of Curriculum Services. A state department advisory committee composed of representatives from curriculum, guidance and counseling, media services, vocational education, and other areas assist the director in determining policies and developing plans for the program.

The faculty is composed of highly qualified secondary and college teachers. In addition to the teaching staff, other personnel on the staff include those working in the areas of counseling, audiovisual coordination, public relations, and student activities. Members of the staff are selected according to their qualifications and recommendations.

Instruction is offered in the following curricular areas: English, foreign language, mathematics, natural sciences, social sciences, art, drama, dance, music, and vocational education. Students are expected to concentrate in one of these areas. The area of concentration is determined by the student's ability, aptitude, and interest. Experiences are presented in such a manner as to be unique and different from the manner in which they are usually presented in the regular program. Course content is "idea centered" and stresses the integration of knowledge. Course credit is not given for work completed in this program nor are grades given. Students are given exploratory experiences in areas outside their major interest. All students are given an opportunity to participate in seminars in a variety of areas. Students may attend concerts, plays, and participate in a full recreation program.

Tuition, room, board, and instructional supplies are provided for each student. There is no charge for any activity provided as a part of the program. Students are responsible for travel expenses to and from the program and for spending money.

Funds for the operation of the program are appropriated by the General Assembly of Georgia as a part of the education budget for the State Department of Education.

## Evaluation of Program

In-depth evaluations of the various instructional components of the program are made periodically. The most recent one, "Evaluation of Career Awareness Component, Georgia Governor's Honors Program: A Follow-up Study of Participants and Their High School Teachers," was completed in June 1977 by E. Paul Torrance, Felice Kaufman, Suzann Gibbs, Orlow Ball, and J. Pansy Torrance.

**THE GOVERNOR'S SCHOOL OF NORTH CAROLINA**
Governor's School West
Salem College
Winston-Salem, North Carolina 27108

Governor's School East
St. Andrews College
Laurinburg, North Carolina 28352

*Reported by:*
Gail W. Howard, Administrative Assistant

*Administrative Responsibility:*
Theodore R. Drain, Director

*For Further Information, Contact:*
Gail W. Howard, Administrative Assistant
The Governor's School of North Carolina
Drawer H, Salem Station
Winston-Salem, North Carolina 27108

### Overview of Program

The Governor's School of North Carolina is a six-week residential program conducted on the campuses of Salem College, Winston-Salem, North Carolina, and St. Andrews College, Laurinburg, North Carolina. Four hundred intellectually gifted North Carolina high school students, rising juniors and seniors, are served at each campus. The program is operated by the State Board of Education through the Director, Division for Exceptional Children, State Department of Public Instruction. A Board of Governors, appointed by the State Board of Education, acts as an advisory body.

During the first three years of its operation, beginning in the summer of 1963, the Governor's School was financed by a grant from the Carnegie Corporation of New York and was matched by contributions from individuals, industries, and foundations of Winston-Salem. The proposal for the special summer program originated with former Governor Terry Sanford. Salem College was selected as the original site. Beginning in the summer of 1978, the program was expanded to the two campuses. The same programs are offered at each campus.

After appraising the program at the end of the first three years of operation, the 1965 General Assembly of North Carolina voted an appropriation to finance the effort toward differential education for gifted and talented students in the state. The School receives annual funding directly from the General Assembly.

The main purposes of the program are as follows:

1. To assist talented and gifted young people to achieve more readily their full potential, to be motivated toward that achievement, and to be motivated to use that potential for achievement in pursuit of an observable product

2. To stimulate local schools toward the establishment and improvement of programs for gifted and talented students by providing leadership in curriculum development and effective teaching techniques

3. To assist the schools of the state by supplying them with certain products of the Governor's School, i.e. specially trained teachers and students and special materials having particular application to the improvement and education of gifted and talented students

4. To conduct and disseminate research which is applicable to the education of gifted and talented students.

## Selection of Students

Gifted and talented students are recommended by their high school principals, teachers, and counselors. These applications form a pool from which each local superintendent submits his quota, based on the total class populations involved. Headmasters of private schools nominate students on the same quota basis.

Students who are selected for the Governor's School must meet the academic criteria established for the North Carolina Gifted and Talented Program. In addition, those selected in the performing arts must personally audition for one of the places on the day set by the Board of Governors. A statewide selection committee of competent judges selects the performing arts students from those invited to audition. The body of academic students comes from those selected by each local superintendent as his two first choices, thus insuring statewide student representation. The remaining students are chosen by a selection committee from the pool of eligible public and private school students. Board policy and dormitory space determine the ethnic and sexual composition of the student body.

## The Program

Twentieth century theories relating to the past and future are given emphasis in the curriculum, which consists of three areas.

AREA I. This curriculum area is where the pupil's special talent or giftedness lies and is the basis upon which he or she was chosen to attend the Governor's School: art, dance, drama, English, French, Spanish, mathematics, both choral and instrumental music, natural science, or social science. About two-thirds of a pupil's class time is devoted to Area I curriculum. Teaching materials used are chosen to acquaint pupils with the latest developments in that specialty, and pupils are encouraged to anticipate and to speculate about possible solution of problems and developments likely to arise in that field in the future.

AREA II. This curriculum area focuses on general conceptual development in which the pupil is expected to expand interests and knowledge beyond his own concentrated specialty to include the whole spectrum of advancing knowledge. Integrative principles of knowledge are emphasized, by which narrow specialties are transcended and seen as incomplete parts of a larger whole. About one-sixth of the student's class time is devoted to Area II curriculum.

AREA III. In this curriculum area, personal and social development is stressed. Through appropriate activities and the insights gained, gifted pupils strengthen their personalities in order to avail themselves of the fullest development of their capacities. About one-sixth of the student's class time is spent in Area III curriculum.

Since the general assembly of North Carolina provides funds for the Governor's School, there are no tuition or room and board fees. Students furnish only their transportation to and from Winston-Salem and Laurinburg and their spending money.

Consultants, some of them nationally recognized, are employed to work with both students and faculty throughout the summer session. An attempt is made to secure consultants who are involved in areas of great relevance to pressing contemporary issues or future developments.

## Evaluation of Program

The North Carolina State Department of Public Instruction has developed a questionnaire by which the student body is asked to evaluate the entire program and its effect on them in terms of: curriculum content, teacher effectiveness, facilities, ancillary programs, and so forth. The results of this evaluation are presented to the students before they complete the program.

Faculty members are asked to evaluate their students at the end of the session. A copy of this report is sent to each student's parents and principal.

Faculty have an opportunity to evaluate the program at each campus in terms of: effectiveness of the curriculum in its three divisions, effectiveness of the administration, appropriateness of the consultants, and so forth. In addition, on-site evaluation committees and consultants are brought in from time to time to observe and comment on the program.

Periodically, the faculty is asked to make self-study reports to the summer directors and to the Division for Exceptional Children. Results of these self-studies have been distributed to the local school systems as a means of having an impact on the schools in the state.

## MENTALLY GIFTED MINOR PROGRAM AT POINT LOMA HIGH SCHOOL
San Diego Unified School District
Point Loma High School
2335 Chatsworth Boulevard
San Diego, California 92106

*Reported by:*
Isabelle Skidmore

*Administrative Responsibility:*
Isabelle Skidmore

*For Further Information, Contact:*
James F. Gauntlett, Principal
Point Loma High School
2335 Chatsworth Boulevard
San Diego, California 92106

### Overview of Program

San Diego City Schools, having long recognized the need for a special program for children within the top one-half of one percent of the student population, began research during the 1948-49 school year on the educational problems of these children. When the newly identified pupils were studied, it was found that only one-half were doing as well in their classes as pupils with average ability and approximately one-half of them had social adjustment problems of some severity.

A committee was formed in the fall of 1952 to develop and implement a program to meet the needs of the gifted child. The board of education approved an experimental project on a year-to-year basis. The program was analyzed and evaluated continuously by parents, teachers, and administrators.

By the summer of 1958, the program had gained stature and had proved itself capable of meeting the needs of these children. As a result, the board of education approved the program for the gifted child as a permanent part of the curriculum of San Diego City Schools.

Since 1958, the program has grown and taken on new dimensions. In 1976-77, programs in the district served approximately seven thousand students in cluster and independent study groupings.

There are, of course, many definitions of giftedness. Using these definitions, most children are gifted in one way or another. The philosophy of the Point Loma High School, therefore, is that every student is unique and should receive an education appropriate to his or her abilities and needs. However, there is a kind of giftedness which should be more narrowly defined as academic aptitude—the kind of ability which is measured by individual or group tests and/or determined by teacher, administrator, and counselor recommendations. It is for students with this kind of talent that the gifted program at Point Loma High School has evolved.

Among Point Loma High School's population of 1,658, there are 215 students who have IQs of 132 or higher as tested individually on a Stanford-Binet. The gifted program has two components: cluster classes for students who have been identified as gifted and for the high academic achiever and independent study, a seminar-reading program for highly gifted students.

### Selection of Students

Admissions procedures for the Independent Study program include the following:

1. Group interview.
2. Application blank.
3. Individual interview.
4. Recommendations from teachers and counselors.
5. The site committee (independent study teachers, vice-principal, head counselor, and district counselor) considers all official records, including grade point average, test scores, comments from teachers, report of individual IQ performance, report from personal interview, recommendations, and readings.

In February, independent study instructors visit feeder junior high schools for a conference with counselors and a group meeting with students eligible by IQ test scores, counselor recommendation, or their own interest. Applications are distributed to interested students at this meeting.

In early March, applications are due from students and are turned over to the junior high school counselors, who forward them to Point Loma High School. In April, the site committee meets to select students for the Independent Study program, and in May, students are notified of the site committee's decisions.

Letters are sent to applicants at their homes indicating acceptance, rejection, or placement on the waiting list. The waiting list is used if openings occur in the fall, or if new information, i.e. summer school attendance, is pertinent.

## The Program

CLUSTER CLASSES. Cluster classes are for the student who has been identified as gifted and for the high academic achiever. Fifty percent of a class must be composed of gifted students in order for the class to be designate "cluster" and to receive special funding. These classes are "qualitatively different" from regular classes in that teaching is characterized by openendedness and flexibility, encouraging independent inquiry, employing individualized learning, and providing multiple resources for students enrolled.

Some of the operational definitions of "qualitatively different" are as follows:

1. Materials are used which are designed specifically for, or are appropriate for, the gifted.
2. Community resources and consultants are used in enrichment activities not regularly a part of the district program.
3. The activity is not a part of the regular advanced curriculum prescribed for that grade level.
4. The activity involves specialized treatment of materials in an intensive or in-depth manner.
5. The activity requires independent study research outside the scheduled class requirements.
6. The activity is accelerated, or self-pacing.
7. The activity involves unusual use of materials and equipment.
8. The activity is part of a pull-out enrichment program designed for the gifted students.

9. The activity can be related to the Structure of the Intellect model.

To qualify for the additional funds needed for this program, students at the various grade levels must enroll in at least one of several academic classes designated by grade level as "cluster classes."

INDEPENDENT STUDY. In the program of independent study at Point Loma High School, students with high intellectual abilities (150 IQ or above with some students accepted with lower intelligence scores if there is room) are assigned to two tutorial advisors who serve forty students in a center, creating a school within a school. The pair of teachers is chosen to include one who specializes in math and science and one who specializes in language, literature, the humanities, and social science.

Independent study is essentially a seminar-reading program encouraging self-motivation and direction. The college preparatory program includes student- and teacher-led seminars, individual research projects, cultural enrichment, intellectual and social activities fostering character development, and encouraged campus and community involvement.

An integral part of the program includes activities and events which enhance classroom and individual study. The following fall into this category: field trips, guest speakers, student exchange between schools, and attendance at theater and film productions.

The atmosphere of the program is conducive to open communication, effective group activities such as family meetings, book-of-the-month discussions, peer teaching, group projects, and the acceptance of individual responsibility.

Characteristics of such highly gifted students of high school age include superior powers of abstraction, conceptualization, synthesis, independent judgment, and a keen interest in productive learning and problem solving. The intention of the Independent Study program is to meet the needs of these students for more responsibility in determining their own courses of study, for learning exercises aimed at employing their high competencies, for broad opportunities for vocational and avocational explorations, and for close interpersonal relationships with adults and students of similar abilities.

From the above characteristics and needs, the following objectives were adopted for the seminar program:

1. To provide a program structure that encourages and allows independent thinking
2. To provide a program structure which fosters excitement and joy in learning
3. To provide a program structure which encourages growth of self-identity
4. To provide a learning program designed to utilize the maximum of each student's high competency level
5. To provide a program structure which will permit greater opportunity for the student to seek out for himself information about possible vocational and avocational choices
6. To provide the student with greater opportunities for increased participation in school and community or peripheral activities.

### Evaluation of Program

Point Loma High School is responsible for filing a written plan which overviews the program of gifted education. The plan is reviewed by a site committee composed of parents, students, and staff, and by a central committee chaired by the director of gifted programs. Each May, the program plan is evaluated by the staff, parents, and students.

## MODEL PROGRAM FOR DEVELOPING CREATIVITY IN SCIENCE
The Bronx High School of Science
75 West 205th Street
Bronx, New York 10468

*Reported by:*
Vincent G. Galasso

*Administrative Responsibility:*
Vincent G. Galasso

*For Further Information, Contact:*
Vincent G. Galasso
The Bronx High School of Science
75 West 205th Street
Bronx, New York 10468

### Overview of Program

The Model Program for Developing Creativity in Science was initiated in 1965, when the first formal research class was established at the Bronx High School of Science. The current format grew out of this initial idea during the latter part of the 1960s. The main objectives of the program are the identification of gifted, motivated students in science and the development of these students so they can carry through an original, creative, independent piece of scientific research. For this purpose, a three-year sequence of courses has been developed. The approaches and strategies employed emphasize giving the students "hands on" experience with a variety of scientific equipment and techniques, exposing these students to the inquiry approach used in science and stimulating them to handle problems in a rational, scientific manner.

The student benefits from this program not only by developing his or her abilities to solve complex scientific problems, but also by developing a positive attitude toward dealing with many other kinds of problems that might arise. Furthermore, it has been demonstrated that college and even medical and graduate school acceptances have been increased when students can provide concrete evidence of having completed independent work.

### Selection of Students

The Bronx High School of Science is a specialized high school for gifted students. Students must pass an examination to be accepted by the school. The entrance exam was designed by the Scholastic Testing Corporation of Bensenville, Illinois, and consists of a verbal and a mathematics segment. The verbal test includes objective questions in vocabulary, sentence completion, and reading comprehension. The reading comprehension is based upon interpretation of scientific and technical materials. The mathematics portion tests concepts, computation, and problem solving.

It is believed, however, that pretesting is not necessary to implement this program. Any comprehensive high school can use this program by allowing one segment of the program to act as a screen for the following part.

The ninth grade curriculum segment of the model project is required of all incoming ninth-year students. From a pool of approximately seven hundred gifted students, a group of one hundred students is selected for special research honors classes which consists of four groups. Selection for the tenth-year segment of this program involves several criteria:

1. Achievement levels in ninth-year science and math
2. Verbal and mathematical aptitudes as demonstrated by the entrance examination score
3. Motivation of the students as indicated by their requesting this program which involves four extra hours of class time per week
4. Creativity in science as determined by the ninth-year science teacher's recommendation, which is based upon his direct observations and evaluative tools.

Teacher evaluation can be especially important in identifying an underachiever as a potentially gifted student, who, given the opportunity, could develop into a highly creative individual. Thus, the basic policy followed in selecting students into the tenth-year research honors course involves identification of students with high achievement and aptitude in science and mathematics who have demonstrated their ability to function creatively in the ninth-year special biology program. The teacher recommendation is based upon practical examinations to determine the student's ability to perform significant laboratory techniques, objective examinations which stress problem solving, and direct observations by the teacher of students functioning in laboratory situations.

Students are selected for the eleventh-year independent research classes from the tenth-year research honors group, based upon their abilities to identify specific creative problems in biology, to design and carry out controlled experiments, and to draw valid conclusions based upon data gathered. Motivation of the student is, of course, crucial in the selection process. The eleventh-year course involves an additional semester of work with no extra credit.

## The Program

In the ninth year, all entering students are given the opportunity to learn the techniques of the scientist by a "hands on" approach. They are taught how to use the microscope and microbiological techniques. Students are led to speculate on what they see and eventually to hypothesize and design simple experiments such as "the effect of temperature on growth rate of various types of bacteria." Students learn how to conduct themselves in a laboratory environment and to cooperate in using materials. The program covers one-half of a year, with eighty-minute periods on two alternate days and one forty-minute period on the last day of the week.

In the eleventh year, the Socratic method of teaching is used with emphasis on recognizing problems and setting up hypotheses. Many open-ended laboratory experiments are performed by the students. For example, during an eighty-minute laboratory experience, the students would be asked to determine the differences between organic and inorganic catalysts. Ongoing experiments are also used. One example is a series of experiments with slime mold in which students, after performing a given group of simple investigations, progress to design and conduct their own experimentation with this organism. Another example is to find the effect of different concentrations of auxin on the growth of oat coleoptiles. Students are given assignments stressing the recognition and selection of problems. Teachers meet with students individually to discuss hypotheses and problem selection for individual research. The tenth-year course lasts forty weeks, eighty minutes (double periods) each day.

In the eleventh year, each student is guided by a teacher or team of teachers about the advisability and practicality of his proposed individual research. Students do extensive library research and learn how to read scientific papers and abstract relevent information. They learn how to use *Biological Abstracts*, the *Index Medicus*, and various specialized journals. The procedure for each project is discussed individually with each student. As necessary, students contact research scientists in hospitals and research institutes. Progress reports are written by each student every six weeks. A scientifically written report is handed in at the end of the year. This course lasts forty weeks. There are two eighty-minute classes on alternate days and one forty-minute class at the end of the week. Each student is scheduled for a lunch period either before or after class. In this way, extra laboratory time is available when needed. The laboratory is available to the students before the start of the school day and at any time during the day if the student has available time. A teacher is always present.

The available materials required for implementation of the program which are expendable correlate with the particular laboratory exercise. Standard laboratory equipment is needed for implementation of the program. This equipment would best be housed in an established biology laboratory room.

## Evaluation of Program

Thus far, evaluation of the program has followed several procedures. Nonstandardized, teacher-developed, and administered instruments are used on a regular basis in the classroom. Scores on standardized examinations, such as the *New York State Biology Regents* examination, the *Advanced Placement Examinations*, and the *Scholastic Aptitude Test* of the College Board have demonstrated the effectiveness of the program. There has also been an increased recognition of our students' accomplishments in scientific competitions, such as the Westinghouse Science Talent Search, the International Science Fair, the Citywide Science Fair, and the New York Academy of Science Otto P. Burgdoff Congress.

**STUDY OF MATHEMATICALLY PRECOCIOUS YOUTH (SMPY)**
The Johns Hopkins University
Charles and Thirty-fourth Streets
Baltimore, Maryland 21218

*Reported by:*
William C. George, Director
Office of Talent Identification and Development

*Administrative Responsibility:*
Dr. Julian C. Stanley, Director

*For Further Information, Contact:*
Dr. Julian C. Stanley, Director of SMPY
Department of Psychology
The Johns Hopkins University
Charles and Thirty-fourth Streets
Baltimore, Maryland 21218

## Overview of Program

The Study of Mathematically Precocious Youth (SMPY) began officially at the The Johns Hopkins University, Baltimore, Maryland, in September of 1971, and unofficially two years earlier. It was originated by Professor Julian C. Stanley. The variety of activities carried on through SMPY is best described in Volumes 1-4 of SMPY's *Studies of Intellectual Precocity* (SIP) series and in a supplemental volume, *Educational Programs and Intellectual Prodigies.*

The SMPY program is doing many different things for large numbers of mathematically superior students and for some verbally able ones, also. Each aspect of the $D^3$ model as set forth in SMPY's first book (*Mathematical Talent: Discovery, Description, and Development*) has been, and is still being, explored in both depth and breadth.

To these three dimensions of SMPY has been added a fourth, dissemination, as its principles, procedures, and programs have been spread across the country. For example, the state of Illinois is presently conducting a statewide talent search based on the

SMPY model. Because of the direct link between SMPY ánd the individual talented child and/or his parents or teachers, the amount of change effected in many school districts is incredibly large. Already, programs exist in Delaware, Illinois, Maryland, Minnesota, Nebraska, Oklahoma, Pennsylvania, and Wisconsin. In effect, SMPY is a catalyst for change that will help the talented individual directly rather than waiting for a school system to eventually develop a program. The main activities of SMPY remain educationally accelerative. This study has not found educational enrichment suitable for math-talented youths over the school years unless it leads to subject-matter and/or grade acceleration.

## Selection of Students

Large numbers of youngsters (approximately seven thousand youths in six talent searches) who reason well mathematically (better than the average male twelfth grader does) and/or verbally are being identified through an appropriately difficult test, the *Scholastic Aptitude Test* of the College Board. The ablest of these youth, primarily seventh graders, are being studied further in order to describe their characteristics better and provide information on which to base special educational efforts on their behalf.

## The Program

This special educational program helps the development of youths who are eager to move ahead faster and better than is permitted in most curricula of public and private schools. Individually prescribed programs for aiding these students are utilized. These opportunities include diagnostic testing followed by prescriptive instruction, association with talented young college students, seminars, special fast-math courses, preparation to take *Advanced Placement Examinations*, early entrance to college, and college courses on a part-time basis for credit during evenings, summers, the regular school year, and correspondence courses.

Activities of SMPY are funded by grants from the Spencer Foundation, the Camille and Henry Dreyfus Foundation, the

Geraldine R. Dodge Foundation, the Educational Foundation of America, and the National Science Foundation.

From time to time, personnel of SMPY conduct special mathematics classes for high scorers in its talent searches. Unfortunately, it is not sufficiently staffed to provide counseling or testing services to persons not coming through its annual contest. It is recommended that parents who believe their child(ren) to be intellectually superior read *Mathematical Talent: Discovery, Description, and Development*; *Intellectual Talent: Research and Development*; *The Gifted and the Creative: Fifty-year Perspective*; *Educating the Gifted: Acceleration and Enrichment*; *Educational Programs and Intellectual Prodigies*; *Women and the Mathematical Mystique*; and general books about the gifted while seeking help from their local school systems. After they exhaust all such resources, SMPY staff members will be pleased to try to answer their specific questions about how to help their mathematically talented youths.

The staff of SMPY has prepared three dissemination packages that are meant for use primarily by the administrative staff of city, county, and state school systems. These materials may also be applicable to single schools that have a staff member reasonably well trained in educational testing. The three packages are: *The First D: Discovery of Talent* (finding intellectually talented youths, especially those who reason extremely well mathematically); *The Second D: Description of Talent* (further study of the intellectually talented youths); and *A Component of the Third D: Development of Talent* (establishing special classes in which mathematics is taught much faster and rigorously than is usual). These dissemination packages were planned and prepared by the staff of SMPY under a grant from the Robert Sterling Clark Foundation.

### Evaluation of Program

Standardized achievement tests and *Advanced Placement Examinations* in appropriate areas are two examples of evaluation instruments used. For further details, see the volumes mentioned in the overview.

## PART E
## PERFORMING ARTS PROGRAMS

One of the two performing arts programs described in this section is conducted in a public junior high school. This program, initiated in 1976, enrolls culturally-diverse, seventh and eighth grade pupils who score high on standardized tests of academic aptitude, creativity, and leadership qualities, and who have a record of outstanding performance in one or more of the arts. Continuation in the program through the ninth grade is limited to students who progress at a rate projected for youth of high aptitude in the performing arts.

While the general goals and objectives of this program provide for a broad range of experiences in the performing arts combined with rigorous study in academic subjects, each student has the option of selecting one of the arts for concentrated study and experience as he enters the third year in the program. Seventh and eighth grade groups meet separately for two two-hour sessions each week, with approximately one-half of the time scheduled after school. Students in the ninth grade meet after school for two three-hour workshops each month.

Self and peer ratings, teacher assessments, and pretest and posttest results are taken into account in the evaluation process.

Funding for this program comes from the regular school budget, augmented by a grant from the Office of the Gifted and Talented, U.S. Office of Education.

The second program is conducted in a rather unique state college of the arts established in 1963. Although students attending this institution come from many states, approximately 75 percent are from the South. Students may enter the program as early as the seventh grade and continue through college graduation. Admission requirements and the selection procedures are very demanding. Each applicant who submits promising credentials and has an established record of performance in the arts is interviewed and auditioned by the staff.

Preparation for a career in one or more of the performing arts is clearly the major goal of the school and of the individual student. The strong academic program required of all who enroll is viewed by students and staff as basic to and supportive of professional proparation in the performing arts. The college is organized into schools of dance, drama, music, and theatre design and technical production. Students are involved continuously in one or more productions.

With emphasis on outstanding performance leading to a career in the arts, it is understandable that the assessment of performance in various productions constitutes the major criterion in the evaluation process in this institution. Self, peer, and staff assessments play an important part in the evaluation of performance.

The primary fiscal support is derived from state appropriations, but tuition and grants from foundations, corporations, and individuals constitute a significant segment of the budget.

# IDENTIFICATION OF HIGH POTENTIAL IN CULTURALLY DIVERSE STUDENTS THROUGH INTEGRATIVE EXPERIENCES IN THEATRE TECHNIQUES AND INDEPENDENT STUDY

Jackie Robinson Middle School
New Haven Public Schools
New Haven, Connecticut 06510

*Reported by:*
Sharyn Esdaile, Susan Hill, and John Dixon

*Administrative Responsibility:*
Mary Hunter Wolf, Director

*For Further Information, Contact:*
Mary Hunter Wolf or Sharyn Esdaile
The Center for Theatre Techniques in Education
1850 Elm Street
Stratford, Connecticut 06497

## Overview of Program

The program was established in 1976 in New Haven, Connecticut. Seventy percent of the school population is comprised of minority students.

The project serves children in the Jackie Robinson Middle School, which has a population of approximately eight hundred students who are predominately black.

The project serves selected students at the seventh and eighth grade levels in the Jackie Robinson School and at the ninth grade level in the James Hillhouse High School. An attempt is made in all grades to have an equal number of boys and girls. Approximately fifty students are served each year.

The program makes available important techniques in the identification of and programming for culturally diverse urban youth who are talented and gifted at the middle and secondary school levels.

The objectives of the project are as follows:

1. To provide an early identification system for students with gifted potential during the middle school years so

that their eligibility for talented and gifted programs at the high school level is pre-established

2. To enable participating students to develop their creative thinking abilities
3. To establish themes drawn from the students' experiences which can be expressed through artistic, dramatic, musical, and literary forms
4. To improve the sense of community among the participating students
5. To improve the ability to concentrate on tasks among participating students
6. To improve the environmental awareness among the participating students
7. To have the students pursue creative projects as a result of participation in theatre techniques
8. To provide the selected students with individual programming for introduction to independent study in academic or arts areas
9. To conduct training sequences in which educators from the New Haven area, the State of Connecticut, the Northeast Region, and from other regions of the country may be trained to use the techniques of the model project
10. To assist educational agencies which made a commitment to adopt the model
11. To provide literature for national dissemination which gives an orientation to the model project.

## Selection of Students

The project consists of a preliminary screening for potential talent, followed by a three-year ongoing support program which develops the selected students through an exploration of creative problem solving and conceptual thinking, new areas of expression, and independent study in one area.

The identification process has two distinct stages. The first stage at the seventh-grade level measures three types of performance: academic, creative, and leadership. One subjective and one objective measure are used for each.

The objective indicator of academic ability is the grade average in academic subjects for the previous school year. The objective indicator of creative ability was derived from the *Torrance Tests of Creative Thinking,* Figure A. The objective indicator of leadership was obtained by peer nomination questionnaire. The subjective indicator in all three areas was obtained from the *Renzulli-Hartman Behavioral Rating Scales.*

The information for the objective indicator was collected for the entire seventh-grade population at Jackie Robinson Middle School. All students were rank ordered on each objective indicator. Subjective information was collected for each student who was again rank ordered on each of the subjective and objective measures. From this rank ordering, the final group, 15 percent of the original population, was selected to participate in the second stage of the identification process.

The second stage of identification involves the student's participation in the theatre techniques program. In a relaxed, open, and encouraging environment, students are given the opportunity to develop the special skills cultivated by theatre techniques. Those students who respond most successfully to the theatre techniques development are encouraged to continue for an additional two years of programming at the eighth and ninth grade levels.

### The Program

The content objectives for the model project are elements of a progression continuing through the three years of the project and are as follows:

1. A sense of community should be created among the members of the participating group. This sense of community will appear in the increased ability of the group to act on problems set before it, in the livelier, relaxed manner with which these individuals interact, and, finally, in the willingness to share ideas and/or materials. The by-product of this workshop atmosphere of community is designed to carry over into the group's normal day-to-day functions.

2. Each member of the group should be introduced to and

incorporate into the self new ways to deepen the powers of concentration. Through practice, the individual will be able to bring forward a state of active readiness without tension or distraction.

3. Each member of the workshop will reawaken his or her own imagination and deepen responses to others through interaction. This deepening will appear in each individual's willingness to contribute to such interaction, to explore problems more acutely, and to risk more sensitive self-expression in the search for solutions.

4. Each member will become more aware of the physical world as well as his or her own physical presence.

In the first year of the program, seventh grade students participate in a general creativity program where particular attention is given to sharpening the senses and the powers of observation, enhancing individual and group resources, and building on the capacity to conceptualize. In their second year of the program, students work in greater depth in several thematic units derived from their interests. At the ninth grade level, the third year of programming, students work specifically in one interest area of their choice, either in the arts or in academics, while continuing to meet, to share, and collectively solve problems with other students from their original group.

Activities of three kinds are selected to meet these needs. The first are developmental, involving exercises, games, and problems. The second is transformational, making use of verbal, graphic, and musical skills. The third is experimental, where emphasis is placed on low risk situations.

Throughout the program, opportunities for specialization in either potential or demonstrated ability areas are available on an individual basis to all participating students. Resource people from the community as well as the Center for Theatre Techniques and the independent study program act as mentors to provide the one-to-one interaction which has been cited as a significant factor in the development of highly gifted and talented people.

Seventh and eighth grade groups meet separately for two two-hour sessions per week. One session takes place after school; the other, scheduled within the school day, necessitates taking students out of their respective classes. Ninth graders meet after school for two three-hour workshops once or twice monthly.

A dissemination plan, maintained and expanded during the three years of federal funding, consisted of community, state, regional, and national sharing of program design through a local advisory board, parent and teacher meetings, participation in state and national conferences, scheduled on-site visitations, a week-long national conference in New Haven, and weekend training sessions in techniques specific to the program.

The program is funded by the U.S. Office of Education, Office of the Gifted and Talented.

## Evaluation of Program

The *Torrance Tests of Creativity Thinking* are administered to students at the beginning and end of each school year. Raw scores are converted to standard scores, and an index of average originality derived from the Torrance scores is an indication of the extent to which the average completed item tends to be unique indicated by appropriate and statistically infrequent responses. These results of the Torrance tests indicate a statistically significant improvement in the index of average originality during the first year of program experience.

A second important indicator of program success relates to the idea of differential education for the gifted. This concept requires that in order for a special program for gifted students to be justified, it should provide something unique that is more appropriate to the needs of gifted students than regular school programming. One way of securing an indication of the unique positive value of special programming is to have students rate their program experience and then rate their general school experiences. A comparison may be made between the two ratings to see which is higher. When the students were asked to give ratings, 64 percent gave the program a higher rating than their general school experience, 23 percent gave both the same rating, and 13 percent gave the school year experience a higher rating. This is a good indication of the differential value of the program for the students selected.

An instructor rating checklist was used for evaluating the success of student participation in more specific activities of the program. Ratings were conducted every eight weeks during the program. Results from these ratings indicate that (1) the responses of students to program activities became more individualized as the program progressed, (2) students tended to generate more creative details in activities as the program progressed, (3) students tended to participate with a greater number of other students, (4) students tended to support each other more, and (5) students were more persistent in completing activities.

**PROFESSIONAL TRAINING FOR CAREERS IN PERFORMING ARTS**
North Carolina School of the Arts
200 Waughtown Street
Winston-Salem, North Carolina 27107

*Reported by:*
Esther Mock, Director of Public Relations

*Administrative Responsibility:*
Robert Suderburg, Chancellor

*For Further Information, Contact:*
Dirk Dawson, Director of Admissions
North Carolina School of the Arts
200 Waughtown Street
Winston-Salem, North Carolina 27107

## Overview of Program

In 1963, the North Carolina legislature created what was, and what has continued to be, a unique school for the professional training of students having exceptional talent in the performing arts which shall be defined as an educational institution of the state, to serve the students of North Carolina and other states, particularly other states of the South.

To implement this mandate, highly qualified professionals established policies to recruit artist/faculty and students of exceptional talent from grades seven through college age. From the beginning, the quality of the faculty and students determined the level of professional training and, in turn, the success of the graduates of the North Carolina School of the Arts in a highly competitive arts world.

As a result, students of exceptional talent in the performing arts receive professional training from highly qualified artist/ faculty and with carefully selected peers to enable them to compete successfully. Top quality is obligatory for a life-work preparation and must be carefully programmed.

A member institution of the University of North Carolina, granting B.F.A. and B.M. degrees, the North Carolina School of the Arts (NCSA) includes four Schools: Dance, Theatre Design and Technical Production, Drama, and Music. Students are trained in these four fields for professional careers. Many famous actors, musicians, and dancers have graduated from the school.

## Selection of Students

Admission to NCSA begins with an audition involving individual performances for a panel of the faculty who have no previous information about the students. They impartially judge talent, accomplishment, potential, commitment to a professional career, and the possibility of success.

Following requests, students are given audition requirements and are provided warm-up periods in advance of performance. Those auditioning in design and production bring portfolios and resumes of previous work. Notification of acceptance is made within two weeks, and appropriate information is requested to include transcripts, *Scholastic Aptitude Test* scores, letters of recommendation, and so forth.

At the North Carolina School of the Arts, the audition/admission process is complicated, comparable to the recruiting of sports teams in order to fill necessary positions. For example, the full music program cannot be adequately offered without talented students for each instrument in the orchestra and in various ensembles as well as solo work. The requirements of the School of Music make special, exacting demands which must be filled for the benefit of all music students, seventh grade through college, in all phases of music.

In the School of Dance, where students also are enrolled at an early age and where approximately one-half are high school students and join professional companies upon graduation, the program offers a unique combination of intensive, professional training, academic studies, and residency unmatched in the United States.

The School of Drama and Theatre Design and Technical Production are college programs. In drama, there is an all-encompassing four-year program. The School of Theatre Design and Technical Production also admits high school students in the visual arts department. Graduates from this program, if committed to theatre design specifically, audition for the college design and production program.

The North Carolina School of the Arts is one of the few schools in this country where undergraduate students are trained in and/or producing sets, costumes, lighting, and stage management for a wide range of performances, thus preparing them for the professional world of theatre, television, radio, films, dance, and music.

## The Program

Rigorous training in appropriately designed studio, class, rehearsal space, and performance halls offers each student full preprofessional experience.

In dance, two classes are offered daily in ballet, modern, and improvisation. In theatre design and technical production, faculty and students design and build the sets, properties, costumes, and lighting for the productions of the other schools, including large and small touring shows. In drama, morning classwork includes voice, movement, and acting; and specific skills such as mime, stage fighting, and singing relevant to afternoon and evening rehearsals.

In music, the curriculum includes three phases: (1) music fundamentals and individual mastery of basic core literature; (2) style and repertoire, specialized skills and electives within the major field; and (3) individual curriculum, with options for preparation for graduate study, strategies for survival and success in performance, career development, special projects, and touring.

In visual arts, which is a two-year exploratory program for high school students, instruction and practice in drawing, two-dimensional design, color theory, painting, sculpture, crafts, and photography are included.

The general studies program, the academic component coordinated with the performing arts, is fully accredited by the state of North Carolina and the Southern Association of Colleges and Schools. There is a deliberate effort by the faculty to make academic work both relevant to the interests and needs of students in the performing arts, and sufficiently comprehensive and rigorous to provide a basis for further work at other educational institutions.

Funding is provided by the state of North Carolina, as for other branches of the greater university system, by tuition charges and by corporate and private support through the North Carolina School of the Arts Foundation, Inc.

### Evaluation of Program

The program evaluation of each school within the North Carolina School of the Arts is the reponsibility of each dean. Program evaluation for general studies is the responsibility of the director of the department, and an accreditation study is conducted every ten years.

However, program evaluation is a continuing process. In addition to major examination ratings, performances also supply evaluative information. The work of each student is evaluated each year by the faculty and deans.

The alumni provide another source of evaluation information to insure that the program is relevant to the employment opportunities for performing artists. Alumni are contacted through a quarterly newsletter and specific questionnaires.

In 1977, an audience evaluation was obtained through questionnaires at performances.

# SECTION II
# NATIONAL LEADERS
# IN GIFTED EDUCATION

Status as a national leader in the education of the gifted and the talented comes as a result of the professional recognition the individual receives for significant contributions in this field. Through their leadership and contributions, the leaders have greatly influenced the focus and direction of gifted education in the United States as well as internationally.

The majority of textbooks on gifted education and related areas have been authored by many of these leaders. Many serve on editorial boards of the journals focusing on the gifted. A substantial number frequently contribute journal articles encompassing research, position statements, program development and evaluation, and state of the art summaries.

State and national organizations have been founded by a few of these national leaders who, along with others, have served or are now serving as officers and on executive and advisory boards. Federal and state legislation has been proposed, drafted, and supported by many of these persons.

Many serve in teaching and research positions in colleges or universities and provide consultant services to school districts directly or through state departments of education.

On a practical level, the leaders have served in a variety of positions in local education agencies as teachers, curriculum specialists, principals, and superintendents. Each has designed, implemented, and evaluated local programs for the gifted in public and/or private schools. Currently, the diversity of their expertise finds them designing teaching methods and models, creating assessment instruments, conducting research studies, and performing a myriad of other important functions. Each continues to make valuable contributions to gifted education.

It should be understood that this listing does not include all persons in the country who are considered worthy of recognition in the field of gifted education. Although many knowledgeable persons in gifted education contributed to the selection procedure utilized, the process itself does not preclude omissions. Furthermore, a few who were nominated by their peers requested that their names not appear for reasons of heavy commitments which leave little time for service beyond their respective positions. No individual was listed without his or her concurrence.

The purpose of listing national leaders and summarizing their contributions and their areas of expertise is to make available information on outstanding persons who have the knowledge, experience, and capabilities to serve schools, agencies, institutions of higher education, and others who have the need for a wide range of consultant services in the areas of gifted and talented education. The national leaders are listed alphabetically, with a description of their professional backgrounds, contributions to the field of gifted education, and publications.

Dr. Alexinia Y. Baldwin
State University of New York
1400 Washington Avenue
Albany, New York 12222

## *Professional Background*

Dr. Alexinia Y. Baldwin holds the Ph.D. degree. She has taught gifted and talented classes in the public schools, has been an instructor at the University of Connecticut's summer freshman program and an adjunct professor at Russell Sage College Evening Division. She was also the coordinator for a national institute which served to train state teams for programming for the gifted. Currently, she is an assistant professor at State University of New York at Albany.

## *Contributions to Gifted Education*

Dr. Baldwin was the president of the Association for the Gifted in 1978-79 and also served as the association's treasurer. She has served as the chairperson of the Committee for the Culturally Different. She is also the first president of Advocacy for Gifted and Talented Education in the state of New York. She has been the director of the International Cooperative Programs for Graduate Study in Manchester, England, and has served as a consultant to the U.S. Department of Health, Education and Welfare, school districts, and professional organizations.

## *Publications in Gifted Education*

Dr. Baldwin has authored or coauthored more than eight articles on tests, open classrooms for the gifted, planning for gifted and talented education, and programming for the gifted. She has also contributed to books dealing with the gifted and edited and coauthored books on the gifted, *Educational Planning for the Gifted: Overcoming Cultural, Geographic and Socio-Economic Impediments* and *The Baldwin Identification Matrix: An Inservice Guide.*

Dr. Walter B. Barbe
*Highlights for Children*
803 Church Street
Honesdale, Pennsylvania 18431

**Professional Background**

Dr. Walter B. Barbe received his B.S., M.A., and Ph.D. from Northwestern University. Dr. Barbe has taught psychology, elementary and special education at such schools as Baylor University, Kent State University, and the University of Tennessee, Chattanooga. Currently, he is the editor-in-chief of *Highlights for Children* as well as being an adjunct professor in the Department for Exceptional Children at Ohio State University.

**Contributions to Gifted Education**

Dr. Barbe is the past president of both the National Association for Gifted Children and the Association for the Gifted.

**Publications in Gifted Education**

Dr. Barbe has written more than seventy-five professional articles on the gifted and has coauthored *Psychology and Education of the Gifted*.

Dr. Jack W. Birch
4625 Fifth Avenue, Apt. 206
Pittsburgh, Pennsylvania 15213

## Professional Background

Dr. Jack W. Birch received the B.S. in special education and secondary education from California State College and the M.Ed. in school psychology and remedial reading from Pennsylvania State University. The Ph.D. in clinical psychology was earned at the University of Pittsburgh. He was among the first to receive certification as a teacher of the gifted from the Pennsylvania Department of Public Instruction. He has teaching, supervisory, and administrative experience from elementary through university levels. Currently, Dr. Birch is professor in educational, developmental, and school psychology and in special education at the University of Pittsburgh. He conducts courses in the preparation of teachers of the gifted and directs doctoral students in the education and psychology of the gifted.

## Contributions to Gifted Education

Dr. Birch was a founder of the Association for the Gifted and is a past president of the Council for Exceptional Children. He was chief advisor to the Carnegie Corporation when it initiated support for a major center on education of the gifted at the University of Virginia through the Southern Regional Education Board. With Carl V. Pegnato, he introduced the efficiency/ effectiveness concept in screening for gifted pupils. In the early 1960s, he directed the first school and system-wide demonstration of early admission to kindergarten for gifted preschoolers.

## Publications in Gifted Education

In 1955, with Earl M. McWilliams, he published the first book on mainstream education for the gifted. Dr. Birch has coauthored an article in *Early School Admission for Mentally Advanced Children* and coauthored *Teaching Exceptional Children in All America's Schools* and *Education of the Gifted and Talented*.

Dr. Carolyn M. Callahan
Department of Foundations
School of Education
University of Virginia
Charlottesville, Virginia 22903

## Professional Background

Dr. Carolyn M. Callahan received her B.A. in mathematics from the University of Connecticut and her M.A. and Ph.D. in educational psychology from the University of Connecticut. She has been an evaluator of the curriculum development project and a lecturer in research methods at the School of Nursing at the University of Connecticut, an instructor at the University of North Carolina, and has taught numerous in-service courses for local school districts. Currently, she is an associate professor in the Department of Foundations in the School of Education at the University of Virginia.

## Contributions to Gifted Education

Dr. Callahan has served as evaluation consultant to gifted programs in Connecticut, Virginia, South Carolina, North Carolina, Louisiana, Maryland, New York, Idaho, Colorado, and Michigan, in addition to consulting on identification and program planning with many other local and state agencies. Dr. Callahan has also served as a review editor of *Teaching Exceptional Children*, *Exceptional Children*, and *Education Unlimited*, and as a reviewer for *Improving Human Performance: A Research Quarterly*. Currently, she is editor of *Journal for the Education of the Gifted*.

## Publications in Gifted Education

Dr. Callahan has written or coauthored nine articles on evaluating creativity training material, teacher perceptions of item types for cognitive categories, and the creative productivity of groups. She has contributed to collections of readings, has authored *What Research Says to the Teacher of the Exceptional Child: Creativity and the Gifted*, and has coauthored two books, *New Directions in Creativity* and *Scales for Rating the Behavioral Characteristics of Superior Students*. Dr. Callahan has also written a chapter, "Gifted Women," for the Seventy-eighth Yearbook of the National Society for the Study of Education.

Dr. John F. Feldhusen, Director
Gifted Education Resource Institute
Purdue University, SCC-G
West Lafayette, Indiana 47906

### Professional Background

Dr. John F. Feldhusen received his B.A., M.A., and Ph.D. from the University of Wisconsin. He has taught English and mathematics in high school and later specialized in creativity research. Currently, Dr. Feldhusen is the director of the Gifted Education Resource Institute and professor in the gifted education graduate program at Purdue University.

### Contributions to Gifted Education

Dr. Feldhusen has done a great many workshops on the gifted and has served as consultant in this area as well. His work has focused on creative enrichment models for gifted education programs.

### Publications in Gifted Education

Dr. Feldhusen has coauthored fourteen professional articles in journals on such subjects as practicum activities, design and evaluation of a workshop on creativity, problem solving for teachers, programmed instruction for the gifted, instructional materials, models, and career education activities in gifted education. He has also coauthored the teacher's edition of *Teaching Children How to Think* and *Teaching Creative Thinking and Problem Solving*.

Dr. Lynn H. Fox, Coordinator
Intellectually Gifted Child Study Group
Evening College and Summer Session
The Johns Hopkins University
Baltimore, Maryland 21218

## Professional Background

Dr. Lynn H. Fox received a B.S. in mathematics education and an M.Ed. in educational psychology from the University of Florida. She earned her M.A. and her doctorate in psychology from the Johns Hopkins University. She has taught mathematics at the junior high school level, including a special system-wide program for mathematically gifted students, worked for the National Center for Educational Statistics, and was a project associate in the Study of Mathematically Precocious Youth while she was a doctoral student at Hopkins. In addition, she has taught graduate courses in gifted education. Dr. Fox is presently an associate professor of education at the Evening College and Summer Session of the Johns Hopkins University, advisor to graduate students enrolled in master's and doctoral degree programs in the gifted at Hopkins, and coordinator of the Intellectually Gifted Child Study Group.

## Contributions to Gifted Education

Dr. Fox has contributed to gifted education primarily in the following areas: sex differences in mathematics, mathematical precocity, the special needs of gifted girls, career education for the gifted, and training for teachers and administrators of gifted programs. She has served as an officer in the National Association of Gifted Children and has been a consultant in gifted education at the local, state, and federal levels.

## Publications in Gifted Education

Dr. Fox has contributed more than seventeen essays to collections on gifted and talented education and has written approximately eleven articles for professional journals. Some of the topics she has written about include the educational development of precocious youth, values and career interests of such students, sex differences in mathematical talent, the mathematically precocious female, career education for gifted preadolescents, and the guidance of gifted youth. She has coedited *Mathematical Talent: Discovery, Description, and Development* and has written a chapter, "Programs for the Gifted and Talented: An Overview," for the Seventy-eighth Yearbook of the National Society for the Study of Education. Her current book (in press) is *Women and the Mathematical Mystique.*

Dr. Mary M. Frasier
Department of Educational Psychology
University of Georgia
Athens, Georgia 30601

## Professional Background

Dr. Mary M. Frasier was an Early Entrant Ford Foundation scholar. She received her B.S. in music education and her M.Ed. in education, with a specialization in guidance and counseling from South Carolina State College, Orangeburg, South Carolina. Her Ph.D. in educational psychology was earned at the University of Connecticut. She has taught in the public schools (middle grades through high school), served as an instructor in Upward Bound, and directed a special services project for disadvantaged college students. Dr. Frasier is presently an assistant professor in the Department of Educational Psychology at the University of Georgia, where she is codirector of the program for the gifted and teaches graduate courses in the education of the gifted.

## Contributions to Gifted Education

Dr. Frasier's contributions to gifted education are primarily in the field of identification and programming for the culturally diverse gifted. Other contributions relate to counseling practices for the gifted and teacher training. Presently, she is a technical assistant to the Georgia State Department of Education for programs for the gifted, and a member of the executive committees of the Association for the Gifted and the National Association for Gifted Children. In 1977-78 she served as president of the Georgia Federation—Council for Exceptional Children. At the national level, she is the gifted consultant for the special needs program area with the National Center for Research in Vocational Education. At the local level, she is the gifted consultant for the science, technology, and environment program of the Clarke County School District.

## Publications in Gifted Education

Dr. Frasier has written journal articles, conference reports, and state reports on gifted education. She has also contributed a chapter on counseling the gifted and another on the disadvantaged minority gifted child.

Dr. Maurice F. Freehill
Department of Educational Psychology
University of Washington
Seattle, Washington 98195

*Professional Background*

Dr. Maurice F. Freehill was certified as a teacher and earned the B.Ed. in Alberta, Canada, and received a master's degree in student personnel and a doctorate in educational psychology from Stanford University. He was a teacher and principal in Alberta and served both special and regular assignments at the university level. Currently, Dr. Freehill is a professor and chairperson in the Department of Educational Psychology at the University of Washington.

*Contributions to Gifted Education*

Dr. Freehill has developed teacher education programs, served on state and district advisory committees, lectured and offered workshops, and supervised graduate students specializing in education of the gifted. Dr. Freehill has also delivered a paper, "The Nurturance of the Intellect," in the Distinguished Lecture Series in Special Education and Rehabilitation at the University of Southern California.

*Publications in Gifted Education*

Dr. Freehill has written approximately seven journal articles on school psychology and the gifted, the methodologic bias about teaching the gifted, school and society in gifted education, and intellectual giftedness. Dr. Freehill has also contributed five essays in volumes devoted to gifted and unusual children. He has written *Gifted Children—Their Psychology and Education* and coedited *The Gifted—Case Studies.*

Dr. Joseph L. French
Department of Special Education
Pennsylvania State University
University Park, Pennsylvania 16801

## Professional Background

Dr. Joseph L. French received a B.S. and M.S. from Illinois State University and an Ed.D. from the University of Nebraska. A faculty member at Pennsylvania State University since 1964, Dr. French was a lecturer in many NDEA Guidance Institutes between 1958 and 1964 while a member of the University of Missouri faculty. A professor of special education and educational psychology at Pennsylvania State University, Dr. French is the professor-in-charge of graduate programs in school and in educational psychology. He has served as head of the Department of Special Education.

## Contributions to Gifted Education

Dr. French is a former president of the Association for the Gifted (TAG) and has represented TAG to the Board of Governors of the Council for Exceptional Children. Also, he chaired the Section for the Gifted in the National Vocational Guidance Association. He was editor of *Education for the Gifted* and its revision. He holds a Certificate of Recognition from TAG and the Office of the Gifted and Talented, U.S. Office of Education. He has served on many USOE advisory panels and as a manuscript reviewer for several publishers. At Pennsylvania State University, he developed the master's degree emphasis for the gifted in education of exceptional children and frequently teaches the introductory course and advanced seminar about the gifted.

## Publications in Gifted Education

Dr. French has written four journal articles on preparation of teachers of the gifted, characteristics of high ability dropouts, aid for the gifted, and has contributed two essays to collections on the gifted, as well as writing a U.S. Office of Education research project. He has also authored *Educating the Gifted*.

Dr. James J. Gallagher, Director
Frank Porter Graham Child Development Center
University of North Carolina
Chapel Hill, North Carolina 27514

## Professional Background

Dr. James J. Gallagher received his B.S. from the University of Pittsburgh and his M.S. and Ph.D. in child and clinical psychology from Pennsylvania State University. He has been the director of psychological services at the Dayton Hospital for Disturbed Children, taught clinical psychology at Michigan State University, and was the associate director for the Institute for Research on Exceptional Children at the University of Illinois. Dr. Gallagher has also been a visiting professor at Duke University. He was the associate commissioner of education (in the Bureau of Education for the Handicapped) and the deputy assistant secretary for planning, research, and evaluation with the U.S. Office of Education. Currently, Dr. Gallagher is the director of the Frank Porter Graham Child Development Center and the Kenan Professor of Education at the University of North Carolina.

## Contributions to Gifted Education

Dr. Gallagher has been a consultant to state and federal agencies and has been the senior investigator for a National Science Foundation Fellowship to study mathematics at Stanford University. He has served as president of the Association for the Gifted and for four years was chairman of the Governor's Advisory Committee on the Gifted for the state of Illinois.

## Publications in Gifted Education

Dr. Gallagher has written articles on gifted education and authored *Teaching the Gifted Child*. He has contributed essays in books on such topics as measurement issues, issues in gifted education, and the diversity of and research on American education. Dr. Gallagher has also coauthored *The Education of Gifted and Talented Students: A History and Prospectus.*

Dr. Juliana T. Gensley
24466 Mulholland Highway
Calabasas, California 91302

## Professional Background

Dr. Juliana T. Gensley received her B.A. from the University of California at Los Angeles (U.C.L.A.), her M.A. from California State University at Los Angeles, and her Ed.D. from U.C.L.A. She has taught in the elementary grades and was the director of the gifted program at Redondo Beach. She has also taught in the summer program at California State University at Northridge and was a professor of education at California State University at Long Beach. Currently, she is a Professor Emeritus at California State University at Long Beach.

## Contributions to Gifted Education

Dr. Gensley is the president of the National Association for Gifted Children from 1979 to 1981 and has served as the program chairman for the 25th and 26th Annual Conventions of the Association. She has been active in training teachers of the gifted. She has also been involved in California's state studies of the gifted.

## Publications in Gifted Education

Dr. Gensley has authored a column in the *Gifted Child Quarterly* since 1970 and is author of the California guidelines for teaching mathematics for the gifted in grades four, five, and six.

Dr. Marvin J. Gold
Post Office Box 66654
Mobile, Alabama 36606

## Professional Background

Dr. Marvin J. Gold obtained his first B.S. from Columbia University in dramatic arts. His second bachelor's degree (in elementary education) was awarded by New Haven State Teachers College (now Southern Connecticut State College). His M.A. in administration and supervision of elementary programs was from New York University. His Ph.D. in gifted child education was granted by George Peabody College. He has taught all levels and grades in public schools and in universities, including Syracuse University, the University of South Florida, and the University of Kentucky. His summer appointments have been at the Universities of Connecticut, Guam, Hawaii, Alabama, McNeese State, and New Orleans, among others. Dr. Gold is presently coordinator of programs for the gifted at the University of South Alabama.

## Contributions to Gifted Education

Dr. Gold is editor and publisher of *G/C/T*, a magazine for parents and teachers of gifted, creative, and talented children. He is also a member of the Alabama State Board of Education, representing the First Congressional District of Alabama. He has been an officer and past president of the Association for the Gifted, the Florida Association for the Gifted, and the Alabama Association for Talented and Gifted. He is a past editor of the newsletter of the Association for the Gifted and *Talents and Gifts*, the journal of the Association for the Gifted. Dr. Gold received the Distinguished Alumnus of the Year Award from Southern Connecticut College in 1973.

## Publications in Gifted Education

Dr. Gold has written approximately ten journal articles on the gifted and contributed to books on topics such as the Lincoln School for the Gifted (Kentucky) and on national programs.

Dr. John Curtis Gowan
1426 Southwind
Westlake Village, California 91361

## Professional Background

Dr. John Curtis Gowan received his A.B. and M.Ed. from Harvard University and his Ed.D. from the University of California at Los Angeles. He has served as a registrar and counselor at private schools and has taught at the university level at such institutions as California State University, Northridge; the University of Hawaii; Southern Connecticut State College; and the University of Canterbury, New Zealand. He is a Professor Emeritus at California State University.

## Contributions to Gifted Education

Dr. Gowan is the former editor of the *Gifted Child Quarterly* and former executive director of the National Association for Gifted Children. He has been the president of both the Association for the Gifted and the National Association for Gifted Children. He is also a Fellow of the American Psychological Association.

## Publications in Gifted Education

Dr. Gowan has written more than one hundred articles on gifted children, teacher evaluation, measurement and guidance, and special education. He is also the author or coauthor of eleven books on the academically talented and the educational implications of creativity. Most recently, he is one of the editors of a revised edition of *Educating the Ablest.*

Mr. John A. Grossi
The Council for Exceptional Children
1920 Association Drive
Reston, Virginia 22091

### Professional Background

Mr. John A. Grossi received his B.A. in English education from St. Leo College and his M.A. in special education and gifted and talented from the University of South Florida. He has taught in public schools and at the college level. Mr. Grossi is presently director of gifted and talented policy information with the Council for Exceptional Children.

### Contributions to Gifted Education

Mr. Grossi has been involved in the development of programs and curriculums for the gifted and talented and in the identification of gifted handicapped children at the preschool level. Mr. Grossi has served as chairperson of the gifted-handicapped committee of the Association for the Gifted from 1976 to 1979. He has served as a consultant at the local, stae, and federal levels.

### Publications in Gifted Education

Mr. Grossi has written articles and books on the gifted and talented and the gifted-handicapped. Most recently, he has authored a model state policy, legislation, and state plan toward the education of the gifted and talented, and is currently coauthoring a book concerning the education of the gifted and talented for local administrators.

Dr. David Munro Jackson
2033 Headlands Circle
Reston, Virginia 22091

### Professional Background

Dr. David M. Jackson received his B.A. (with highest honors) in history and his M.A. in education from the University of Illinois, and his Ph.D. in curriculum and administration from the University of Chicago. He has been a teacher and principal in public and independent schools, a principal of the University of Illinois High School, and an associate dean of education at the University of Illinois. He has taught at the University of Illinois at Chicago Circle. He was the executive director of the National/ State Leadership Training Institute on the Gifted and Talented. Currently, he serves as president of the Gifted-Talented Institute, Reston, Virginia.

### Contributions to Gifted Education

Dr. Jackson has been involved in planning for the gifted at state and national levels in the United States and abroad. He has worked in the ERIC Clearinghouse on Handicapped and Gifted Children. He has been the director of program development for gifted children in the Office of the Illinois Superintendent of Public Instruction, and an associate superintendent for research, planning, and development in the Office of the Illinois Superintendent of Public Instruction. He has been a consultant on gifted education to the Brazilian Ministry of Education and to the government of Iran.

### Publications in Gifted Education

Dr. Jackson has authored or coauthored numerous articles on curriculum revision and programs and provisions for gifted children. He has also written documents on Illinois programs and contributed to a resource manual on gifted and talented. He has most recently written a chapter, "The Emerging National and State Concern for Educating the Gifted and Talented," for the Seventy-eighth Yearbook of the National Society for the Study of Education.

Ms. Joyce Juntune
National Association for Gifted Children
635 Twenty-third Avenue NW
New Brighton, Minnesota 55112

## Professional Background

Ms. Joyce Juntune received her B.A. from Bethel College, St. Paul, Minnesota, and her M.A. from Saint Cloud State University. She has done additional graduate work at Mankato State University and the University of Minnesota. She has taught in the public schools and at Saint Cloud State University and the College of Saint Thomas in St. Paul. She has also been a staff member at the Creative Problem Solving Institute at Buffalo. Currently, she is the executive director of the National Association for Gifted Children.

## Contributions to Gifted Education

Ms. Juntune is the past president of the Minnesota Council for Gifted and Talented and a member of the board for this group and the National Association for Gifted Children. She has been a consultant to school districts on gifted education and has worked on both state and national levels in developing materials for local parent groups. She has also led several parent training sessions.

## Publications in Gifted Education

She has been the guest editor for the *Gifted Child Quarterly* and has edited curriculum guides for developing thinking on mathematics, reading, social studies, language arts, and science. She has also authored three books, *The REACH Theory Book*, the *Creative Problem Solving Guide*, and *Thinking Activities on the Theme of Caring*.

Ms. Sandra N. Kaplan
National/State Leadership Training Institute on the
Gifted and Talented
316 West Second Street
Suite PH-C
Los Angeles, California 90012

## Professional Background

Ms. Sandra N. Kaplan has been a resource teacher for the gifted and has taught courses on the gifted on the university level. Currently, Ms. Kaplan is the assistant director of the National/State Leadership Training Institute on the Gifted and Talented.

## Contributions to Gifted Education

Ms. Kaplan has been a consultant on the state and national levels in gifted education. She has also administered programs for the gifted in California. She is a contributing editor of *Whole Classroom*, a magazine in education.

## Publications in Gifted Education

Ms. Kaplan is the coauthor of a number of books. These include *Big Book of Independent Study* and *Think Ins*. She is also the author of *Providing Programs for the Gifted: A Handbook*.

Dr. Felice A. Kaufmann
Department of Special Education
Auburn University
Auburn, Alabama 36830

## Professional Background

Dr. Felice A. Kaufmann received her B.A. in child development from Rockford College, her M.A. in special education for the gifted from Teachers College of Columbia University, and her Ph.D. in educational psychology and gifted education at the University of Georgia. She has directed gifted programs for public schools and a demonstration program at the University of Georgia. She has been an intern at the Office of Gifted and Talented, U.S. Office of Education. She was also a research assistant to Dr. E. Paul Torrance at the University of Georgia. Dr. Kaufmann is presently an assistant professor in special education and the gifted at Auburn University.

## Contributions to Gifted Education

Dr. Kaufmann's contributions to gifted education are in the field of creativity, problem solving, local programming, and parent education. She has presented workshops in these areas at state, local, and national conferences. She has also been a Fellow of the Graduate Leadership Education Project and a consultant in gifted education at the state and local levels.

## Publications in Gifted Education

Dr. Kaufmann has coauthored a journal article and a book on the evaluation of an experimental course in educational psychology. She is the author of *Your Gifted Child and You.*

Dr. Joe Khatena
Department of Educational Psychology
Mississippi State University
Drawer EP
Mississippi State, Mississippi 39762

## Professional Background

Dr. Joe Khatena received a Certificate in Education, a B.A. Honors in English from the University of Malaya, an M.Ed. in educational psychology from the University of Singapore, and his Ph.D. in psychology from the University of Georgia. He held two university scholarships and received two university awards. Dr. Khatena was a teacher in the Singapore public schools, a lecturer of English at the Singapore Teacher's Training College, and has taught psychology and education at East Carolina University and Marshall University. He is a Fellow of the American Psychological Association and is cited in ten biographical works. Dr. Khatena is presently a professor in and head of the Department of Educational Psychology at Mississippi State University.

## Contributions to Gifted Education

Dr. Khatena has been a president of the National Association for Gifted Children. He is on the editorial board of the *Gifted Child Quarterly* and has served as guest editor of two issues on the subject of creativity. He has received a Certificate of Recognition from the Office of Gifted and Talented, U.S. Office of Education, and a Robert Sterling Clark Foundation travel grant to speak at the First World Conference for the Gifted. Dr. Khatena has also served nationally as a consultant in gifted education, and while in West Virginia he was consultant and evaluator of Project Talented and Gifted and served as the chairman of the committee to establish state standards for teachers of the gifted. In addition, he was chairman of the U.S. Office of Education Region II Advisory Committee on Gifted and Talented.

## Publications in Gifted Education

Dr. Khatena has written three evaluation reports on Project Talented and Gifted, and over one hundred journal articles on various aspects of gifted education and creativity. He has also coauthored the publication of *Thinking Creatively with Sounds and Words* and the *Khatena-Torrance Creative Perception Inventory*, and he has coedited *Educating the Ablest*. Dr. Khatena is also the author of *The Creatively Gifted Child: Suggestions for Parents and Teachers.*

Dr. Alfred L. Lazar
Department of Special Education
California State University
Long Beach, California 90840

## Professional Background

Dr. Alfred L. Lazar attended Indiana State University, the University of Illinois, Redlands University, California State University at Los Angeles, University of Southern California, and California Western University. He holds the Ed.D. degree. He has taught special education courses in the elementary school and psychology at the community college and university levels. He is currently a professor of special education at California State University at Long Beach, where he was also the associate dean of the School of Education. He is also an adjunct professor at Pepperdine University.

## Contributions to Gifted Education

Dr. Lazar has been a consultant to school districts, state departments of education, industry, and the military. He was the president of the California Association of the Gifted and founder and first editor of the *CAG Communicator*, for which he has served as a treasurer and a member of the executive board. He is a Life Member of the Council for Exceptional Children. Dr. Lazar was the associate editor of *Exceptional Children* and editor of *The Journal for Special Educators*. In addition, he is a correspondent for *ETC, The Journal for General Semantics*, and is on the advisory board of *The Pointer*.

## Publications in Gifted Education

Dr. Lazar has published more than a dozen articles on creative teaching, attitudes of and toward the gifted, and intelligence and creativity. He has also authored or coauthored three studies of exceptional children, psycholinguistic teaching, and educational psychology.

Dr. Harold C. Lyon, Jr.
Office of Gifted and Talented
U.S. Office of Education
Washington, D.C. 20202

## Professional Background

Dr. Harold C. Lyon, Jr., received his bachelor's degree from West Point and his doctorate from the University of Massachusetts. A licensed psychologist, Dr. Lyon has served as the Abraham Maslow Professor at Antioch College and has taught at Georgetown University in humanistic psychology. He was also the Horace Mann Lecturer at the University of Massachusetts and the assistant to the president at Ohio University. Currently, Dr. Lyon is the director of education for the gifted and talented in the U.S. Office of Education.

## Contributions to Gifted Education

Dr. Lyon has served as the assistant deputy and deputy associate commissioner of education in the U.S. Office of Education. He worked with The White House Task Force on the Gifted in 1968.

## Publications in Gifted Education

Dr. Lyon has written *Learning to Feel—Feeling to Learn, It's Me and I'm Here,* and *Tenderness is Strength.* He is coauthoring *On Becoming a Teacher* with Dr. Carl Rogers. He has published numerous articles in periodicals on gifted education.

Dr. C. June Maker
Department of Special Education
University of New Mexico
Albuquerque, New Mexico 87131

### Professional Background

Dr. C. June Maker received her B.S. in elementary education from Western Kentucky University and her M.S. in special education for the gifted from Southern Illinois University. She completed a Ph.D. in special education and educational psychology with an emphasis in gifted education at the University of Virginia. Dr. Maker has taught in elementary schools and demonstrated teaching strategies with the gifted. She has served as a regional supervisor of programs for the gifted and as an administrative intern in the Office of the Gifted, U.S. Office of Education. Currently, Dr. Maker is an assistant professor of special education at the University of New Mexico. She was the principal investigator in a research project to identify the coping and learning strategies of handicapped scientists.

### Contributions to Gifted Education

Dr. Maker is presently teaching courses in curriculum development for the gifted and talented as well as courses in creativity and identification of the gifted. She is developing an exemplary master's degree program in education of the gifted as well as codirecting two experimental summer enrichment programs for gifted children. These programs serve as sites for practicum experiences for students in the master's degree and certification programs at the University of New Mexico. Her major contributions to gifted education are in the areas of teaching strategies for the gifted and provisions for the gifted-handicapped. She has developed general stratgies and materials for teaching the gifted and for teaching the gifted-handicapped. She serves on two advisory boards for programs for the gifted and is a review editor for *Teaching Exceptional Children* and the *Journal for Education of the Gifted*. Dr. Maker also serves on the board of directors and is secretary of the National Association for Gifted Children. She is a member of the gifted-handicapped committee and the chairperson of the committee on the culturally different gifted for the Association for the Gifted.

### Publications in Gifted Education

Dr. Maker has written journal articles on exceptional children and the gifted-handicapped. She has also written two books entitled *Providing Programs for the Gifted Handicapped* and *Training Teachers of the Gifted and Talented*. She is currently writing a second book on the gifted-handicapped and one on curriculum development for the gifted.

Dr. Mary Nacol Meeker
Structure of the Intellect Institute
343 Richmond
El Segundo, California 90245

## Professional Background

Dr. Mary Nacol Meeker received her B.S. and M.S. in psychology and an Ed.D. in educational psychology from the University of Southern California, where she taught for three years. She was director of training for school psychology at Loyola University of Los Angeles for seven years. Dr. Meeker has worked with the Japanese government and with most state departments of education. Currently, she is the director of the Structure of the Intellect Institute in El Segundo, California.

## Contributions to Gifted Education

Dr. Meeker is the recipient of an award from the U.S. Office of Education for her work with the structure of the intellect as a predictor of education in the next century. In 1962, she translated psychological structure of the intellect theory into structure of the intellect as application to education and has written workbooks and tests to diagnose and prescribe for development of intellectual abilities in all children. She has worked with the California State Department of Education in their programs for the gifted.

## Publications in Gifted Education

Dr. Meeker has written books and chapters on the gifted, the structure of the intellect, and testing and screening of students. She has authored *The Structure of the Intellect: Its Interpretation and Uses.*

Dr. T. Ernest Newland
702 South Race Street
Urbana, Illinois 61801

## Professional Background

Dr. T. Ernest Newland received his B.A. in French and education and psychology from Wittenberg College and his M.A. and Ph.D. in psychology and education from Ohio State University. Dr. Newland has taught gifted and talented education courses and was chief of special education with the Pennsylvania Department of Public Instruction. Dr. Newland was the director of the school psychology program at the University of Illinois at Urbana-Champaign where he is currently a Professor Emeritus in educational psychology.

## Contributions to Gifted Education

In addition to contributions in school psychology, Dr. Newland has done considerable clinical work with gifted children involving their educational adjustments. He has been active in presenting legislation to include the gifted as exceptional. He has been a selection officer for the Peace Corps and served the Teacher Corps as an evaluation consultant. Dr. Newland was president of the Association for the Gifted.

## Publications in Gifted Education

Dr. Newland has written numerous professional articles and contributed to works on the gifted and talented student dealing with such specific topics as observations and essential qualifications of teachers of the mentally superior, defining mentally superior in terms of social need, psychological assessment of exceptional children, and assessing the cognitive capability of exceptional children. Most recently, Dr. Newland has written a book entitled *The Gifted in Socio-Educational Perspective.*

Dr. Albert I. Oliver, Jr.
Graduate School of Education
University of Pennsylvania
Philadelphia, Pennsylvania 19104

### Professional Background

Dr. Albert I. Oliver, Jr., received his A.B. cum laude from Bates College, his M.Ed. from the University of New Hampshire, and his Ed.D. in curriculum development from the University of Colorado. He has also studied at Harvard University. Dr. Oliver was a high school teacher and administrator in several New England schools before becoming a curriculum specialist at the University of Pennsylvania. He has also been a visiting lecturer at the Universities of California and Colorado. He is presently a professor of education and coordinator of the educational leadership program at the University of Pennsylvania.

### Contributions to Gifted Education

Dr. Oliver is the past president of the Pennsylvania Association for the Study and Education of the Mentally Gifted and was the first president of the Association for the Gifted. He has been the chairman of the Middle States Commission on Secondary Schools and was chairman of the Pennsylvania State Committee on Secondary Schools Mathematics. At the University of Pennsylvania, Dr. Oliver is a consultant for the Educational Service Bureau and was coordinator of the teacher intern program for educating the gifted. He has also worked with curriculum development in secondary school mathematics for the gifted in Colorado.

### Publications in Gifted Education

Dr. Oliver has written journal articles on the gifted pupil and was a major contributor to *Administration: Procedures and School Practices for the Academically Talented in the Secondary School*. His text, *Curriculum Improvement,* is in its second edition, and he has also written a book entitled *Maximizing Minicourses.*

Dr. Sidney J. Parnes
160 Monroe Drive
Williamsville, New York 14221

## Professional Background

Dr. Sidney J. Parnes received his B.S., M.Ed., and Ph.D. from the University of Pittsburgh. Dr. Parnes has conducted workshops and taught at State University College at Buffalo, both on campus and in extension programs. Currently, he is president of the Creative Education Foundation and chairman of the annual creative problem-solving institutes. He is a professor and director of the Interdisciplinary Center for Creative Studies, State University College at Buffalo.

## Contributions to Gifted Education

Dr. Parnes is a member of the advisory board of the *Journal of Creative Behavior* and has conducted a wide variety of management and creativity workshops for schools, business, industry, and government. He has spoken at regional, state, national, and world conferences on the gifted, and was a special consultant and workshop leader for the U.S. Office of Education's "First National Student Symposium on the Education of the Gifted and Talented."

## Publications in Gifted Education

Dr. Parnes is the author of the *Creative Behavior Guidebook* and the *Creative Behavior Workbook*, and coauthor of *Guide to Creative Action* and *Creative Actionbook*. In addition, he is author of five more texts related to the gifted and an article on guiding creative action.

Dr. A. Harry Passow
Teachers College
Columbia University
New York, New York 10027

### Professional Background

Dr. A. Harry Passow received his B.A. in science and mathematics, his M.A. in administration and guidance from the State University of New York at Albany, and his Ed.D. in supervision and curriculum development from Columbia University. Dr. Passaw has taught in high school, but has been at Teachers College, Columbia University for most of his professional career. He founded and directed the Talented Youth Project. Dr. Passow is currently the Jacob H. Schiff Professor of Education and the director of the Division of Educational Institutions and Programs at Teachers College, Columbia University.

### Contributions to Gifted Education

Dr. Passow's contributions to education of gifted and talented have been in research and policy making. As founder and director of the Talented Youth Project of Teachers College's Horace Mann-Lincoln Institute, he headed up research and experimentation in numerous school systems across the country on various aspects of education of the gifted, consulted on panel for the *Marland Report*, and has served as monitor for the Astor Foundation on the Astor Gifted Child Project. He has conducted numerous workshops, institutes, and programs on gifted and talented. He is also the associate director of the Teachers College's project, Graduate Leadership Education Program in the Gifted and Talented, sponsored by the U.S. Office of Education, Office of the Gifted and Talented.

### Publications in Gifted Education

Dr. Passow has written twenty-two books, 135 articles, and chapters in books on topics including education of the gifted, the disadvantaged, secondary curriculum, and urban and comparative education. He is the editor of the Seventy-eighth Yearbook of the National Society for the Study of Education entitled *The Gifted and the Talented: Their Education and Development.*

Ms. Jo Patterson, Consultant
Gifted Education
Board of Education
Memphis City Schools
2597 Avery Avenue
Memphis, Tennessee 38112

**Professional Background**
    Ms. Jo Patterson received her B.A. cum laude and M.Ed. from Memphis State University and has completed work toward her doctorate at the University of Tennessee. She has taught in public schools and was the general supervisor of elementary education in Memphis. She is currently a consultant for gifted education in the Division of Special Education with the Memphis Board of Education.

**Contributions to Gifted Education**
    Ms. Patterson has served on the national nominating committee of the Association for the Gifted (TAG), has been state membership chairman, and has served a three-year term as secretary of the association. She is vice-president of TAG and president-elect (1980-1981). She designed and implemented CLUE, a program for the gifted in grades 1-9 in Memphis. She has served as a consultant for school systems throughout the United States. She has done workshops for teachers of the gifted in Memphis through Memphis State University and workshops at other universities including Colorado State University, University of Alaska, and Western Michigan University.

Dr. Joseph S. Renzulli
Bureau of Educational Research
University of Connecticut
Storrs, Connecticut 06268

**Professional Background**
  Dr. Joseph S. Renzulli received his B.S. from Glassboro State
College, his M.Ed. from Rutgers University in educational
psychology, and his Ed.D. in educational psychology from the
University of Virginia. He has taught mathematics, science, and
reading in the public schools and has been a school psychologist
as well. He has been a director of training at the Institute for
Educational Program Evaluators and a coordinator of research
and evaluation for high risk disadvantaged youth at the University of Connecticut. Currently, Dr. Renzulli is a professor of
educational psychology and the director of the program for
teaching the talented at the University of Connecticut. He is also
the associate director of the Bureau of Educational Research at
that institution.

**Contributions to Gifted Education**
  Dr. Renzulli has served as a consultant to the city of Boston for
their programs for the culturally disadvantaged, to the U.S.
Office of Education on legislation for the gifted and talented, and
to Station WBZ-TV (in Boston) for the children's television
program, *Earth Lab*. He has served as the vice-president and
president of the Association for the Gifted of the Council for
Exceptional Children. He has served as the chairman of three
different committees of the Council for Exceptional Children. He
is also on the board of directors of the National Association for
Gifted Children. Dr. Renzulli is an associate editor of *Exceptional
Children*, the *Gifted Child Quarterly*, the *Roeper Review*, the
*Journal of the Association for the Gifted*, and the *Journal of Law
and Education*.

**Publications in Gifted Education**
  Dr. Renzulli has authored more than twenty books, mono-
graphs, or chapters in books. He has written *The Enrichment
Triad Model: A Guide for Developing Defensible Programs for*

*the Gifted and Talented, Riders on the Earth,* and coauthored *The Learning Styles Inventory: A Measure of Student Preference for Instructional Techniques.* Dr. Renzulli has also authored or coauthored more than forty articles in professional journals on such topics as developing creativity training activities, talent potential in minority students, instructional management systems, an enrichment triad model, problems in the assessment of creativity, and training programs in the language arts.

Dr. Joseph P. Rice
2100 Twenty-first Street
Sacramento, California 95818

## Professional Background

Dr. Joseph P. Rice received his B.A. in science and psychology from American International College, his M.Ed. in pupil personnel services from Springfield College (Massachusetts), and his Ph.D. in administration, counseling, and child development from the University of Connecticut. He also had credentials in school psychology. He has taught in community colleges and been a school psychologist. He was chief of the Bureau of Mentally Exceptional Children of the California State Department of Education, and in that role he served as the state consultant in the education of the mentally gifted and directed the California Project Talent. He served as the associate commissioner of education with the Massachusetts State Department of Education. Currently, he is associate director of the California Migrant Teacher Assistant Corps, a federal project.

## Contributions to Gifted Education

Dr. Rice has taught extension courses in special education and curriculum construction; conducted workshops for teachers and parents of gifted students and for state and school district pupil personnel workers; and evaluated technical assistance projects involving eighteen state departments of education. He has also evaluated a bilingual, cross-cultural project for the San Mateo County Board of Education.

## Publications in Gifted Education

Dr. Rice has written more than ten journal articles on exceptional children, parent-teacher conferences, opinions of gifted students regarding secondary school programs, and the types of problems referred to a central guidance agency at different grade levels. He has authored a book entitled *The Gifted: Developing Total Talent.*

Dr. Marshall P. Sanborn
Department of Counseling and Guidance
University of Wisconsin-Madison
Madison, Wisconsin 53706

## Professional Background

Dr. Marshall P. Sanborn received his A.B. in English, speech, and drama from Colorado State College of Education at Greeley. After teaching for several years in high schools in Nebraska and Colorado, he was awarded a research assistantship at Iowa State Teachers College (now University of Northern Iowa), where he completed his M.A. in counseling and guidance. He then served as guidance director for Routt County School District Re2 in Colorado. He completed his Ph.D. in education at the University of Iowa. While at Iowa, he was a research assistant for the Iowa Testing Programs and a part-time instructor in the counselor education program. Currently, he is a professor in the Department of Counseling and Guidance, School of Education, University of Wisconsin-Madison.

## Contributions to Gifted Education

Dr. Sanborn was the associate director and director of the Research and Guidance Laboratory for Superior Students (now GIFTS), 1963-1974. He has been a consultant to the U.S. Office of Education, Office of Gifted and Talented, and a member of the National Invitational Seminar on Career Education for the Gifted, University of Maryland, and a member of the National Invitational Conference on Disadvantaged Gifted, Durham, North Carolina. Dr. Sanborn has conducted in-service training workshops for teachers of the gifted in most regions of the United States. As a Fulbright lecturer in Spain, he has employed principles developed at GIFTS for summer in-service training of Spanish educators.

## Publications in Gifted Education

Dr. Sanborn has written some twenty publications—books, articles, reports—on research and demonstration work with the gifted. He has written a chapter, "Counseling and Guidance Needs of Gifted and Talented," for the Seventy-eighth Yearbook of the National Society for the Study of Education and has also authored "A Statewide Program in the Discovery and Guidance of Gifted and Talented Students" for *Educational Programs and Intellectual Prodigies.*

Mr. Irving S. Sato
National/State Leadership Institute on
   the Gifted and Talented
316 West Second Street
Suite PH-C
Los Angeles, California 90012

## Professional Background

Mr. Irving S. Sato received both his B.Ed. (with honors) and his Fifth Year Diploma in education from the University of Hawaii and his M.S. from the University of Southern California. He has taught in elementary and secondary schools as well as on the university level. He has served as a consultant for gifted and creative student programs in Colorado and education of the mentally gifted in the California State Department of Education. Currently, he is the director of the National/State Leadership Institute on the Gifted and Talented.

## Contributions to Gifted Education

Mr. Sato has been a speaker at numerous meetings, conferences, and workshops for educators and parents of the gifted, including presentations at the annual international meetings of the Council for Exceptional Children and the annual meetings of the National Association for Gifted Children. He has been an associate director for the development of California's Statewide Framework and Exemplary Curriculum Guides and was the director of a federal project on gifted child education and was an advisor to the U.S. Office of Education. He was also a consultant to the government of Iran. Mr. Sato was the associate field editor of *Teaching Exceptional Children.*

## Publications in Gifted Education

Mr. Sato has published more than a dozen articles on gifted education, including such topics as the arts, training, giftedness, and creativity. He was the coeditor of *The Gifted Pupil* and is the coauthor of *Developing a Written Plan for the Education of Gifted and Talented Students.*

Dr. Dorothy A. Sisk
University of South Florida
College of Education
Tampa, Florida 33620

### Professional Background

Dr. Dorothy A. Sisk received her B.S. in education from Mount Union College and her M.A. in education from California State College. She earned the Ed.D. in special education from the University of California at Los Angeles. She began her professional career in the public schools in Garden Grove, California, as an elementary classroom teacher and later as a teacher of elementary gifted students. She served as both a teaching assistant and as a research assistant at the University of California at Los Angeles and as a consultant for gifted education to the Inglewood Unified School District in Los Angeles. She served as the coordinator of teacher training programs for the gifted at the University of South Florida and as a visiting lecturer at various colleges and universities. From 1976 to 1979, she was the director of the Office of Gifted and Talented with the U.S. Office of Education. Currently, she is a professor of special education at the University of South Florida.

### Contributions to Gifted Education

Dr. Sisk's service as a consultant to state, federal, and international agencies has been extensive. Her contributions to professional organizations include chairing the section of gifted education at annual international meetings for the Council for Exceptional Children and serving as program chairperson, president, and international chairperson at annual meetings of the Association for the Gifted. She has served as vice-chairperson and is currently serving on the World Executive Committee of the World Council for Gifted and Talented Children.

### Publications in Gifted Education

Dr. Sisk has written numerous technical reports for the Office of Education, professional organizations, state departments of education, and intermediate school units. She has written or coauthored several articles on such topics as the culturally disadvantaged, orthopedic disabilities, self-concept and creativity, teaching the gifted and talented teacher, and communication skills for the gifted.

Dr. Richard Stahl
Department of Special Education
Appalachian State University
Boone, North Carolina 28607

## Professional Background

Dr. Richard Stahl received a B.A. in psychology and an M.A. in special education with an emphasis in gifted and talented from the University of South Florida at Tampa. Dr. Stahl received his Ph.D. from Florida State University in educational administration. Dr. Stahl has directed Saturday and summer enrichment programs and is currently an associate professor and coordinator of gifted and talented programs at Appalachian State University.

## Contributions to Gifted Education

Dr. Stahl has served as a consultant at the national, state, and local levels. He is the state secretary for the North Carolina Association for Gifted and Talented Education. He founded and edits the *NCAGT Quarterly*. He also founded and directs the Appalachian State University summer and Saturday enrichment programs.

## Publications in Gifted Education

Dr. Stahl has written several journal articles dealing with gifted education.

Dr. Julian C. Stanley
Director of SMPY
Department of Psychology
The Johns Hopkins University
Baltimore, Maryland 21218

## Professional Background

Dr. Julian C. Stanley received his Ed.D. in educational psychology and measurement from Harvard University. He has taught high school science and mathematics and has taught psychology at a junior college. Dr. Stanley taught education and educational psychology at Harvard University, George Peabody College, and the University of Wisconsin, where he was chairman of the educational psychology department and the director of the Laboratory of Experimental Design. Currently, Dr. Stanley is a professor of psychology and the director of the Study of Mathematically Precocious Youth at the Johns Hopkins University.

## Contributions to Gifted Education

Dr. Stanley is a former president of the American Research Association, National Council on Measurement in Education, and the Divisions of Educational Psychology and of Evaluation and Measurement of the American Psychological Association. He is the recipient of the E. L. Thorndike Award for his contribution to education.

## Publications in Gifted Education

Dr. Stanley has coedited four volumes, *Mathematical Talent: Discovery, Description, and Development, The Gifted and the Creative: A Fifty-year Perspective, Educational Programs and Intellectual Prodigies,* and *Educating the Gifted: Acceleration and Enrichment.* He has also edited another volume on gifted education and written a journal article on educational non-acceleration.

Dr. Abraham J. Tannenbaum
Teachers College
Columbia University
New York City, New York 10027

### Professional Background

Dr. Abraham J. Tannenbaum received his B.A. in English from Brooklyn College and his M.A. in guidance and educational administration and his Ph.D. in social and educational psychology from Columbia University. He has taught in the public schools in New York and has served as a supervisor of instruction there and a supervisor of student teaching for Brooklyn College, where he also taught education courses. Dr. Tannenbaum has taught at Yeshiva University, where he was an associate dean of the Graduate School of Education. Currently, he is a professor of education at Teachers College, Columbia University.

### Contributions to Gifted Education

Dr. Tannenbaum was a Fulbright-Hays visiting professor at Hebrew University, Jerusalem, and director of the federally funded Graduate Leadership Education Project and is recipient of a U.S. Office of Education contract to prepare a series of information products on gifted and talented education. He has been a member of the Cooperative Research Review Board and a research consultant to the Language Laboratory Research Project, Project Head Start, and Mobilization for Youth (New York City). Dr. Tannenbaum has been the president of the Metropolitan Association for the Study of the Gifted and an associate editor of the *Journal of Social Issues*. He also served a term as president of the Council for Children with Behavioral Disorders.

### Publications in Gifted Education

Dr. Tannenbaum has written or coauthored more than a dozen articles on gifted education, psychological and sociological considerations, school dropouts, tutoring programs, and group care of immigrant adolescents in Israel. He has contributed more than seven articles and chapters to books on gifted education and authored or edited books and journals on the disadvantaged; the gifted; values, attitudes, and behaviors in social science and society; and alienated youth. Dr. Tannenbaum has also coedited a book of readings on education of the disadvantaged. He has also coauthored a three-volume work entitled *A Taxonomy of Instructional Treatments* and written a chapter, "Pre-Sputnik to Post Watergate Concern about the Gifted," for the Seventy-eighth Yearbok of the National Study of Education. He is currently writing a book on the nature and needs of the gifted.

Dr. E. Paul Torrance
Department of Educational Psychology
University of Georgia
Athens, Georgia 30601

## Professional Background

Dr. E. Paul Torrance received his B.A. in English at Mercer University, his M.A. in educational psychology at the University of Minnesota, and his Ph.D. at the University of Michigan in educational psychology. He has taught at all educational levels and been a counselor and counseling bureau director; he has been a researcher and research director in Georgia, Kansas, Colorado, Nevada, and Minnesota. He has served as consultant to a variety of organizations. Dr. Torrance is currently Alumni Foundation Distinguished Professor of Educational Psychology at the University of Georgia and director of the Georgia Studies of Creative Behavior.

## Contributions to Gifted Education

Dr. Torrance has been honored by the National Association for Gifted Children, the Association for the Gifted, Psi Chi, and American Personnel and Guidance Association for his pioneering work in identifying and developing creative talent.

## Publications in Gifted Education

Dr. Torrance has published approximately twenty-five books, several tests, and at least one thousand articles on gifted education. His latest books are *Discovery and Nurturance of Giftedness in the Culturally Different,* and *The Search for Satori and Creativity.*

Dr. Donald J. Treffinger
160 Monroe Drive
Williamsville, New York 14221

### Professional Background

Dr. Donald J. Treffinger received his B.S. in education from the State University College at Buffalo and his M.S. and Ph.D. in educational psychology from Cornell University. He has taught in the elementary and junior high schools and at Purdue University, Cornell University, and the University of Kansas. Currently, Dr. Treffinger is professor of creative studies at the State University College at Buffalo.

### Contributions to Gifted Education

Dr. Treffinger has been very active in teacher training programs and research. He is editor of the *Gifted Child Quarterly*, a book review editor and member of the editorial board of the *Journal of Creative Behavior*, and a member of the editorial board of the *Journal for the Education of the Gifted*. He has served as a resource leader at the Creative Problem Solving Institute, Buffalo, and a member of numerous committees and review panels on educational research and gifted education. He is a member of the executive board of the National Association for Gifted Children. Dr. Treffinger has also presented at numerous conferences and professional meetings.

### Publications in Gifted Education

Dr. Treffinger has authored or coauthored more than fifty articles in professional journals, written many reviews, and contributed several chapters to volumes devoted to gifted education. Recent books of which he is author or coauthor include *Reach Each You Teach, Encouraging Creative Learning, It's A Gas to be Gifted*, and *Creative Thinking and Problem Solving in Gifted Education*.

Dr. Virgil S. Ward
School of Education
Peabody Hall
University of Virginia
Charlottesville, Virginia 22903

## Professional Background

Dr. Virgil S. Ward received his B.A. from Wofford College, his M.Ed. from Duke University, and his Ph.D. in educational psychology from the University of North Carolina. Dr. Ward has taught English in high school and education at Wofford College and the University of Virginia, where he currently is professor of education and past chairman of the Department of Foundations of Education.

## Contributions to Gifted Education

Dr. Ward has been a consultant at the national, state, and local levels. He has served as the president of the Association for the Gifted and as a member of the board of directors for the National Association of the Gifted. He was the Virginia representative to the Council for Exceptional Children. Dr. Ward has delivered approximately fifty conference papers and addresses on curricula for the gifted, the Governor's School of North Carolina, and the gifted in world perspective. He has consistently urged a strong theoretical base—scientific and philosophical—for differential education for the gifted.

## Publications in Gifted Education

Dr. Ward has written approximately thirty-five essays and research papers on professional education, the role of theory in education, and education of the gifted and disadvantaged. He has authored a book entitled *Educating the Gifted: An Axiomatic Approach*. He was director of the Southern Regional Project for Education of the Gifted, and contributed widely to the National Education Association's Project on the Academically Talented Secondary School Student.

Dr. Frank E. Williams
3670 Dallas Road, NW
West Salem, Oregon 97304

## Professional Background

Dr. Frank E. Williams received his B.S. in engineering from the University of Colorado, his M.A. in science education from Stanford University, and his Ph.D. in educational psychology at the University of Utah. Dr. Williams was a research associate at the University of Utah and a former director of the National Schools Project at Macalester College. He has served as an educational consultant to numerous school districts across the country. Currently, Dr. Williams is an adjunct professor at Oregon College of Education and director of the Annual Northwest Conferences on the Gifted.

## Contributions to Gifted Education

Dr. Williams has been a consultant and evaluator to the Anchorage, Alaska, project; SORD consortium in Southern Oregon; and Impact Project in Des Moines, Iowa. He is founder of the Oregon Association for the Gifted and Talented. He has produced teacher training packets, a delivery system model and a complete kit on creative-productive thinking, including checklists and scales for identification of gifted students and programs.

## Publications in Gifted Education

Dr. Williams has written fifty-three articles for professional journals, created the Williams' Model involving processes and strategies for gifted education, produced a *Total Creativity Program Kit*, a *Classroom Ideas Book*, and a textbook, *Teachers Without Fear*.

Mrs. Mary Hunter Wolf
Center for Theatre Techniques in Education
1850 Elm Street
Stratford, Connecticut 06497

## Professional Background

Mrs. Mary Hunter Wolf has been a Broadway director and producer and established the professional training program for the American Theatre Wing. Currently, she is the president of the Center for Theatre Techniques in Education and the director of the model project, Talent Search and Development, which has been expanded to include the identification of potentially gifted students in visual and performing arts.

## Contributions to Gifted Education

Mrs. Wolf has been a member of the Connecticut Advisory Council on Special Education and the chairperson of the Task Force on Gifted Education in that state; she has also served as a consultant to the Task Force on Gifted Education for the City of New Haven, Johnson State College's graduate program on gifted education, and helped to develop the graduate curriculum on gifted education for Fairfield University. She is a reader and consultant at policy conferences for the U.S. Office of Education, Office of the Gifted. In addition, she has served as a panelist and consultant for the summer leadership training institute conferences.

## Publications in Gifted Education

Mrs. Wolf has authored *Concept H4: Identification of Students Gifted in the Performing Arts* and *American Education: Identifying Talent Among the Disadvantaged.* She is also the coauthor of a book entitled *Talent Search and Development.*

# SECTION III
## STATE CONSULTANTS

The growth in the number of state consultants for gifted and talented education has increased significantly over the past several years and parallels the resurgence of a national interest and concern for gifted and talented youth. Presently, virtually all of the states have designated a person or persons with responsibility for gifted and talented education, with the majority of states employing a full-time consultant.

While the scope of responsibilities of state consultants varies considerably from state to state, there are general functions and responsibilities that are common to most and are similar to those of state consultants in other program areas. These general responsibilities are comprehensive in scope and include, but are not limited to, the following.

1. Determining the state's needs through periodic assessments of state-wide programs and services for the gifted and talented.

2. Determining appropriate goals or objectives based upon needs assessments in terms of the unique educational requirements of the state's gifted and talented student population.

3. Developing an annual state plan based upon the stated goals or objectives for gifted and talented education.

4. Assisting in the formulation and supervision of the state's policies and procedures guiding all aspects of the educational provisions for gifted and talented education.

5. Preparing and presenting position papers in support of legislation needed to initiate, revise, and expand state-wide programs and services for gifted and talented education.

6. Serving as the liaison person in the communications network among the various national, regional, state, and local

171

constituencies for gifted and talented education.

7. Gathering, evaluating, and disseminating information on all aspects of gifted and talented education.

 ' 8. Providing consultant services and assistance to intermediate and local educational agencies in the implementation and evaluation of programs and services for the gifted and talented.

As a group, the state consultants for gifted and talented education have made significant contributions to the literature through various print and nonprint media.

A majority of the consultants have provided invaluable service as officers of, advisors to, and members of various state professional associations and organizations. Several have provided active leadership in national organizations and associations for gifted and talented education.

All of the consultants have worked to secure increased state funding for gifted and talented education in their respective states, and several have given support to the passing of federal legislation.

At the practical level, the consultants have a rich and varied experiential background as teachers, principals, curriculum specialists, and other supervisory and administrative positions at both school and school district levels.

By virtue of their pivotal state position, their professional preparation, their experiential background, and their professional expertise, the state consultants represent an indispensable resource to parents, teachers, supervisors, and administrators in all areas of concern in gifted and talented education. These individuals are presented by state and name in alphabetical order.

## ALABAMA

Ms. Cynthia Ratliff Aguero, Education Specialist
Gifted and Talented Education
State Department of Education
416 State Office Building
Montgomery, Alabama 36130

### Professional Background

Ms. Cynthia Ratliff Aguero received her B.S. in psychology and sociology and an M.A. in special education and gifted education from the University of South Florida. She has taught in the public schools and has been a coordinator of student teachers and a demonstration teacher. At the University of South Florida, she was an undergraduate advisor and supervisor of undergraduate teaching interns. She was formerly a learning specialist and teacher of the gifted for the Pinellas County School System in Clearwater, Florida, and is currently an education specialist for the gifted and talented with the Alabama State Department of Education.

### Contributions to Gifted Education

Ms. Aguero has been on programs for the gifted and exceptional children at the state and national levels. She has served as a consultant to principals, advising them about testing programs for the gifted, and she has worked with individual teachers and parents. She has also conducted workshops and in-service meetings on the curriculum for the gifted.

### Publications in Gifted Education

Ms. Aguero has coauthored a state grant on the development of the gifted curriculum for the Florida State Department of Education and Florida Learning Resource Systems and has provided research data and informational surveys on exceptional students.

**ARIZONA**

Ms. Eleanor Martini TeSelle, Director
Gifted Education
Division of Special Education
State Department of Education
1535 West Jefferson
Phoenix, Arizona 85007

*Professional Background*
Ms. Eleanor Martini TeSelle received her B.A. and M.A. from Arizona State University. She has done further graduate work at the University of Nevada and at the University of Southern California. She has taught in a one-room school and has taught creative writing and journalism in California and English in Phoenix, Arizona. She has been a principal, a curriculum center director, and a director of special projects with the Mesa School District. Currently, she is a consultant with the Arizona State Department of Education.

*Contributions to Gifted Education*
Ms. TeSelle was the first woman president of the Arizona School Administrators and is the president-elect for Soroptimist International of Mesa. She has presented papers on gifted education to various groups, including the American Educational Research Association, Arizona School Administrators, and the American Association of School Administrators. She has also been a reader for gifted programs for the U.S. Office of Education, Office of Gifted and Talented.

# ARKANSAS

Dr. Clifford D. Curl, Consultant
Programs for the Gifted and Talented
Special Education Section
State Department of Education
Arch Ford Education Building
Little Rock, Arkansas 72201

## *Professional Background*

Dr. Clifford D. Curl received his A.B. degree in piano performance at Pasadena College, California, and the M.S. degree in elementary education from Emporia State University, Kansas. He earned the Ed.D. degree in special education administration with emphasis in gifted education from the University of Kansas, Lawrence. He has had extensive teaching experience in elementary and secondary schools and has served as guest lecturer in several colleges and universities. Dr. Curl has served as a consultant in gifted education at the local, state, and national levels. Dr. Curl is presently consultant for the gifted at the Arkansas State Department of Education.

## *Contributions to Gifted Education*

Dr. Curl's contributions to gifted education have focused on administration, programming, and the curriculum.

## *Publications in Gifted Education*

Dr. Curl has coauthored a work on a self-directed course of study for gifted, talented, and creative learners for the National/State Leadership Training Institute on the Gifted and Talented.

**CALIFORNIA**

Dr. Jack A. Mosier, Manager and Director of
  Federal Projects
Gifted and Talented Education Management Team
State Department of Education
721 Capitol Mall
Sacramento, California 95814

*Professional Background*
  Dr. Jack A. Mosier received his B.S. and M.A. in education from
the University of Southern California. He earned his Ed.D. in
gifted education from Brigham Young University. His professional career includes teaching at the public school and
university levels, serving as an administrator in the public
schools, and serving as a consultant in gifted education at the
local, state, and national levels. Currently, he is the manager of
the California program for gifted and talented education and is
assuming the position of federal project director for school year
1979-80.

*Contributions to Gifted Education*
  Dr. Mosier's contributions to gifted education are primarily in
program planning and implementation. He is responsible as
manager for 340 school districts in California (rural and urban),
serving over 160,000 identified, state-funded gifted students. The
federal project will serve California, Oregon, and Washington in
training forty-two program support coordinators.

*Publications in Gifted Education*
  Dr. Mosier has written articles for journals and newsletters, has
participated as a member of the management team for gifted
education in California in presenting papers and workshops, and
has authored works on the gifted.

## CALIFORNIA

Dr. Paul Plowman, Consultant
Gifted and Talented Education Management Team
State Department of Education
721 Capitol Mall
Sacramento, California 95814

### *Professional Background*

Dr. Paul Plowman received a B.A. in political science from Carleton College and an M.A. in political science from the University of Wisconsin. He received his Ed.D. in general school administration from Stanford University. In public and private schools, he has been employed as counselor, educational consultant, and principal. Dr. Plowman is presently a California state consultant in the education of the gifted and talented. He is a member of the gifted and talented education management team of the California State Department of Education.

### *Contributions to Gifted Education*

Dr. Plowman has made numerous presentations at professional conferences; advised school districts, state departments of education, and college personnel on organizing and improving programs for gifted and talented children and youth; and prepared many articles and guidelines which have aided program development. He has worked with personnel in the U.S. Office of Education and in various states to coordinate program development at the national level and among the states. Since 1962, Dr. Plowman has been instrumental in California and nationally in developing, implementing, and improving "qualitatively different" and "uniquely appropriate" programs for gifted and talented children. He tested, refined, and disseminated information concerning enrichment, acceleration, special classes, and counseling-instructional program options through California's Project Talented, a U.S. Office of Education cooperative research project (1962-65); produced a state framework and twenty-eight exemplary curriculum and teaching guides through a U.S. Office of Education, Title V contract (1968); trained three thousand teachers of gifted in ninety-two workshops in fourteen regions of

California, PL 93-380 (1976-78); and designed and is directing a PL 93-380 project: Integrative Education for Gifted Children and Youth, Their Parents, Their Teachers, and Their Counselors (1978-79). Dr. Plowman has also assisted the commissioner of the U.S. Office of Education in preparing a report to Congress (1971); served as a consultant to the Texas State Legislature (1974); was employed as a visiting scholar and supervising teacher at the University of Washington (1975); made a major speech on "Futuristic Views of Gifted Child Education" at the Second World Conference on the Education of the Gifted (1977); and gave a presentation on "Extraordinary Leadership" at a U.S. Office of Education—State of Illinois sponsored conference in Chicago in 1978.

### Publications in Gifted Education

Dr. Plowman has written a book on behavioral objectives in terms of teacher success through student performance, has contributed essays to volumes on the gifted, and has published numerous journal articles on such topics as encouraging the academic development of the talented, programming for the gifted child, refinement of programs for the gifted through a process of evaluation, and futuristic views of gifted child education. He has written extensively on California programs for the gifted.

## COLORADO

Dr. Gerald K. Villars, Senior Consultant and
    State Coordinator
Programs for the Gifted and Talented
State Department of Education
201 East Colfax Avenue
Denver, Colorado 80203

### Professional Background

Dr. Gerald K. Villars received his B.A. in history and economics from Macalester College and an M.A. in history and literature from the University of Colorado. He has also studied the humanities as a John Hay Fellow at Yale University. His Ph.D. is in curriculum and instruction, with an emphasis in organization development from the University of Colorado. Presently, he is a senior consultant with the Colorado State Department of Education, providing technical assistance in developing programs for gifted and talented students in Colorado.

### Contributions to Gifted Education

Dr. Villars is a charter member of the Minnesota Council for the Gifted and the editor of the Council's first monograph on the gifted. He has contributed to gifted child education by providing technical assistance to Colorado school districts and other interested agencies, emphasizing the importance of employing systematic change strategies in developing comprehensive and full-time programming for gifted and talented students.

### Publications in Gifted Education

Dr. Villars has written on issues and recommendations dealing with programming for the gifted and on diverse approaches to developing individual student talent.

**CONNECTICUT**

Mr. William G. Vassar, Director
Programs for the Gifted
State Department of Education
305 State Office Building
Hartford, Connecticut 06115

### Professional Background

Mr. William G. Vassar received his B.A. magna cum laude from American International College, his M.Ed. from Springfield College, and an Advanced Graduate Study Certificate in educational administration from the University of Massachusetts, where he is presently a doctoral candidate. Mr. Vassar has taught in elementary and high school; he was also a junior high school principal. In addition, he has been a visiting lecturer and adjunct professor at numerous colleges and universities in Massachusetts and Connecticut. For one and one-half years, he was the senior supervisor for the academically talented for the Massachusetts State Department of Education. Since 1966, he has been the state director for gifted and talented programs with the Connecticut State Department of Education.

### Contributions to Gifted Education

Mr. Vassar has been the president of both the Association for the Gifted, Division of International Council for Exceptional Children, and the National Association for Gifted Children. He is now the president of the Council of State Directors of Gifted Programs. He has been a consultant to state departments of education in over ten states and to the National Education Association's project on the academically gifted. He has served as the coordinator of the 50-state study for President Johnson's White House Task Force on the Gifted and Talented and is a consultant to the U.S. Office of Education's commission for the study of gifted and talented. Mr. Vassar has appeared before various Senate and House subcommittees on education. Finally, he has served as a resource consultant to over fifteen colleges and universities.

### Publications in Gifted Education

Mr. Vassar has published forty-two articles and seven monographs on the gifted and talented.

## DISTRICT OF COLUMBIA

Dr. Patsy B. Blackshear, Coordinator
Gifted and Talented Education Programs
Public Schools of the District of Columbia
415 Twelfth Street, NW, Room 1207
Washington, D.C. 20004

### Professional Background

Dr. Patsy B. Blackshear received a bachelor's degree in mathematics education and a master's degree in special education. She holds an Advanced Graduate Study Certificate in supervision and special education. She holds a Ph.D. from the University of Maryland. She has worked in the Washington, D.C., public schools for the last ten years, holding positions as teacher of mathematics and special education, supervisor of in-service training of teachers of mathematics and special education, and school coordinator for the Washington, D.C., Teacher Corps program. Currently, she is the coordinator of the gifted and talented education program for the Washington, D.C., public schools.

### Contributions to Gifted Education

During her tenure as coordinator for the gifted and talented education program, Dr. Blackshear has developed pilot programs for the academically and potentially gifted students in the Washington, D.C., public schools.

**FLORIDA**

Ms. Joyce Runyon
Consultant for the Gifted
State Department of Education
204 Knott Building
Tallahassee, Florida 32304

### *Professional Background*
Ms. Joyce Runyon earned her B.A. in psychology from Maryville College (Tennessee) and an M.S. in special education from the University of Tennessee at Knoxville. In addition, she has completed work beyond her master's degree at several institutions, including the University of Georgia, Syracuse University, and San Francisco State University. She has taught in programs for the mentally retarded, emotionally disturbed, homebound, and gifted child. She has been a director of exceptional student education in the public schools. Currently, she is the consultant for the gifted for the Florida State Department of Education.

### *Contributions to Gifted Education*
Ms. Runyon has been active in the development and programming for the gifted, including program organizational structures and curriculum and instruction. She has served three terms as the president of the National Council of State Directors of Programs for the Gifted.

### *Publications in Gifted Education*
Ms. Runyon has written a resource manual for gifted education and contributed two chapters in books on the gifted.

## GEORGIA

Ms. Margaret O. Bynum, Director
Programs for the Gifted
State Department of Education
State Office Building
Atlanta, Georgia 30334

### Professional Background

Ms. Margaret O. Bynum received her B.A. in elementary education from the University of Montevallo and her M.S. in special education, with an emphasis in gifted education, from Syracuse University. She has taught in the public schools and at the university level; she was also a high school librarian. She served as the director of the Governor's Honor Program for nine years. Currently, she is the director for programs for the gifted in the Georgia State Department of Education.

### Contributions to Gifted Education

Ms. Bynum has served as the national membership chairman and president of the Association for the Gifted. For two years, she was the secretary for the Council for State Directors of Programs for the Gifted. She has also served on national committees for gifted education in addition to being a consultant for numerous school systems and several states.

### Publications in Gifted Education

Ms. Bynum has written articles on identifying the gifted and the Governor's Honor Program. She has contributed to a manual on program improvement in gifted education. She also has written guidelines for in-service education for the gifted and talented.

**IDAHO**

Ms. Genelle L. Christensen, Coordinator
Programs for Gifted and Talented
State Department of Education
Len B. Jordan Building
Boise, Idaho 83720

### *Professional Background*

Ms. Genelle L. Christensen received her B.A. in education from Illinois State University and an M.A. in guidance and counseling from the University of Illinois. She was granted an Advanced Certificate in Education (sixth year) from the University of Illinois. She taught in special education, was a classroom teacher, and directed federal projects in Illinois. Ms. Christensen is currently state coordinator of programs for gifted and talented in Idaho and is the consultant in special education for the Idaho State Department of Education.

### *Contributions to Gifted Education*

Ms. Christensen has been an educational consultant to Science Research Associates, the University of Illinois, and the University of Oregon. She has also served as a consultant at federal, state, and local levels in various educational areas, particularly in the education of exceptional children and youth. She was instrumental in the development of state guidelines for the gifted and talented and in writing a resource manual for gifted and talented education for Idaho.

### *Publications in Gifted Education*

Ms. Christensen has written articles on the importance of the counselor in gifted and talented education and on exceptionalities in this field.

## ILLINOIS

Ms. Joyce Van Tassel, Director
Gifted Program
State Department of Public Instruction
100 North First Street
Springfield, Illinois 62777

### Professional Background

Ms. Joyce Van Tassel received a B.E. in English and Latin, an M.A. in English and an M.E. in education, all from the University of Toledo. She has taught on the high school and university levels. She has administrated gifted programs at the local and state levels as well as worked in a variety of gifted programs with students and teachers. In addition, she has served as a consultant to the local, state, and national levels. Ms. Van Tassel is presently the director of gifted education with the Illinois State Department of Public Instruction.

### Contributions to Gifted Education

Ms. Van Tassel has contributed to the field through service work on behalf of the Association for the Gifted, setting up a local parents' group, organizing a university-based Saturday enrichment program, and presenting material pertinent to program development at many conferences and meetings.

### Publications in Gifted Education

Ms. Van Tassel has written four articles dealing with the gifted. These concern the role of libraries in gifted child education, the talent search for the gifted in Illinois, local level gifted programs, and the gifted child.

# INDIANA

Mr. Charles E. Whaley, Director
Gifted Education
Division of Curriculum
Department of Public Instruction
Room 229, State Capitol Building
Indianapolis, Indiana 46204

## Professional Background

Mr. Charles E. Whaley received his B.S. and an M.S. in secondary and alternative education in addition to an Ed.S. in secondary and currriculum education from Indiana University. He has taught in both elementary and secondary schools and in both traditional and alternative school settings. He is currently the director of gifted education with the Indiana State Department of Public Instruction.

## Contributions to Gifted Education

Mr. Whaley has designed and implemented curricular programs focusing on the study of global futures as they apply to the gifted and talented student. He has also served as a consultant to local educational agencies, universities, and professional groups in Indiana.

## Publications in Gifted Education

Mr. Whaley has written articles on the study of global futures and the gifted child.

**KENTUCKY**

Mr. Joseph T. Clark, Coordinator
Gifted and Talented
Division of Program Development
Bureau of Instruction
Department of Education
1809 Capitol Plaza Tower
Frankfort, Kentucky 40601

### Professional Background

Mr. Joseph T. Clark received his B.A. in English and his M.A. in secondary education from the University of Kentucky. He is currently enrolled in a doctoral program in educational administration and supervision at the University of Kentucky. He has taught at the junior and senior high school levels and has also served as a consultant for the reading and language arts program at the state level and for the Right to Read program. Mr. Clark currently serves as coordinator of the Kentucky program for gifted and talented education with the Kentucky State Department of Education. In this position, he coordinates both the administrative and curricular aspects of the state program by working with local school districts.

### Contributions to Gifted Education

Mr. Clark has conducted numerous training sessions for teachers in creativity and learning processes for the gifted. He has also been involved in workshops on motivating the reluctant learner.

## LOUISIANA

Mrs. Ruth Castille, Section Chief
Gifted and Talented Education
State Department of Education
P. O. Box 44064, Capitol Station
Baton Rouge, Louisiana 70804

### *Professional Background*

Ms. Ruth Castille received her B.S. in mathematics, science, and chemistry, and her M.S. in mathematics and educational administration from the University of Southwestern Louisiana. She earned an educational specialist degree in psychology and administration and supervision from the same institution. She has completed additional graduate hours in varied fields from several out-of-state universities and is presently working toward her Ph.D. in administration and supervision of programs for the gifted at Louisiana State University. She has taught science, mathematics, and chemistry at the secondary level, and has been a guidance counselor, teacher of psychology and education, and an educational coordinator for an Upward Bound program at the university level. She has also taught in an experimental program for the academically gifted. Currently, she is the section chief with two full-time coordinators for gifted and talented programs with the Louisiana State Department of Education.

### *Contributions to Gifted Education*

Ms. Castille has been a member of the South Carolina ten-state project on gifted and talented in-service leadership training and a member of the Region VI program on leadership training. She has participated in numerous workshops and conferences nationally and locally and has also directed twenty conferences on gifted and talented education. She has been instrumental in providing unique state identification criteria for the academically gifted student and also for the talented student. She has authored many articles on gifted education.

## MAINE

Ms. Patricia O'Connell, Consultant
Gifted Education
Department of Educational and Cultural Services
State Department of Education
Augusta, Maine 04333

### Professional Background

Ms. Patricia O'Connell received her B.A. in anthropology from Beloit College, Wisconsin, and an M.A.T. in education from George Washington University. She was selected as a George Washington University Educational Policy Fellow. She has worked with public and private schools and is presently the state consultant for gifted education with the Maine State Department of Education.

### Contributions to Gifted Education

Ms. O'Connell's contribution to gifted education is in initiating programs in gifted education in Maine. She drafted and successfully saw enacted the first state legislation dealing with education for the gifted student.

### Publications in Gifted Education

Ms. O'Connell has written state guidelines for the applications of gifted programs and the identification of gifted students.

## MARYLAND

Dr. Janice L. Wickless, Coordinator
Gifted and Talented Programs
Division of Instruction
State Department of Education
P. O. Box 8717
Baltimore-Washington International Airport
Baltimore, Maryland 21240

### *Professional Background*

Dr. Janice L. Wickless received her B.S. in elementary education from Towson State College and an M.Ed. in curriculum and elementary education from the University of Maryland. She earned an Ed.D. in supervision and curriculum improvement at Teachers College, Columbia University. She has taught in public schools and has served as a supervisor and consultant in a local school system. Dr. Wickless is presently coordinator of gifted and talented programs, Division of Instruction, Maryland State Department of Education.

### *Contributions to Gifted Education*

Dr. Wickless has served on the state advisory committee for gifted and talented programs in Maryland. In her role as coordinator for gifted and talented programs, she has assisted local school systems with planning programs, developing screening and identification procedures, and teacher training activities.

**MASSACHUSETTS**

Ms. Roselyn Frank, Consultant
Gifted and Talented
State Department of Education
31 St. James Avenue
Boston, Massachusetts 02111

*Professional Background*
   Ms. Roselyn Frank received her B.A. cum laude in elementary education from Chatham College and an M.Ed. from the University of Pittsburgh. She has taught in the public schools · and has done research in learning theory and cognitive styles. Currently, she is a state consultant for gifted and talented children with the Massachusetts State Department of Education.

*Contributions to Gifted Education*
   Ms. Frank has served as a consultant to school districts on designing and implementing innovative programs through grants under Title IV and III of the Elementary and Secondary Act. She is the project director of the Leadership Training Program for the Student Advisory Council Network, which was chosen as a national model by the U.S. Office of the Gifted and Talented.

*Publications in Gifted Education*
   Ms. Frank is a senior author of the position paper, *The Education of the Gifted and Talented*, that was adopted by the Massachusetts Board of Education. She has directed the compilation of the comprehensive state *Resource Guide for the Education of Gifted and Talented Students*. In addition, Ms. Frank has supervised the preparation of an early childhood packet, a parent package, and a booklet on the education of the disadvantaged gifted.

## MICHIGAN

Ms. Nancy C. Mincemoyer, Consultant
Gifted and Talented Programs
State Department of Education
P. O. Box 30008
Lansing, Michigan 48909

### *Professional Background*

Miss Nancy C. Mincemoyer received her B.S. in elementary education and special education from Clarion State College, Clarion, Pennsylvania. Her M.A. degree was earned from Ohio State University in exceptional children and in learning and behavior disorders. She has taught special education students, served as a learning disabilities supervisor and consultant, served as a gifted and talented consultant, and coordinator in a county school office in Ohio. Currently, she is the state consultant for gifted and talented programs with the Michigan State Department of Education.

### *Contributions to Gifted Education*

Miss Mincemoyer's contributions to the field include direct involvement with local schools in program development. She has also done consultant work in the areas of program development, identification, teaching strategies, curriculum, and evaluation. She is a committee member of a variety of advisory councils and task forces. She has given presentations at a number of conferences, including the May 1978 Conference on the Disadvantaged Gifted, Washington, D.C.

**MINNESOTA**

Mrs. Lorraine B. Hertz, Program Specialist
Gifted Education
State Department of Education
641 Capitol Square Building
St. Paul, Minnesota 55101

### Professional Background
Mrs. Lorraine B. Hertz received her B.S. in nutrition and elementary education, her M.A. in education psychology, with an emphasis in gifted education, and a specialist degree in special education from the University of Minnesota. She is currently enrolled in the Ph.D. program there in educational administration. She has been a dietitian with the Department of Child Welfare at the University of Minnesota. She has also taught in public schools in St. Paul. Presently, she is a program specialist in gifted education with the Minnesota State Department of Education.

### Contributions to Gifted Education
Mrs. Hertz has been a member of the staff of the National/State Leadership Training Institute on the Gifted and Talented at Wilmington, North Carolina, and has been a consultant to institutes in Chester County, Pennsylvania; Austin, Texas; and Baton Rouge, Louisiana. She is the editor of *Dialogue Annual Newsletter for Teachers of High Potential Students.*

### Publications in Gifted Education
Mrs. Hertz is the author of studies on problems teachers encounter with their gifted students and models for conducting regional teacher workshops on the education of high potential children.

**MISSISSIPPI**

Ms. Betty Walker, Consultant
Gifted Education
State Department of Education
Walter Sillers Building
P. O. Box 771
Jackson, Mississippi 39205

## Professional Background

Ms. Betty Walker received her B.M.Ed. in vocal music education from Northeast Louisiana University. She taught junior high chorus in Lake Charles, Louisiana, for six years. During 1976-77, she worked with Dr. Dorothy Sisk at the University of South Florida as a graduate assistant in gifted education and in Washington, D.C., as an intern in the Office of the Gifted and Talented. After she received her M.A. in gifted child education, she served as resource consultant for the gifted at Educational Service Unit No. 2 in Fremont, Nebraska, in Exemplary Systems Unique for Rural Gifted Program. She was also part of a four-member team which taught graduate courses in gifted education through the University of Nebraska. Currently, Ms. Walker is state consultant for gifted education with the Mississippi State Department of Education.

## Publications in Gifted Education

Ms. Walker has designed a learning module entitled *Middle East Peace Talks*, the concept of which has been accepted by a journal.

## MISSOURI

Dr. Nell S. Sanders, Director
Gifted and Alternative Program Section
Department of Elementary and Secondary Education
State Department of Education
Jefferson State Office Building
Jefferson City, Missouri 65101

### Professional Background

Dr. Nell S. Sanders received a B.S. in elementary education, an M.S. in educational administration, and a Ph.D. in elementary and secondary school programs from Florida State University. She has taught accelerated classes in language arts and social sciences in the public schools and was a resource teacher for the Leon County Gifted Child Program. She has also taught at the university level at Livingston University and Lincoln University (Missouri). Presently, she is the director of the gifted and alternative program section with the Missouri State Department of Education.

### Contributions to Gifted Education

Dr. Sanders has been a consultant for Title IV-C programs under the Elementary and Secondary Education Act in Florida and to various other agencies. She was a research consultant with the Missouri Department of Higher Education and served as the coordinator of the self-study for the National Council for Accreditation of Teacher Education at Lincoln University (Missouri).

### Publications in Gifted Education

Dr. Sanders has written a dissertation on the nomination of gifted students by teachers, has published a study of postsecondary developmental studies programs in Missouri, and has coauthored a variety of manuals for writing proposals for Title IV-C of the Elementary and Secondary Education Act.

**MONTANA**

Ms. Judi Fenton, Consultant
Gifted Education
State Department of Public Instruction
106 Capitol Building
Helena, Montana 59601

## Professional Background

Ms. Judi Fenton received her B.A. in elementary education with emphasis in language arts and received her M.A. in school administration from the University of Montana. She has taught in the public elementary schools for twelve years. In addition, Ms. Fenton worked for two years as a member of the gifted advisory committee and as a teacher in the gifted and talented academic program in Missoula, Montana. Ms. Fenton presently serves as the consultant for gifted and talented education with the Montana State Department of Public Instruction.

## Contributions to Gifted Education

Ms. Fenton is actively engaged in gifted education programs and policies in Montana.

## NEBRASKA

Dr. Anne B. Crabbe, Supervisor
Gifted and Talented
State Department of Education
301 Centennial Mall
Lincoln, Nebraska 68509

### Professional Background
Dr. Anne B. Crabbe received her B.S. from the University of Wisconsin, her M.A. from the University of Iowa, and her Ed.D. from the University of Nebraska. Dr. Crabbe has taught in the public schools and at the University of Iowa and the University of Nebraska. She is currently the supervisor of programs for gifted children with the Nebraska State Department of Education.

### Contributions to Gifted Education
Dr. Crabbe has been the facilitator for educators of gifted and talented children in Nebraska. She has served as the director of the national Future Problem Solving program.

### Publications in Gifted Education
Dr. Crabbe has written *Guidelines for Developing a Program for the Gifted and Talented, Survey of Nebraska's Gifted Programs, An Introductory Booklet on the Gifted and Talented, A National Survey of Programs for the Gifted and Talented, The Handbook for Training* (future problem solving), *Myth-Information* (rationale for gifted and talented programs), *Potentially Yours, Future Problem Solving* (a videotape for training), and *Future Problem Solving* (an overview for the gifted, creative, and talented).

## NEVADA

Mrs. Jane Early, Consultant
State Department of Education
400 West King Street
Capitol Complex
Carson City, Nevada 89710

### Professional Background

Mrs. Jane Early received her B.A. in elementary education from San Francisco State College and her M.Ed. in special education from the University of Nevada at Reno, where she is presently a doctoral candidate in educational administration. Mrs. Early also pursued graduate studies in elementary education at Sacramento State College. She taught in the public school in addition to teaching the educationally handicapped and trainable retarded/ multiple handicapped. In Nevada she has coordinated activities for the deaf, blind, deaf-blind, and gifted and talented as well as for students with learning disabilities and the physically handicapped. She is presently the consultant in special education with the Nevada State Department of Education.

### Contributions to Gifted Education

Mrs. Early has written and administered grants for handicapped personnel preparation and provided consultant service to parents, teachers, and administrators in special and gifted and talented education. She is a field reader for the Division of Training Programs, Bureau of Education for the Handicapped, U.S. Office of Education and serves on advisory committees for the deaf-blind. She is also an education consultant with the Nevada Mental Health Institute. She has presented seven conference papers on such topics as educational programs for the gifted and talented, selection of exceptional pupil programs in Nevada, learning disabilities, and assessing the needs of institutionalized children.

### Publications in Gifted Education

Mrs. Early has written journal articles on gains for the gifted and on learning disabilities. She has also written on Nevada plans for gifted and talented, regulations for the administration of statutes relating to the education of aurally and visually handicapped minors, and on standards and instructions for the administration of special education programs.

**NEW JERSEY**

Dr. Theodore J. Gourley, Coordinator
Gifted and Talented Education
State Department of Education
225 West State Street
Trenton, New Jersey 08625

## Professional Background

Dr. Theodore J. Gourley received his B.A. in history from Wilkes College, his M.A. in special education from Trenton State College, and his Ed.D. in special education administration from Temple University. He has taught special education for the handicapped and advanced classes for the gifted at elementary and middle school levels. He has administrative and program development experience in elementary and secondary schools at the local, county, state, and regional levels in all areas of special education, both for the handicapped and gifted. He has also taught educational psychology and special education at the college level. Currently, Dr. Gourley is the coordinator for gifted and talented education with the New Jersey State Department of Education.

## Contributions to Gifted Education

Dr. Gourley has developed state guidelines for implementing mandated gifted and talented education in New Jersey. He has organized and planned in-service training, working with higher education in developing graduate programs in gifted and talented education; he has also directed four educational improvement centers for consultants. He was the director of the Northeast Exchange, a five-state consortium to develop gifted and talented education, coordinating various special education projects. He was also the director of the nationally validated project, Institute for Creative Education, developing the curriculum in creative thinking which involve hundreds of teachers in elementary and secondary schools, as well as the Olympics of the Mind program, also for creative students. Dr. Gourley has developed and presented workshops on the gifted.

### Publications in Gifted Education

Dr. Gourley has written a regular column on grantsmanship for a semi-monthly publication. He has written thirty articles for professional journals on such topics as New Jersey's programs for the gifted, the gifted as a special population group, learning disabilities, vocational education for special education students, and new outlooks for the gifted. He has also authored a work on programs for handicapped pupils in county vocational technical schools and a guidebook on programs for the gifted throughout the country.

## NORTH CAROLINA

Miss Cornelia Tongue, Coordinator
Gifted and Talented Programs
State Department of Public Instruction
Education Building
Raleigh, North Carolina 27611

### Professional Background

Miss Tongue received her A.B. in secondary social studies at the Woman's College of the University of North Carolina (now University of North Carolina at Greensboro) and her master's degree at the University of North Carolina at Chapel Hill. She has also studied at North Carolina State University and Duke University. She taught in the public schools of North Carolina for many years prior to coming to the state agency. Miss Tongue is presently coordinator of the gifted and talented program for the state of North Carolina as a staff member in the Division for Exceptional Children, State Department of Public Instruction.

### Contributions to Gifted Education

Miss Tongue has expanded and opened the state program to culturally different children, has developed the state certification program, has written widely, and has developed program alternatives for the state. Currently, she is the president-elect of the Council of State Directors of Programs for the Gifted, having recently completed a term as secretary-treasurer of the Council. She is currently treasurer of the Association for the Gifted. She has conducted workshops for and served as a consultant to universities and many state agencies and has presented papers at many regional and national conferences.

### Publications in Gifted Education

Miss Tongue has written journal articles on social studies and programs on education for the gifted as well as coauthoring publications on identification of the gifted pupil, resources for teachers of the gifted, and programs on hands-on career education for gifted and talented students. She has also edited two groups of papers presented at conference sessions devoted to the gifted and talented and a volume on identifying academic talent from biographical data. She has been a film and book consultant as well.

## NORTH DAKOTA

Ms. LaDonna Whitmore, Coordinator
Gifted and Talented Education
State Department of Public Instruction
State Capitol Building
Bismarck, North Dakota 58501

### Professional Background

Ms. LaDonna Whitmore received her B.A. in elementary education from Valley City State College and an M.A. in administration from the University of North Dakota in 1976. She has taught in public schools in several states and in six foreign countries. Ms. Whitmore taught in the gifted program at Moorhead, Minnesota, for two years prior to teaching at the University of North Dakota, where she also served as a consultant for the education of gifted children at the preservice and in-service levels of education. She is currently the state coordinator for the development of gifted and talented programs with the North Dakota State Department of Public Instruction.

### Contributions to Gifted Education

Ms. Whitmore is active in gifted education programs and policies in North Dakota.

**OHIO**

Mr. George Fichter, Educational Consultant
Programs for the Gifted and Talented
State Department of Education
808 State Office Building
Columbus, Ohio 43215

## Professional Background

Mr. George Fichter received his B.S. in education and an M.A. in speech pathology and psychology from Kent State University and has taken postgraduate studies at Ohio State University. Mr. Fichter also possesses a Certification of Completion from the National/State Leadership Training Institute on the Gifted and Talented at Aspen, Colorado. He has served as consultant in gifted education at the local, state, and federal levels. He has been consultant to the state of West Virginia and the U.S. Office of Education. He has taught in the public schools, at Kent State University, and at the Ohio State University. Mr. Fichter has also lectured extensively in the area of gifted and talented education and has served as a board member of the U.S. commissioner of education's national advisory committee on gifted education. He was a program review panel member for the Office of Gifted and Talented, U.S. Office of Education, and has served in numerous organizations concerning speech and hearing. Currently, he is the educational consultant with the Ohio State Department of Education for programs for the gifted and talented.

## Contributions to Gifted Education

Mr. Fichter plans and directs the Martin W. Essex School for the Gifted, a statewide annual summer experience for selected students. His main contribution is in program initiation at the local school level. He has provided direction, coordination, and technical assistance to hundreds of local districts throughout Ohio as they started or modified programs for the gifted and talented. These coordination efforts include total community involvement in a comprehensive program for gifted and talented students.

## *Publications in Gifted Education*

Mr. Fichter has published an article on programs for gifted and talented students.

## OKLAHOMA

Mr. Larry Huff, Coordinator
Gifted and Talented Education
State Department of Education
Oliver Hodge Memorial Education Building
2500 North Lincoln Boulevard
Oklahoma City, Oklahoma 73105

### Professional Background

Mr. Larry Huff received his B.A. with a major in social studies from Northeastern Oklahoma State University and earned an M.A. in special education from the University of Oklahoma. He has also earned twenty-nine hours beyond his master's degree in educational psychology. Before joining the state education agency, Mr. Huff taught high school for seven years. He is currently the coordinator of gifted and talented education with the Oklahoma State Department of Education.

### Contributions to Gifted Education

During Mr. Huff's employment with the Oklahoma State Department of Education, gifted and talented education programs have increased tremendously. In the last three years, these programs have grown from 8 to 120.

## OREGON

Mr. Robert J. Siewert, Specialist
Gifted and Talented Education
State Department of Education
942 Lancaster Drive, NE
Salem, Oregon 97310

### *Professional Background*

Mr. Robert J. Siewert received his B.A. in secondary education from Western Washington State College and an M.S. in special education from Portland State University. He has also done graduate work beyond his master's degree, including gifted education. He taught both handicapped and gifted children and served as a gifted program coordinator for a large suburban school district. He has served also as a private consultant in gifted education at the local and state levels. He has taught at Portland State University and Lewis and Clark College in Portland, Oregon. Currently, he is a state specialist for the talented and gifted program with the Oregon State Department of Education.

### *Contributions to Gifted Education*

Mr. Siewert has been active in program development at both the local and state levels, including all aspects of a comprehensive program for the gifted. His responsibilities as a specialist in gifted education include reviewing policies and procedures in Oregon. He served as president of the Student Council for Exceptional Children at Portland State University and was a member of the advisory committee for the Casey Foundation. He also served as director of a Title VI project and two federal grant programs under the Elementary and Secondary Education Act.

### *Publications in Gifted Education*

Mr. Siewert has written a handbook on talented and gifted programs and a source book for parents of talented and gifted children. In addition, he has written about underachieving and disadvantaged gifted students and directed a contract which has resulted in the publication of ten technical assistance and parent information booklets in the field of gifted education.

## PENNSYLVANIA

Ms. Jean G. Farr, Program Director
Right to Education, Gifted and Talented
State Department of Education
P. O. Box 911
Harrisburg, Pennsylvania 17126

### Professional Background

Jean Gatling Farr received her bachelor's degree in education from Madison College (Virginia) and has completed graduate coursework at the University of Virginia, Pennsylvania State University, and Temple University. She has taught in the public schools and has served as a principal as well. Employed by Bucks County, she taught, designed, and implemented programs for the gifted. Ms. Farr is currently program director of gifted education with the Pennsylvania State Department of Education.

### Contributions to Gifted Education

Ms. Farr has worked exclusively with gifted youngsters in Pennsylvania for eighteen years. In working for the Pennsylvania State Department of Education, Ms. Farr serves as a technical assistant whose services are available to the 505 school districts, 29 intermediate units, colleges and universities, and parents. She aids these agencies in implementing programs for the gifted in both elementary and secondary schools. She was recently tapped for membership in Delta Kappa Gamma, an international honorary sorority for educators.

### Publications in Gifted Education

Ms. Farr is the author of several articles for professional journals as well as a coauthor of *A Guide for Parents—Mentally Gifted Children and Youth.*

## RHODE ISLAND

Ms. Carolyn Hazard, Consultant
Program Development
State Department of Education
CIC Building
235 Promenade Street
Providence, Rhode Island 02908

### *Professional Background*

Ms. Carolyn Hazard received a B.A. and an M.A. in history from the University of Rhode Island. She served as the director of admissions for the Newport School of Girls, Newport, Rhode Island, and is currently the program development consultant for gifted education for the Rhode Island State Department of Education.

### *Contributions to Gifted Education*

In addition to coordinating Rhode Island activities in gifted education, Ms. Hazard has conducted numerous workshops in gifted education and is chairperson of the Northeast Exchange Coordinating Council, a project funded through a U.S. Office of Education grant.

## SOUTH CAROLINA

Mr. James H. Turner, Coordinator
Programs for the Gifted and Talented
State Department of Education
Rutledge Building, Room 803
1429 Senate Street
Columbia, South Carolina 29201

### Professional Background

Mr. James H. Turner received his B.A. in history education and an M.Ed. in secondary education from the University of South Carolina. He has taught, coached, and served as an administrator in South Carolina public schools. In addition, Mr. Turner has served as a consultant in gifted education at the local, state, and federal levels. Mr. Turner is presently coordinator of programs for the gifted with the South Carolina State Department of Education.

### Contributions to Gifted Education

Mr. Turner has coordinated the development of programs in South Carolina since the program was initiated in 1973. He has served as director of a ten-state Title V project on the gifted and talented, as well as being a director of four other gifted and talented projects funded by the U.S. Office of Education, emphasizing planning and teacher training. He has also made presentations about South Carolina's programs for the gifted at several state and national conferences.

### Publications in Gifted Education

Mr. Turner has assisted in the development of publications on identification, programming, and in-service work in gifted and talented education through a Title V grant. He has also authored several department of education publications on gifted and talented programs. He has written an article on the gifted and talented as an indispensable resource and coauthored a handbook on guidelines for in-service education of the gifted and talented.

**SOUTH DAKOTA**

Mr. Robert R. Geigle, Consultant
Gifted and Talented Programs
State Department of Public Instruction
Division of Elementary and Secondary Education
Section for Special Education
Richard F. Kneip Building
Pierce, South Dakota 57501

### Professional Background

Mr. Robert R. Geigle received his B.S. and M.A.T. in elementary education from Augustana College (South Dakota) in 1969 and 1973, respectively. He received an administrator's certification in 1978 from Northern State College. Mr. Geigle taught for seven years at the elementary school level in Herreid and Winner, South Dakota. For three years, he served as a principal and teacher in Pollack, South Dakota.

### Contributions to Gifted Education

Mr. Geigle is a member of the Council for Exceptional Children, the Association for the Gifted, and the National Association for the Gifted. He has been instrumental in organizing parent and community groups as advocates for gifted programs.

### Publications in Gifted Education

Mr. Geigle has published guidelines for gifted education in South Dakota and articles in state publications.

## TENNESSEE

Dr. Joel P. Walton, Director
Exceptional Children Services
State Department of Education
Cordell Hull Building
436 Sixth Avenue, North
Nashville, Tennessee 37219

### Professional Background

Dr. Joel P. Walton received his B.S. in elementary education and his M.A. in supervision from Memphis State University. He earned his Ph.D. from the University of Mississippi. He has served as a teacher, principal, and supervisor in the public schools and has taught at the college level as well. He has been a chairman and dean and currently is chief of the curriculum service for the handicapped with the Tennessee State Department of Education.

### Contributions to Gifted Education

Dr. Walton has served for six years as a consultant in gifted education with Tennessee State Department of Education and has also been a consultant to the U.S. Office of Education.

**TEXAS**

Mrs. Ann Greer Shaw, Program Director
Educational Programs for Gifted and Talented Students
Texas Education Agency
201 East Eleventh Street
Austin, Texas 78711

*Professional Background*
   Mrs. Ann Greer Shaw received a B.A. in Spanish and social science at Texas Woman's University and her M.A. in Latin American Studies at the University of Texas at Austin. She has taught in public schools at the secondary level and has held supervisory positions in foreign language education, the Head Start program, and in instructional media, as well as serving as a textbook editor and consultant. She has participated in six institutes on gifted education. She is presently director of programs for gifted and talented students with the Texas Education Agency.

*Contributions to Gifted Education*
   Mrs. Shaw has directed the Texas leadership clusters project and the Texas regional consortia project. Both projects are staff development programs aimed at developing leadership skills in gifted education for regional and local school district personnel.

*Publications in Gifted Education*
   Mrs. Shaw has written on foreign languages and the gifted and supplied recommendations and reports on the gifted to the governor and the Texas Education Agency.

**UTAH**

Mrs. Jewel J. Bindrup, Director
Gifted and Talented Education
State Department of Education
250 East Fifth South Street
Salt Lake City, Utah 84111

*Professional Background*
  Mrs. Jewel J. Bindrup has a B.S. and M.S. from Utah State University and has completed other graduate work at the University of Utah. She was awarded two fellowships, the John Hay Humanities Fellowship from Northwestern University and the College Entrance Examination Board Fellowship from the University of Nevada. She presently has a dual appointment as state director for the gifted and talented and specialist in English education with the Utah State Department of Education.

*Contributions to Gifted Education*
  Since 1972 as state director, Mrs. Bindrup has planned and promoted education for the gifted in state sponsored workshops and has assisted other funded projects in Utah as funding becomes available through the state legislature.

**WASHINGTON**

Ms. Mary Henri Fisher, Director
Gifted Programs
Department of Public Instruction
Old Capitol Building
Olympia, Washington 98504

*Professional Background*

Ms. Mary Henri Fisher received her B.A. from Meredith College and her M.Ed. from North Carolina State University. She has also studied at New York State University at Buffalo and the University of North Carolina at Chapel Hill. She was an elementary school teacher and learning laboratory coordinator before becoming a consultant for the gifted and talented in the Division of Exceptional Children for the North Carolina State Department of Public Instruction. She served as the director of the summer teacher training institute at the North Carolina Governor's School. At present, she is the director of gifted programs with the Washington State Department of Public Instruction.

*Contributions to Gifted Education*

Ms. Fisher has been the liaison person on a state task force on secondary education, consultant to many states in the area of the gifted, and a participant in a number of institutes. She has been involved in national and regional organizations dealing with gifted children for eight years. She has participated in and developed a TV program on the gifted, served on national committees related to the gifted, and participated in numerous gifted conferences.

*Publications in Gifted Education*

Ms. Fisher has written an article on teacher training institutes for the gifted and is presently involved in the development of portable in-service labs for teachers of the gifted.

## WEST VIRGINIA

Ms. Barbara Jones, Curriculum Specialist
Gifted Education
Division of Special Education and Support Services
State Department of Education
Capitol Complex, Room 315-B
Charleston, West Virginia 25305

### Professional Background

Ms. Barbara Jones received her B.A. in English from Morris Harvey College and her M.A. in history from Marshall University. A G.L.E.P. Fellow throughout her doctoral study at the University of Georgia, she has extensive experience as a teacher in the public schools and at the university level. Ms. Jones has served as a consultant in gifted education at the local, regional, state, and federal levels. Ms. Jones is currently curriculum specialist for the gifted with the West Virginia State Department of Education.

### Contributions to Gifted Education

Ms. Jones has been a catalyst in the development of services for the gifted throughout the state of West Virginia. She was responsible for the development of a kindergarten, elementary, and secondary program in the state's largest county: participated in the organization of the Children's College; served as coordinator of a regional summer workshop in the performing arts for gifted secondary student; developed a Master of Arts degree program with specialization in the gifted for West Virginia University; and represented the gifted and talented on an advisory council for a grant under Title IV of the Elementary and Secondary Education Act. She has served as a consultant to both the Office of Career Education and the Office of the Gifted and Talented of the U.S. Office of Education and as a member of the committee for the culturally diverse of the Association for the Gifted.

**WISCONSIN**

Mr. Thomas F. Diener, Supervisor
Gifted and Talented Programs
State Department of Public Instruction
126 Langdon Street
Madison, Wisconsin 53702

### Professional Background

Mr. Thomas F. Diener received his B.S. in elementary education from Milwaukee State Teachers College and an M.S. in guidance and counseling and school administration from the University of Wisconsin-Madison. He has served as a teacher, counselor, and principal in the Milwaukee public schools. He has been a state supervisor with the Wisconsin State Department of Public Instruction since 1966 and the supervisor of gifted programs for the state of Wisconsin since 1976. Mr. Diener is also the director of the Wisconsin component of a multi-state consortium on education for the gifted and will be the director of the 404C project, attempting to better serve the culturally diverse gifted and talented.

### Contributions to Gifted Education

Mr. Diener's contributions are largely within the state of Wisconsin, working with local education agencies in developing and implementing programs for the gifted, especially through utilization of Title IV-C funds under the Elementary and Secondary Education Act.

# SECTION IV
# LOCAL RESOURCE PERSONS

In response to the renewed interest of the past few years in special programs for the gifted and the talented, both professional and lay persons at school and community levels in each state of the nation have acquired the preparation and experience that equips them to serve as consultants to personnel who request professional assistance in the initiation, development, and evaluation of programs for the gifted and the talented.

The local resource persons included in this chapter were identified by state consultants and/or others knowledgeable in gifted education within each of the states. Represented in the group of resource people are parents, administrators, teachers, legislators, college and university professors, counselors, psychologists, and civic leaders. Areas of interest and competence these people represent include parent advocacy and education, screening and identification, program development and curriculum, subject matter areas, and legislation. Their contributions can be realized through all aspects of programming for the gifted and talented.

The names of local resource persons, their professional positions, their locations, and their areas of gifted education are listed by state.

## ALABAMA

**Norma H. Bell**
Director, Special Education
Huntsville City Schools
P. O. Box 1256
Huntsville, Alabama 35807
*Gifted Education Areas*
Program Development
Program Supervision
Student Identification

**Charlotte A. Donaldson**
Teacher, Gifted
Rocky Ridge Elementary
  School
2876 Old Rocky Ridge Road
Birmingham, Alabama 35243
*Gifted Education Areas*
Social Studies
Student Identification

**Gayle H. Gear**
Associate Professor
The University of Alabama in
  Birmingham
Building 4/243
Birmingham, Alabama 35294
*Gifted Education Areas*
Program Development
Student Identification

**Leslie B. Helton**
Director, Gifted and Talented
Jefferson County Board of
  Education
1810 25th Court South
Birmingham, Alabama 35209
*Gifted Education Areas*
Mentor Program
Program Development
Program Evaluation

**Felice A. Kaufmann**
Assistant Professor
Auburn University
1230 Haley Center
Auburn, Alabama 36830
*Gifted Education Areas*

Creative Problem Solving
Program Development
Teaching Methods

**James R. Nelson**
Executive Director
Alabama School of Fine Arts
280 North Eighteenth Street
Birmingham, Alabama 35203
*Gifted Education Areas*
Program Objectives
Student Identification
Visual Arts

**Carol L. Schlichter**
Associate Professor
University of Alabama
P. O. Box 2592
University, Alabama 35486
*Gifted Education Areas*
Curriculum Development
Instructional Strategies

**Joy M. Stewart**
Coordinator, Gifted Program
Birmingham Public Schools
P. O. Drawer 10007
Birmingham, Alabama 35203
*Gifted Education Areas*
Program Development
Program Objectives
Teaching Methods

**Sandra F. Vanlandingham**
Teacher, Gifted
Highlands Elementary School
West Powell Street
Dothan, Alabama 36301
*Gifted Education Areas*
Program Development
Student Identification

**Jonathan W. Vare**
Teacher, Gifted and Talented
Vestavia Hills Schools
2020 Pizitz Drive
Vestavia Hills, Alabama 35020
*Gifted Education Areas*
In-service Education

Program Development
Program Evaluation
Program Objectives

**R. Gene Wiggins**
Professor
Alabama Agricultural and
  Mechanical University
2204 Linde Street
Huntsville, Alabama 35810
*Gifted Education Areas*
Program Development
Teaching Strategies
Teacher Training

## ALASKA

**Amy E. Budge**
Coordinator, Gifted
and Talented
Kenai Peninsula Borough
School District
P. O. Box 1200
Soldotna, Alaska 99669
*Gifted Education Areas*
Parent Advocacy
Teacher Training
Student Identification

**Joseph S. Caldarera**
Director, Special Education
School Psychologist
Lower Kuskokwim School
District
P. O. Box 305
Bethel, Alaska 99559
*Gifted Education Areas*
Individually Prescribed
Instruction
Program Development,
Culturally Different
Student Identification,
Culturally Different

**Sydney D. Hole**
Facilitator, Gifted and Talented
Auke Bay School
P. O. Box 808
Douglas, Alaska 99824
*Gifted Education Areas*
Grouping Practices
Language Arts
Program Development

**Patricia B. Horter**
Coordinator, Gifted and Talented
Anchorage Schools
505 West Second Avenue, No. 202
Anchorage, Alaska 99501
*Gifted Education Areas*
Consciousness Study
Student Identification,
Native Americans
Teaching Methods

**Peter E. Larson**
Director, Secondary Education
Kenai Peninsula Borough
School District
P. O. Box 1200
Soldotna, Alaska 99669
*Gifted Education Areas*
Program Development
Student Identification
Teaching Methods

# ARIZONA

**Willard Abraham**
Professor
Arizona State University
Tempe, Arizona 85281
*Gifted Education Areas*
Parent Education
Program Development
School and Public Relations
Student Identification

**Sanford J. Cohn**
Professor
Department of Special
    Education
Arizona State University
Tempe, Arizona 85281
*Gifted Education Areas*
Program Development
Program Evaluation
Longitudinal Studies
Student Identification

**Mary J. Cook**
Teacher, Gifted
Paradise Valley School District
7145 North Seventh Avenue
Phoenix, Arizona 85021
*Gifted Education Areas*
Program Development
Program Objectives

**Lucille N. Ellsworth**
Teacher, Gifted
Lafe Nelson School
1101 Eleventh Street
Safford, Arizona 85546
*Gifted Education Areas*
Grouping Practices
Mathematics
Reading
Teaching Methods

**Robert E. Hall**
Consultant, Gifted and
    Talented
Tempe Elementary School
P. O. Box 27708

Tempe, Arizona 85282
*Gifted Education Areas*
Parent Advocacy
Program Development
Teaching Methods

**Donna M. Johnson**
Teacher, Gifted
Kingman High School
400 Grandview
Kingman, Arizona 86401
*Gifted Education Areas*
Chemistry
Program Development
Student Identification

**Lenora M. Kleinstiver**
Principal
Safford Unified School District
2013 Eighth Avenue
Safford, Arizona 85546
*Gifted Education Areas*
Program Objectives
Reading
Student Identification

**Bobbie S. Kraver**
Coordinator, Gifted and
    Talented Education
Washington Elementary School
    District
8610 North Nineteenth Avenue
Phoenix, Arizona 85021
*Gifted Education Areas*
Alternative Programs
Parent Advocacy
Program Development

**Joyce B. Maughan**
Director and Psychologist,
    Gifted Program
Kyrene District No. 28
8700 South Kyrene Road
Tempe, Arizona 85284
*Gifted Education Areas*
In-service Education
Program Development
Student and Parent Counseling
Student Identification

**Anne D. Murphy**
Teacher, Gifted
Paradise Valley School
  District
Phoenix, Arizona 85032
*Gifted Education Areas*
Program Development
Program Objectives
Teaching Methods

**Herbert J. Prehm**
Professor and Chairperson
Department of Special
  Education
Arizona State University
Tempe, Arizona 85281
*Gifted Education Areas*
Program Development
Program Evaluation

**Maxine C. Saperstein**
President
Arizona Association for
  Gifted and Talented
1745 West Laurie Lane
Phoenix, Arizona 85021
*Gifted Education Areas*
Parent Advocacy
State and National Advocacy

**Dennis Schuman**
Teacher
Aire Libre School
1017 Village Circle Drive
  North
Phoenix, Arizona 85022
*Gifted Education Areas*
Program Evaluation
Literature
Teaching Methods

## ARKANSAS

**Martha A. Jones**
Chairman
Arkansas Gifted and Talented
   Advisory Council
2318 Jefferson
Texarkana, Arkansas 75502
*Gifted Education Areas*
Parent Advocacy
Parent and Child
   Relations

**Emily D. Stewart**
Assistant Professor
Department of Education
University of Arkansas at
   Little Rock
Little Rock, Arkansas 72204
*Gifted Education Areas*
Enrichment Triad
Learning Styles
Regular Classroom Provisions

## CALIFORNIA

**Pat L. Barnes**
Coordinator, Mentally Gifted
  Minors Program
Oceanside Unified School
  District
2080 Mission Avenue
Oceanside, California 92054
*Gifted Education Areas*
Curriculum
Differentiated Instruction
Program Development

**Robert Bell**
Coordinator, Gifted
San Diego County Department
  of Education
6401 Linda Vista Road
San Diego, California 92111
*Gifted Education Areas*
Creative Problem Solving
Structure of the Intellect
Student Identification
Teaching Methods

**Eugene F. Brucker**
Director, Guidance
San Diego City Schools
4100 Normal Street
Room 3126
San Diego, California 92103
*Gifted Education Areas*
Budget Development and
  Accountability
Program Development
School and Public Relations

**Barbara J. Clark**
Professor
Department of Special Education
California State University,
  Los Angeles
Los Angeles, California 90032
*Gifted Education Areas*
Holistic Learning
Learning Environments
Nurturing Giftedness

**James A. Curry**
Training Coordinator
National/State Leadership
  Training Institute—
  Gifted/Talented
316 West Second Street, Ph-C
Los Angeles, California 90012
*Gifted Education Areas*
Curriculum Development
In-service Education
Program Planning
Teaching Strategies

**Jeanna L. Delp**
Principal
Garden Grove Unified
  School District
10311 Stanford Avenue
Garden Grove, California 92640
*Gifted Education Areas*
Grouping Practices
Program Development
Teaching Methods

**Bruce L. Devries**
Director, Curriculum and
  Extended Learning
Ukiah Unified School District
  Office
445 South Dora
Ukiah, California 95482
*Gifted Education Areas*
Program Development
Student Identification
Student Underachievers

**Joyce M. Hardy**
Administrator, Gifted Child
  Program
Mt. Diablo Unified School
  District
1936 Carlotta Drive
Concord, California 94519
*Gifted Education Areas*
Program Development
Program Objectives
Staff Interpersonal Relations

**Barbara W. Hartloff**
Specialist, Gifted
Newport-Mesa Unified School
  District
425 East Eighteenth Street
Costa Mesa, California 92627
*Gifted Education Areas*
Creative Problem Solving
Curriculum Development
Leadership Development

**David P. Hermanson**
Supervisor, Gifted
San Diego City Schools
4100 Normal Street
San Diego, California 92103
*Gifted Education Areas*
Program Development
Program Evaluation
Program Objectives
Student Identification

**Imogene Hill**
Teacher, Gifted and Talented
Deterding School
6 Cattail Court
Sacramento, California 95833
*Gifted Education Areas*
Curriculum Development
Program Development
Teacher and Parent Education

**Julie F. Hume**
District Coordinator, Special
  Services
Tustin Unified School District
300 South C Street
Tustin, California 92680
*Gifted Education Areas*
Problem Solving and Critical
  Thinking
Program Development
Self-concept Development

**Margaret B. Humphrey**
Director, Gifted and Talented
Shasta County Superintendent
  of Schools

1644 Magnolia Avenue
Redding, California 96001
*Gifted Education Areas*
Individually Prescribed
  Instruction
Staff Development
Student Identification

**Elizabeth I. Kearney**
Director of Gifted, Staff
  Development, and Public
  Relations
Pasadena Unified School
  District
351 South Hudson
Pasadena, California 91109
*Gifted Education Areas*
Program Development
Program Evaluation
Program Objectives
Student Identification

**Yvonne W. Kuhlman**
Director, Gifted (retired)
San Mateo City Schools
50 Peninsula Avenue
San Mateo, California 94401
*Gifted Education Areas*
Creative Writing
Program Development
Program Objectives

**Carole A. Laidlaw**
Assistant Principal
Capistrano Unified School
  District
32972 Calle Perfecto
San Juan Capistrano,
  California 92675
*Gifted Education Areas*
Children's Literature
In-service Education
Program Design
Program Evaluation

**Ann R. Lord**
Elementary Principal and
  Coordinator, Mentally

Gifted Minors Program
Fremont Unified School
District
40775 Fremont Boulevard
Fremont, California 94538
*Gifted Education Areas*
In-service Education
Program Development
Student Identification

**Ruthe A. Lundy**
Coordinator, Elementary
Education
Palo Alto Unified School
District
25 Churchill Avenue
Palo Alto, California 94306
*Gifted Education Areas*
Program Development
Social Studies
Teaching Strategies

**Charlotte E. Malone**
Director, Education Programs
University Extension X-001
University of California,
San Diego
La Jolla, California 92093
*Gifted Education Areas*
Program Development
Staff Development
Student Guidance

**David M. Moorhouse**
Coordinator, Mentally Gifted
Minors Program
Palos Verdes Peninsula
Unified School District
38 Crest Road West
Rolling Hills, California 90274
*Gifted Education Areas*
Program Development
Program Objectives
Teaching Methods

**James L. Olivero**
Director, Professional Staff
Development

Association of California
School Administrators
4020 Birch Street, Suite 111
Newport Beach, California 92660
*Gifted Education Areas*
Program Development
Program Evaluation
Program Objectives

**Sally J. Patton**
Consultant and College
Professor
P. O. Box 1377
San Mateo, California 94401
*Gifted Education Areas*
Curriculum Development
Humanities
Teaching Methods

**Diane C. Peterson**
Guidance Consultant and
School Psychologist
Mt. Diablo Unified School
District
1936 Carlotta Drive
Concord, California 94519
*Gifted Education Areas*
Social and Emotional Problems
Structure of the Intellect
Student Identification

**Judith J. Roseberry**
Supervisor, Mentally Gifted
Minors Program
Garden Grove Unified School
District
10331 Stanford Avenue
Garden Grove, California 92640
*Gifted Education Areas*
Curriculum Development
Parent and Child Relations
Student Underachievers
Teacher Training

**Richard D. Sholseth**
Consultant, Gifted and
Talented
Office of the Los Angeles

County Superintendent
of Schools
9300 East Imperial Highway,
  Room 210
Downey, California 90242
*Gifted Education Areas*
Critical Thinking Skills
Program Supervision
Teaching and Learning
  Strategies

**Robert E. Swain**
Program Specialist, Gifted
San Juan Unified School
  District
4825 Kenneth Avenue, Room 1
Carmichael, California 95608
*Gifted Education Areas*
Program Development
Program Evaluation
Program Objectives
Teaching Methods

**Betty A. Tetzke**
Teacher and Team Leader,
  Gifted Program
Standley Junior High School
6298 Radcliffe Drive
San Diego, California 92122
*Gifted Education Areas*
English
Program Development
Program Objectives
Social Sciences
Student Counseling

**Claire D. Tremaine**
Coordinator, Mentally Gifted
  Minors Program
Gross Mont Union High School
  District
1725 Hillsdale Road
El Cajon, California 92024
*Gifted Education Areas*
Program Development
Program Evaluation
Teaching Methods

**Leah G. Welte**
Supervisor, Mentally Gifted
  Minors Program
Saddleback Valley Unified
  School District
25631 Diseno Drive
Mission Viejo, California 92691
*Gifted Education Areas*
Program Development
Program Evaluation
Teaching Methods

**Gail G. Wickstrom**
Principal and Coordinator,
  Mentally Gifted Minors
  Program
Lowell Joint School
  District
11019 South Valley Home Avenue
Whittier, California 90603
*Gifted Education Areas*
Critical Thinking Skills
Enrichment Programs
Language Arts
Student Underachievers

## COLORADO

**Carole A. Anderson**
Teacher, Gifted
Weld County School
    District No. 6
811 Fifteenth Street
Greeley, Colorado 80631
*Gifted Education Areas*
Expressive Skills
Program Development
Teaching Methods

**Delbert L. Barcus**
Instructional Consultant
Denver Public Schools
900 Grant Street
Denver, Colorado 80203
*Gifted Education Areas*
Community Involvement
Program Development
Program Objectives

**Rita M. Dickinson**
Psychologist, Educational
    Consultant and Researcher
Dickinson-Associates, Inc.,
    Consultants
P. O. Box 1209
Evergreen, Colorado 80439
*Gifted Education Areas*
Longitudinal Studies
Program Design

**Marian T. Giles**
Executive Director
Giles Institute for Educational
    Research
3021 North Hancock Street
Colorado Springs, Colorado 80907
*Gifted Education Areas*
Program Development
Student Identification
Teacher Training, Methods
    and Materials

**Edward B. Larsh**
Director of Dissemination
U.S. Office of Education

1961 Stout Street
Denver, Colorado 80294
*Gifted Education Areas*
Fine Arts
Program Evaluation
Teaching Methods

**Raymond A. McGuire**
Associate Superintendent,
    Instructional Services
Aurora Public Schools
1085 Peoria Street
Aurora, Colorado 80011
*Gifted Education Areas*
Program Objectives
Student Identification
Teaching Methods

**Harry J. Morgan**
Coordinator, Gifted and Talented
Jefferson County Public Schools
1209 Quail Street
Lakewood, Colorado 80226
*Gifted Education Areas*
Career Exploration
Program Prototypes, Elementary
Student Selection

**Kenneth R. Seeley**
Professor
School of Education
University of Denver
Denver, Colorado 80208
*Gifted Education Areas*
Program Development
Program Evaluation

**Linda F. Silverman**
Assistant Professor
School of Education
University of Denver
1 Buchtel Chapel
Denver, Colorado 80208
*Gifted Education Areas*
Elementary Curriculum
Student Counseling
Student Identification

**Paul J. Staiert**
Director, Research
Arapahoe County School
   District No. 6
6558 South Acoma Street
Littleton, Colorado 80120
*Gifted Education Areas*
Program Development
Program Evaluation
Student Identification
Student Screening

**Robert E. Zach**
Director, Gifted and Talented
Poudre School District R-1
2407 La Porte Avenue
Fort Collins, Colorado 80521
*Gifted Education Areas*
Composition
Creative Writing
Humanities
Mentorships

## CONNECTICUT

**Sigmund Abeles**
Education Consultant
Connecticut State Department
  of Education
P. O. Box 2219
Hartford, Connecticut 06115
*Gifted Education Areas*
Program Development
Science
Teaching Methods

**Arnold Fassler**
Director
Special Education Resource
  Center
275 Windsor Street
Hartford, Connecticut 06120
*Gifted Education Areas*
Consulting

**June K. Goodman**
Vice-Chairman, State Board
  of Education
Connecticut State Department
  of Education
Hartford, Connecticut 06101
*Gifted Education Areas*
Lobbying

**Donald P. La Salle**
Director
Talcott Mountain Science
  Center
Montevideo Road
Avon, Connecticut 06001
*Gifted Education Areas*
Program Development
Science
Student Identification
Teaching Methods

**Randolph J. Nelson**
Professor
Department of Counselor
  Education and Human
  Resources
University of Bridgeport

Bridgeport, Connecticut 06602
*Gifted Education Areas*
Career Education
Student Identification
Student Guidance and
  Counseling

**Rudolph G. Pohl**
Associate Professor
Editor, *Gifted/Talented
  Education*
Southern Connecticut State
  College
New Haven, Connecticut 06515
*Gifted Education Areas*
Alternative Programs
Independent Study
Program Development
Student Identification,
  Primary Grades

**Edwin E. Stein**
Dean
University of Hartford
200 Bloomfield Avenue
West Hartford, Connecticut 06117
*Gifted Education Areas*
Program Evaluation
Program Objectives
Student Identification

**Alan J. White**
Director, Project BRIDGE
Area Cooperative Educational
  Services
800 Dixwell Avenue
New Haven, Connecticut 06511
*Gifted Education Areas*
Curriculum, Handicapped
Program Development

**Victoria Wilson**
Graduate Student
Bureau of Educational
  Research
University of Connecticut
Storrs, Connecticut 06268
*Gifted Education Areas*

Grouping Practices
Program Development
Teaching Methods

**DELAWARE**

**Thomas K. Pledgie**
Supervisor, Exceptional
   Children
Delaware Department of
   Public Instruction
Townsend Building
Dover, Delaware 19901
*Gifted Education Areas*
Program Development
Program Implementation
Student Identification

**Lucille K. Sherman**
Supervisor, Academically
   Gifted
New Castle County School
   District
3606 Concord Pike
Wilmington, Delaware 19899
*Gifted Education Areas*
Program Development
Student Identification
Student Selection
Teaching Methods

**Leroy C. Thompson**
Supervisor, Special Education
New Castle County School
   District - Area I
Pennsylvania Avenue
Claymont, Delaware 19703
*Gifted Education Areas*
Program Development
Program Objectives
Student Identification

**Melody G. Young**
Teacher and President of Gifted
   Child Association of
   Delaware
New Castle County School
   District
204 Gordy Place
New Castle, Delaware 19720
*Gifted Education Areas*
Legislation

Parent Advocacy
Parent Counseling

## DISTRICT OF COLUMBIA

**Linda B. Addison**
Project Coordinator
School of Education
Howard University
Washington, District of
  Columbia 20059
*Gifted Education Areas*
Program Development
Student Leadership
Teacher Training

**Hattie H. Davis**
Teacher, Gifted and Talented
Seaton School
Tenth Street and Rhode
  Island Avenue NW
Washington, District of
  Columbia 20001
*Gifted Education Areas*
Program Development
Staff Development
Student Identification
Teacher Training

**Maurice G. Eldridge**
Principal and Director,
Ellington School of the Arts
Thirty-fifth and R Streets NW
Washington, District of
  Columbia 20007
*Gifted Education Areas*
Program Administration
Program Development
Program Objectives

**Florence E. Hesser**
Director
The Reading Center
George Washington University
2001 G Street
Suite 429
Washington, District of
  Columbia 20052
*Gifted Education Areas*
Program Development
Reading

Student Identification

**Phyllis D. Hines**
Teacher, Gifted and Talented
Seaton School, Room 311A
Tenth and Rhode Island Avenue NW
Washington, District of
  Columbia 20002
*Gifted Education Areas*
Program Development
Program Implementation
Program Evaluation
Student Identification

**Martha N. Rashid**
Professor
Department of Education
George Washington University
2201 G Street
Washington, District of
  Columbia 20052
*Gifted Education Areas*
Cognitive Skills
Creativity
Teacher Training

**Marie C. Thompson**
Director, Humanistic Studies
Howard D. Woodson Senior
  High School
Fifty-fifth and Eads Streets NE
Washington, District of
  Columbia 20019
*Gifted Education Areas*
Program Development
Classical and English
  Literature
Teaching Methods

**Roswell Whitaker**
Principal
Public Schools of the
  District of Columbia
Bell Career Center
3145 Hiatt Place NW
Washington, District of
  Columbia 20010
*Gifted Education Areas*

Program Administration
Program Development
Program Objectives

**James H. Williams**
Associate Professor
School of Education
Howard University
Washington, District of
 Columbia 20059
*Gifted Education Areas*
Program Evaluation
Program Objectives
Student Identification,
 Cross-cultural
Teacher Training

# FLORIDA

**Camille C. Barr**
Principal
The PATS Center,
  McReynolds School
1408 East Blount Street
Pensacola, Florida 32503
*Gifted Education Areas*
Program Administration
Program Development
Public Relations
Student Identification

**Reta F. Gardner**
Chairperson and Staffing
  Specialist, Gifted
  Education
Marion County School Board
P. O. Box 670
Ocala, Florida 32670
*Gifted Education Areas*
Program Development

**Diane D. Grybek**
Supervisor, Gifted
Hillsborough County Schools
411 East Henderson Avenue
Tampa, Florida 33602
*Gifted Education Areas*
Grouping Practices
Program Development
Student Identification
Teaching Methods

**Norma H. Kahn**
Coordinator, Gifted
St. Petersburg Junior College
P. O. Box 13489
St. Petersburg, Florida 33733
*Gifted Education Areas*
Enrichment Activities
Parent Education
Program Administration

**Judith S. Kasweck**
Coordinator, Gifted
Brevard County, Florida
1274 South Florida Avenue

Rockledge, Florida 32955
*Gifted Education Areas*
Grouping Practices
Program Development
Program Objectives

**Jacqueline O. McCormick**
Teacher, Gifted
Pine View School
Sarasota School System
2525 Tami Sola
Sarasota, Florida 33577
*Gifted Education Areas*
Program Development
Social Studies
Teaching Methods

**Pamela S. C. Mayer**
Associate Superintendent
Orange County Public Schools
P. O. Box 271
Orlando, Florida 32802
*Gifted Education Areas*
Program Development
Program Implementation
Student Counseling

**James F. Miley**
District Coordinator
Division of Exceptional
  Student Education
Dade County Public Schools
6700 Southwest 115 Street
Miami, Florida 33156
*Gifted Education Areas*
Program Development
Program Objectives
Science
Student Identification

**Sarah C. Neeley**
Manager, Gifted
Leon County Schools
415 Canal Street
Tallahassee, Florida 32301
*Gifted Education Areas*
Program Development
Student Identification

**Vernetta H. Ovitz**
Educational Prescriptor,
  Gifted
Polk County Office
P. O. Box 391
Bartow, Florida 33830
*Gifted Education Areas*
Program Objectives
Social Studies
Student Identification
Teaching Methods

**Lucille A. Peterson**
Supervisor, Gifted
Pinellas County Schools
1890 Gulf-to-Bay Boulevard
Clearwater, Florida 33516
*Gifted Education Areas*
Program Development
Program Evaluation
Program Objectives

**Jennifer G. Smith**
Coordinator, Gifted
District School Board of
  Pasco County
2609 U.S. Highway 41 North
Land O' Lakes, Florida 33539
*Gifted Education Areas*
Program Development

**Frances R. Wasson**
Director, Gifted
Okaloosa District
  Learning Center
120 Lowery Place, Southeast
Fort Walton Beach, Florida 32548
*Gifted Education Areas*
Program Development
Student Underachievers
Teaching Methods

**John D. Woolever**
Principal
Pine View School
2525 Tami Sola Street
Sarasota, Florida 33577
*Gifted Education Areas*

Program Administration
Curriculum Development
Science

**Etoyal G. Yelverton**
Supervisor
Exceptional Student Section
Duval County School System
1450 Flagler Avenue
Jacksonville, Florida 32207
*Gifted Education Areas*
Program Development
Program Evaluation
Program Objectives
Student Identification

## GEORGIA

**Genelda Bass**
Assistant Professor
Head, Gifted Program
Regional Education Center
Valdosta State College
Valdosta, Georgia 31601
*Gifted Education Areas*
Program Development
Program Evaluation
Program Objectives
Student Identification

**George E. Colyer**
Coordinator, Certification
  Program for Teachers of
  the Gifted
West Georgia College
Carrollton, Georgia 30118
*Gifted Education Areas*
Environmental Theatre
Program Design
Teacher Training

**Anne M. Edwards**
Teacher and Coordinator, Gifted
Bulloch County Schools
Vocational Building
Highway 80 West
Statesboro, Georgia 30458
*Gifted Education Areas*
Program Development
Program Objectives
Teaching Methods

**JoBeth R. Griffin**
Teacher, Gifted
Putnam County Board of
  Education
Route 4, Box 62
Eatonton, Georgia 31024
*Gifted Education Areas*
Instructional Materials
Program Development
Teaching Methods

**Marjorie W. Hatten**
Consultant, Gifted

Heart of Georgia Cooperative
  Educational Services
  Agency
P. O. Box 368
Eastman, Georgia 30411
*Gifted Education Areas*
Program Development
Program Evaluation
Student Identification

**Leo J. Kelly**
Callaway Professor
Valdosta State College
Valdosta, Georgia 31601
*Gifted Education Areas*
Program Development
Program Evaluation
Program Objectives

**Leonard J. Lucito**
Professor
Department of Special Education
Georgia State University
University Plaza
Atlanta, Georgia 30303
*Gifted Education Areas*
Instructional Methods
Program Development
Program Objectives
Student Identification

**Jean B. Mays**
Consultant, Gifted
Okefenokee Cooperative
  Educational Services Agency
Route 5, Box 406
Waycross, Georgia 31501
*Gifted Education Areas*
Program Development
Program Objectives
Student Identification

**Gervaise W. Perdue**
Coordinator, Gifted
Houston County Board of
  Education
305 Watson Boulevard
Warner Robins, Georgia 31093

*Gifted Education Areas*
Program Development
Student Identification
Teaching Methods

**Jack C. Stewart**
Associate Professor
School of Education
Columbus College
Columbus, Georgia 31907
*Gifted Education Areas*
Parent Counseling
Program Development
Program Objectives

**Joseph J. Walker**
Professor
Georgia State University
University Plaza
Atlanta, Georgia 30303
*Gifted Education Areas*
Program Development
Teacher Training
Teaching Methods

# IDAHO

**John W. Briggs**
Consultant, Mathematics
Idaho State Department
of Education
Len B. Jordan Building
650 West State Street
Boise, Idaho 83720
*Gifted Education Areas*
Program Development
Mathematics
Teaching Methods

**Bert A. Burda**
Consultant, Music and
Fine Arts
Idaho State Department of
Education
Len B. Jordan Building
650 West State Street
Boise, Idaho 83720
*Gifted Education Areas*
Fine Arts

**Trudy Y. Comba**
Professor and Coordinator of
Early Childhood Programs
Boise State University
1910 University Drive
Boise, Idaho 83725
*Gifted Education Areas*
Program Development
Early Childhood
Creative Development, Preschool

**Winnie W. Freeman**
Teacher, Gifted
Joint School District No. 2
911 Meridian Street
Meridian, Idaho 83642
*Gifted Education Areas*
Grouping Practices
Program Development
Student Identification

**Gail E. Hanninen**
Project Director
Panhandle Child Development

Association, Inc.
418 Coeur D'Alene Avenue
Coeur D'Alene, Idaho 83814
*Gifted Education Areas*
Handicapped
Preschool Gifted
Student Identification

**Candace V. Kane**
Teacher-Facilitator, Gifted
Blaine County No. 61
Box 1200
Hailey, Idaho 83333
*Gifted Education Areas*
Program Evaluation
Literature
Theatre

**Jack J. Kaufman**
Teacher Educator
College of Education
University of Idaho
Moscow, Idaho 83843
*Gifted Education Areas*
Student Identification,
Handicapped
Vocational Special Needs

**Richard Kay**
Consultant
Idaho State Department of
Education
Len B. Jordan Office Building
650 West State Street
Boise, Idaho 83720
*Gifted Education Areas*
Energy and Environmental
Education
Science

**Richard W. Leonard**
Director, Special Education
Cloverdale School
1616 North Cloverdale Road
Boise, Idaho 83702
*Gifted Education Areas*
Program Development

**Leila R. Lewis**

Consultant, Career Education
and Pupil Personnel
Idaho State Department of
Education
Len B. Jordan Office Building
650 West State Street
Boise, Idaho 83720
*Gifted Education Areas*
Career Education
Program Development
Student Counseling

**Henrik G. Lundgren**
Director, Special Education
Idaho Falls School District
No. 91
690 John Adams Parkway
Idaho Falls, Idaho 83401
*Gifted Education Areas*
Program Development
Program Objectives
Student Identification

**Mike P. Mitchell**
State Senator
Legislature of the State of
Idaho
316 Skyline Drive
Lewiston, Idaho 83501
*Gifted Education Areas*
Legislation
Program Evaluation

**A. Lee Parks**
Associate Professor
Department of Special
Education
University of Idaho
Moscow, Idaho 83843
*Gifted Education Areas*
Program Development
Program Evaluation
Rural Programs
Self-management

**Fred Russell**
Special Education
Consultant

Idaho State Department of
Education
Len B. Jordan Office
Building
650 West State Street
Boise, Idaho 83720
*Gifted Education Areas*
Individually Prescribed
Instruction
Program Evaluation

**Thomas V. Trotter**
Director, Special Services
Independent School District
No. 1
1026 Ninth Avenue
Lewiston, Idaho 83501
*Gifted Education Areas*
Program Administration
Program Development
Student Identification

**Gerald R. Wallace**
Dean (retired)
School of Education
Boise State University
1910 University Drive
Boise, Idaho 83725
*Gifted Education Areas*
Program Development
Program Evaluation
Teacher Training

**Percival A. Wesche**
State Representative,
District No. 13
House Education Committee
Legislature of the State
of Idaho
323 Nineteenth Avenue South
Nampa, Idaho 83651
*Gifted Education Areas*
State Funding
State Legislation

## ILLINOIS

**Linda D. Avery**
Specialist, Special
  Education
Illinois State Board of
  Education
100 North First Street
Springfield, Illinois 62777
*Gifted Education Areas*
Policy Development
Program Development
Program Evaluation

**J. Thomas Burk**
Associate Director
Region VI Area Service
  Center for Gifted
1505 Caseyville Avenue
Belleville, Illinois 62221
*Gifted Education Areas*
Creative Problem Solving
Consultation Theory
Curriculum Development
In-service Education

**John R. Ferrell**
Director
Region VII Area Service Center
  for Gifted
202 West Main Street
Benton, Illinois 62812
*Gifted Education Areas*
Program Development
Parent Involvement
Student Identification
Teaching Methods

**Barbara G. Ford**
Assistant Professor
Department of Learning and
  Development
Northern Illinois University
236 Graham Hall
DeKalb, Illinois 60115
*Gifted Education Areas*
Instructional Materials
Program Development

Program Evaluation
Teaching Methods

**Raymond Grinter**
Director
Region VI Area Service Center
  for Gifted
1505 Caseyville Avenue
Belleville, Illinois 62221
*Gifted Education Areas*
Grouping Practices
Program Objectives
Student Identification

**Marie Plozay**
Director, Gifted Program
Community Unit School
  District No. 220
Administration Building
310 East James Street
Barrington, Illinois 60010
*Gifted Education Areas*
Grouping Practices
Program Development
Student Identification
Teaching Methods

**Lorraine Plum**
Consultant, Gifted
Elgin School District U-46
4 South Gifford
Elgin, Illinois 60120
*Gifted Education Areas*
Instructional Materials
Program Development
Student Identification
Teaching Methods

**Glenn W. Poshard**
Consultant
Area Service Center for
  Educators of the Gifted
200½ West Main Street
Marion, Illinois 62918
*Gifted Education Areas*
Program Development
Student Discipline
Student Identification

**Leonard E. Roberts**
Superintendent of Schools
Lombard District No. 44
150 West Madison Drive
Lombard, Illinois 60148
*Gifted Education Areas*
Program Administration

**Adrienne Samuels**
Consultant, Gifted
5111 Crain Street
Skokie, Illinois 60077
*Gifted Education Areas*
Parent Counseling
Program Development
Student Identification

**Sandra J. Schmulbach**
Director
Region I-North Area Service
   Center for Gifted Youth
4 South Gifford
Elgin, Illinois 60120
*Gifted Education Areas*
Creative Writing
Program Development
Program Implementation
Student Identification

**Robert C. Todd**
Coordinator
District 18-South Area Service
   Center for Gifted
1633 West Ninety-fifth Street
Chicago, Illinois 60643
*Gifted Education Areas*
Program Development
Student Identification,
   Checklists

# INDIANA

**Sandra P. Black**
Director, Project Triad
Vigo County School
  Corporation
961 Lafayette Avenue
Terre Haute, Indiana 47804
*Gifted Education Areas*
Critical Thinking Skills
Enrichment Triad Model
  Implementation
Program Development

**Bennie M. Collins**
Supervisor, Gifted and
  Talented
Gary Community School
  Corporation
2700 West Nineteenth Avenue
Gary, Indiana 46404
*Gifted Education Areas*
Program Development
Program Objectives
Student Identification

**Joyce E. Fletcher**
Project Director, Gifted and
  Talented
Indianapolis Public Schools
901 North Carrollton
Room 209
Indianapolis, Indiana 46204
*Gifted Education Areas*
Program Development
Program Objectives
Student Identification
Teaching Methods

**Carl H. Keener**
Professor
Burris Laboratory School
Ball State University
Muncie, Indiana 47306
*Gifted Education Areas*
Human Futuristics
Program Development

**Dorothy C. Lawshe**
Administrative Assistant
Educational Services
Gary Community School
  Corporation
620 East Tenth Place
Gary, Indiana 46404
*Gifted Education Areas*
Program Development

**Arlene L. Munger**
Director
Developing Exceptional
  Talent and Ability
Monroe County Community
  School System
University Middle School
Room 146
Bypass and Tenth Street
Bloomington, Indiana 47401
*Gifted Education Areas*
Alternative Programs
Community Resources
Student Identification

**Robert Seitz, Jr.**
Professor
Ball State University
Teachers College 722
Muncie, Indiana 47306
*Gifted Education Areas*
Program Development
Program Evaluation
Program Organization
Student Identification

**Dan C. Wertz**
Assistant Superintendent
Bartholomew Consolidated
  School Corporation
2650 Home Avenue
Columbus, Indiana 47201
*Gifted Education Areas*
Program Development
Program Implementation
Student Identification

## IOWA

**Jean P. Beard**
Consultant
Green Valley Area Education
  Agency 14
Green Valley Road
Creston, Iowa 50801
*Gifted Education Areas*
Program Development
Awareness
Teaching Methods

**Ann O. Boultinghouse**
Consultant
Keystone Area Education
  Agency
1473 Central Avenue
Dubuque, Iowa 52001
*Gifted Education Areas*
Creative Writing
Critical Thinking Skills
Program Development

**Joy C. Corning**
School Board Member
Area Education Agency 7
516 West Eighth
Cedar Falls, Iowa 50613
*Gifted Education Areas*
Community Public Relations
Parent Organizations
Local Funding

**Patricia A. Cutts**
Consultant, Gifted and Talented
Area Education Agency 7
3712 Cedar Heights Drive
Cedar Falls, Iowa 50613
*Gifted Education Areas*
Literature
Program Development
Student Identification

**Martha R. Dean**
Educational Consultant
402 West Stone Avenue
Fairfield, Iowa 52556
*Gifted Education Areas*

Curriculum Development
Student Identification
Early Childhood

**Marilyn R. Dow**
Consultant, Gifted and
  Talented
Area Education Agency 7
3712 Cedar Heights Drive
Cedar Falls, Iowa 50613
*Gifted Education Areas*
Creative Writing
Program Development
Teaching Methods

**Jonathan D. Edwards**
Coordinator, Gifted and Talented
Heartland Education Agency
1932 Southwest Third Street
Ankeny, Iowa 50021
*Gifted Education Areas*
Creativity Programming
Program Development
Student Identification

**Janice N. Friedel**
Coordinator, Secondary
  Curriculum
Lakeland Area Education Agency 3
Cylinder, Iowa 50528
*Gifted Education Areas*
Program Development
Program Objectives
Social Studies

**Karen S. Garvin**
Consultant, Gifted and
  Talented
Area Education Agency 7
3712 Cedar Heights Drive
Cedar Falls, Iowa 50613
*Gifted Education Areas*
Grouping Practices
Program Development
Teaching Methods

**Mary B. Giese**
Consultant, Gifted
Northern Trails Area

Education Agency
Box M
Clear Lake, Iowa 50401
*Gifted Education Areas*
Creativity
Program Development
Teaching Methods

**Emma L. Godfrey**
Teacher, Gifted
Council Bluffs Community
  Schools
207 Scott Street
Council Bluffs, Iowa 51501
*Gifted Education Areas*
Art
Puppetry
Student Identification, Child
Teaching Methods

**Ella M. Gogel**
President
Board of Directors
Area Education Agency 7
2216 Main Street
Cedar Falls, Iowa 50613
*Gifted Education Areas*
Parent Advocacy
Parent Counseling

**David C. Grindberg**
Director, Educational
  Services
Western Hills Area
  Education Agency 12
1520 Morningside Avenue
Sioux City, Iowa 51106
*Gifted Education Areas*
Program Development
Program Evaluation
Program Objectives

**Roger L. Hanson**
Consultant, Talented and
  Gifted
Loess Hills Area Education
  Agency
P. O. Box 1109

Council Bluffs, Iowa 51502
*Gifted Education Areas*
Curriculum Design
Enrichment Triad Model
  Implementation
Program Development

**Wilbur C. House**
Principal
Crescent Park Elementary
Sioux City Community School
  District
1114 West Twenty-seventh Street
Sioux City, Iowa 51103
*Gifted Education Areas*
Program Objectives
Student Identification

**Eleanor R. Johnston**
Coordinator, Gifted and
  Talented
Keystone Area Education Agency
1473 Central Agency
Dubuque, Iowa 52001
*Gifted Education Areas*
Student Leadership
Self-concept

**George L. Magrane**
Consultant
Area Education Agency 15
P. O. Box 498
Ottumwa, Iowa 52501
*Gifted Education Areas*
Science and Environmental
  Education
Teaching Methods

**Janet M. McCumsey**
Consultant, Gifted and
  Talented
Area Education Agency 7
3712 Cedar Heights Drive
Cedar Falls, Iowa 50613
*Gifted Education Areas*
Program Development
Student Identification
Teaching Methods

**Melissa McEwen**
Consultant, Rural Gifted
Area Education Agency 4
102 South Main
Sioux Center, Iowa 51250
*Gifted Education Areas*
Program Development
Parent Communications
Student Identification

**James O. Schnur**
Associate Dean
College of Education
University of Northern Iowa
211 Education Center
Cedar Falls, Iowa 50613
*Gifted Education Areas*
Program Evaluation
Handicapped Learner
Student Identification

**Janice M. Yoder**
Consultant, Gifted and
    Talented
Mississippi Bend Area
    Education Agency
2604 West Locust Street
Davenport, Iowa 52722
*Gifted Education Areas*
Creative Thinking
Student Identification
Teaching Methods

# KANSAS

**Lorenne B. Gurley**
Coordinator, Gifted
Wichita Public Schools
640 North Emporia
Wichita, Kansas 67214
*Gifted Education Areas*
Individually Prescribed
    Instruction
In-service Education
Program Development

**Myrliss A. Hershey**
Associate Professor
Corbin Education Center
Wichita State University
Wichita, Kansas 67208
*Gifted Education Areas*
Affective Needs
Creative Writing
Individually Prescribed
    Instruction

**Linda Homeratha**
Director, Gifted
Unified School District No. 497
1837 Vermont
Lawrence, Kansas 66044
*Gifted Education Areas*
Program Development
Staff Development
Student Identification

## KENTUCKY

**Delores M. Beck**
Curriculum Coordinator
Paducah Independent Schools
2607 Kentucky Avenue
Paducah, Kentucky 42001
*Gifted Education Areas*
Program Development
Program Evaluation
Student Identification

**Larry M. Burke**
Director, Exceptional
  Children
Pike County School District
P. O. Box 2408
Pikeville, Kentucky 41501
*Gifted Education Areas*
Program Development
Program Implementation
Student Identification

**Marilynn V. Chandler**
Supervisor, Exceptional
  Children
Pulaski County Board of
  Education
University Drive
Somerset, Kentucky 42501
*Gifted Education Areas*
Program Coordination
Resource Programming
Student Identification

**John E. Dunn**
Principal
Daviess County Middle School
1415 East Fourth Street
Owensboro, Kentucky 42301
*Gifted Education Areas*
Grouping Practices
Program Administration
Program Development

**Gayle W. Ecton**
Superintendent
Owen County Board of Education
Box 475

Owenton, Kentucky 40359
*Gifted Education Areas*
Disadvantaged Gifted
Program Development
Residential Programs

**Violet A. Farmer**
Teacher, Gifted and
  Talented
Berea Independent School
  District
Peach Bloom Hill
Berea, Kentucky 40403
*Gifted Education Areas*
Program Development
Student Identification
Teaching Methods

**Floyd J. Hines**
Teacher and Coordinator, Gifted
Leslie County School District
Box 377
Hyden, Kentucky 41749
*Gifted Education Areas*
Program Development
Program Objectives
Teaching Methods

**Tricia Jones**
Director, Special Education
Boone County Schools
8330 U.S. 42
P. O. Box 37
Florence, Kentucky 41042
*Gifted Education Areas*
Creativity
Program Development
Longitudinal Studies

**Susan L. Leib**
Director, Gifted and Talented
Pulaski County School
  District
Box P
Somerset, Kentucky 42501
*Gifted Education Areas*
Program Development
Program Objectives
Student Identification

**Dove A. McNabb**
Principal
Jackson Elementary School
Twenty-first and Park Avenue
Paducah, Kentucky 42001
*Gifted Education Areas*
Creative Writing
Grouping Practices
Program Development
Student Identification

**Norman D. Osborne**
Assistant Superintendent
Fayette County Board of
  Education
701 East Main Street
Lexington, Kentucky 40502
*Gifted Education Areas*
Program Development
Program Objectives
Student Identification

**Marti L. Pearce**
Teacher, Gifted
Cumberland Trace Elementary
Route 11
Box 137
Bowling Green, Kentucky 42101
*Gifted Education Areas*
Language Arts
Program Development
Student Identification

**Cynthia J. Raker**
Teacher, Gifted and Talented
Garden Springs Elementary
  School
Lexington, Kentucky 40504
*Gifted Education Areas*
Program Development
Teacher Training

**James R. Young**
Superintendent
Russellville City Schools
Seventh and Summer Streets
Russellville, Kentucky 42276
*Gifted Education Areas*

Program Development
Program Objectives
Teaching Methods

## LOUISIANA

**Kippy I. Abrams**
Assistant Professor and
  Chairperson
Special Education Programs
Department of Education
Tulane University
New Orleans, Louisiana 70118
*Gifted Education Areas*
Research
Student Identification

**Frances H. Anderson**
Guidance Counselor
Polk Elementary School
Fort Polk, Louisiana 71459
*Gifted Education Areas*
Fine Arts
Program Development
Program Objectives

**Harold Bartlett**
Supervisor, Special Education
Webster Parish School Board
P. O. Box 520
Minden, Louisiana 71055
*Gifted Education Areas*
Program Development
Program Objectives
Student Identification

**Gayle G. Camus**
Teacher, Gifted
Orleans Parish School Board
703 Carondelet Street
New Orleans, Louisiana 70130
*Gifted Education Areas*
Language Arts
Teaching Methods

**Kay R. Coffey**
President
Association for Gifted and
  Talented Students
1627 Frankfort Street
New Orleans, Louisiana 70122
*Gifted Education Areas*
Advocacy

**Elizabeth D. Evans**
Teacher, Gifted
Westminster Elementary School
8935 Westminster Drive
Baton Rouge, Louisiana 70809
*Gifted Education Areas*
Language Arts
Teaching Methods

**Dean O. Frost**
Supervisor, Gifted and
  Talented
Baton Rouge Public Schools
1016 Mont Rose Boulevard
Lafayette, Louisiana 70804
*Gifted Education Areas*
Creative Activities

**Ellen P. Gilbert**
Supervisor, Special Education
Orleans Parish School Board
708 Carondelet Street
New Orleans, Louisiana 70130
*Gifted Education Areas*
Program Administration
Program Development

**Marlene F. Hillebrandt**
Coordinator, Gifted and
  Talented
Calcasieu Parish School Board
809 Kirby Street
Lake Charles, Louisiana 70601
*Gifted Education Areas*
Creative Writing
Program Development
Student Identification

**Barbara T. Miller**
Consultant, Gifted and
  Talented
Jefferson Parish Public
  School System
519 Huey P. Long Avenue
Gretna, Louisiana 70053
*Gifted Education Areas*
Program Development
Student Identification
Teaching Methods

**Wamul R. Owens**
Supervisor, Special
  Educational Services
Ouachita Parish School Board
P. O. Box 1642
Monroe, Louisiana 71201
*Gifted Education Areas*
Art
Program Development
Student Identification

## MAINE

**Jeannie M. Hamrin**
Assistant Professor
University of Southern Maine
506 Bailey Hall
Gorham, Maine 04038
*Gifted Education Areas*
Program Development
Student Identification
Teaching Strategies

**Patricia A. Kleine**
Coordinating Teacher, Gifted
John R. Graham School
MRB Box 246
Bangor, Maine 04401
*Gifted Education Areas*
Program Development
Program Objectives
Teaching Methods

**Merle R. Nelson**
Representative
State of Main
State House
Augusta, Maine 04333
*Gifted Education Areas*
Program Development
Student Identification
Teaching Methods

**Lenore H. Worcester**
Assistant Professor
University of Maine at Orono
305 Shibles Hall
Orono, Maine 04469
*Gifted Education Areas*
Student Identification
Student Underachievers
Teaching Methods

# MARYLAND

**Ruth H. Burkins**
Supervisor, Secondary Schools
Harford County Public Schools
45 East Gordon Street
Bel Air, Maryland 21014
*Gifted Education Areas*
Differentiated Instruction
Program Development
Student Identification

**Lynn C. Cole**
Specialist, Gifted and Talented
Maryland State Department of
  Education
P. O. Box 8717
Baltimore and Washington
  International Airport
Baltimore, Maryland 21240
*Gifted Education Areas*
Creativity
Creative Problem Solving
Program Development
Reading

**Gwendolyn J. Cooke**
Coordinator, Gifted and
  Talented
Baltimore City Public Schools
2300 North Calvert Street
Room 219
Baltimore, Maryland 21218
*Gifted Education Areas*
Language Arts
Program Development
Student Identification
Teaching Methods

**James L. Fisher**
Principal
Catoctin High School
Thurmont, Maryland 21788
*Gifted Education Areas*
Fine Arts
Program Administration
Program Development

**William C. George**
Director
Office of Talent Identification
  and Development
The Johns Hopkins University
104 Merryman Hall
Baltimore, Maryland 21218
*Gifted Education Areas*
Mathematics
Program Development
Student Identification

**Jane Hammill**
Coordinator, Gifted
Prince George's County
  Public Schools
Upper Marlboro, Maryland 20870
*Gifted Education Areas*
Program Administration
Program Development

**John M. Schaffer**
Director
Gifted and Talented Summer
  Centers
Maryland State Department
  of Education
P. O. Box 8717
Baltimore and Washington
  International Airport
Baltimore, Maryland 21240
*Gifted Education Areas*
Music
Program Development
Program Objectives

**Linda H. Smith**
Consultant, Gifted
3802 St. Paul Street
Baltimore, Maryland 21218
*Gifted Education Areas*
Individually Prescribed
  Instruction
Program Development
Student Identification

**Waveline T. Starnes**
Educational Planner, Gifted

and Talented
Montgomery County Public
  Schools
850 Hungerford Drive
Rockville, Maryland 20850
*Gifted Education Areas*
Curriculum Development
Instructional Strategies
Staff Development

# MASSACHUSETTS

**Ann M. Bradford**
Teacher, Gifted
Granger School
31 South Westfield Street
Feeding Hills, Massachusetts 01030
*Gifted Education Areas*
Community Resources
Program Development
Program Implementation

**Maryellen Cunnion**
Director
Project PRISM
37 West Main Street
Norton, Massachusetts 02766
*Gifted Education Areas*
Student Identification
Theories of Intelligence
Teacher Training

**Anthony F. DeCesare**
Teacher and Program Director
Oxford Project Talent
Oxford Public Schools
Oxford, Massachusetts 01540
*Gifted Education Areas*
Program Development
Student Identification
Teaching Methods

**Clista M.E. Dow**
Teacher, Gifted and Talented
Sharon Intermediate School
South Main Street
Sharon, Massachusetts 02067
*Gifted Education Areas*
Curriculum Development
In-service Education
Teaching Strategies

**Frances D. Leach**
Teacher, Gifted
West Junior High School
271 West Street
Brockton, Massachusetts 02401
*Gifted Education Areas*
Curriculum Design

Independent Study
Social Studies
Teaching Strategies

**Marcia G. Lebeau**
Teacher and Consultant, Gifted
Chelmsford High School
200 Richardson Road
North Chelmsford,
  Massachusetts 01863
*Gifted Education Areas*
Leadership Development
Program Development
Social Studies
Teaching Methods

**Diana O. Reeves**
Director and Teacher, Gifted
Medfield Junior High School
88 South Street
Medfield, Massachusetts 02052
*Gifted Education Areas*
Curriculum Design
Critical Thinking Skills
Program Development
Student Identification

**Gertrude M. Webb**
Professor of Education
Curry College
Blue Hill Avenue
Milton, Massachusetts 02186
*Gifted Education Areas*
Grouping Practices
Program Development
Program Evaluation

## MICHIGAN

**Barbara J. Davis**
Coordinator, Talented
Eaton Intermediate School
  District
1790 East Packard Highway
Charlotte, Michigan 48813
*Gifted Education Areas*
Creative Thinking
Learning Styles
Student Identification

**Terre A. Davis**
Principal
Sparta Middle School
565 Maple
Sparta, Michigan 49345
*Gifted Education Areas*
Program Administration
Program Development
Student Identification
Teaching Methods

**Patricia K. Diederich**
Assistant Director of
  Elementary Schools
Grand Rapids Public Schools
134 Bostwick NE
Grand Rapids, Michigan 49503
*Gifted Education Areas*
Program Development
Student Identification

**Barbara B. Lavery**
Teacher and Coordinator,
  Gifted
Lincoln Consolidated Schools
7425 Willis Road
Ypsilanti, Michigan 48197
*Gifted Education Areas*
Program Development
Gifted, Early Childhood

**Allan L. McDonald**
Resource Teacher, Gifted
  Program
Dearborn Public Schools
18700 Audette

Dearborn, Michigan 48124
*Gifted Education Areas*
Classroom Management
Creative Writing
Teaching Strategies

**Phyllis H. Maul**
Consultant, Gifted and
  Talented
Kalamazoo Valley Intermediate
  School District
1819 East Milham Road
Kalamazoo, Michigan 49002
*Gifted Education Areas*
Alternative Programs
Program Development
Teaching Strategies

**Annemarie M. Roeper**
Headmistress
Roeper City and Country
  School
Bloomfield Hills, Michigan 45013
*Gifted Education Areas*
Developmental Psychology
Program Administration
Student Identification

**Nancy Skinner**
Special Education Program
  Aide
Garden City Public Schools
33411 Marquette
Garden City, Michigan 48135
*Gifted Education Areas*
State Organization

**Robert L. Trezise**
Consultant
Michigan State Department
  of Education
P. O. Box 30008
Lansing, Michigan 48909
*Gifted Education Areas*
Program Implementation
Reading
Student Identification

## MINNESOTA

**Paul M. Goodnature**
Teacher, Gifted
Albert Lea Central Senior
  High School
504 West Clark Street
Albert Lea, Minnesota 56007
*Gifted Education Areas*
American Studies
Teaching Methods

**Flora Hausman**
Teacher and Coordinator,
  Gifted
Howe Elementary District No. 1
3733 Forty-third Avenue S
Minneapolis, Minnesota 55406
*Gifted Education Areas*
Grouping Practices
Program Development

**Daniel P. Keating**
Associate Professor
Institute of Child Development
University of Minnesota
51 East River Roadon
Minneapolis, Minnesota 55455
*Gifted Education Areas*
Program Planning
Research
Student Identification

**Bella Kranz**
Associate Professor
Moorhead State University
Moorhead, Minnesota 56560
*Gifted Education Areas*
Program Development
Student Identification
Teaching Methods

**Joseph B. Michel**
Teacher, Gifted
Richfield Public Schools
7001 Harriet Avenue South
Richfield, Minnesota 55423
*Gifted Education Areas*
Program Development

Science
Teacher Training

**Joyce C. Olson**
Teacher and Coordinator, Gifted
  and Talented
Osseo Senior High School
317 Second Avenue NW
Osseo, Minnesota 55369
*Gifted Education Areas*
Program Development
Student Identification

**Gerald P. Thilmany**
Coordinator, Gifted and
  Talented
Duluth Board of Education
Lake Avenue and Second
  Street
Duluth, Minnesota 55802
*Gifted Education Areas*
Program Development
Parent Workshops
Student Identification

## MISSISSIPPI

**Lela A. Alcorn**
Director
Special Educational Services
Columbia Municipal Separate
  School District
613 Bryant Avenue
Columbia, Mississippi 39429
*Gifted Education Areas*
Program Development
Program Objectives
Student Identification

**Mary A. Baird**
State Reading Supervisor
Mississippi State Department
  of Education
P. O. Box 771
Jackson, Mississippi 39601
*Gifted Education Areas*
Language Arts
Reading

**Joan A. Brumfield**
Supervisor, Special Education
McComb Public Schools
695 Minnesota Avenue
McComb, Mississippi 39648
*Gifted Education Areas*
Grouping Practices
Program Development
Teaching Methods

**Mitchell A. Campbell**
Teacher, Gifted
Olive Branch High School
6530 Blocker Street
Olive Branch, Mississippi 38654
*Gifted Education Areas*
Creative Writing
Curriculum Development
Student Identification

**Mary M. Carmean**
Graduate Student
Department of Special Education
University of Southern
  Mississippi

Hattiesburg, Mississippi 39401
*Gifted Education Areas*
Program Development
Student Identification
Teaching Methods

**Mollie M. Cranford**
Teacher, Gifted
F. B. Woodley Elementary
  School
2006 O'Ferrall Street
Hattiesburg, Mississippi 39401
*Gifted Education Areas*
Program Development
Teaching Methods
Student Identification

**Emily Collins**
Psychometrist and Coordinator,
  Gifted
Moss Point Municipal
  Separate School District
Box 727
Moss Point, Mississippi 39563
*Gifted Education Areas*
Critical Thinking Skills
Student Identification,
  Culturally Different

**Veronica V. Dampier**
Director, Gifted and
  Talented
Hinds Agricultural High
  School
Box 89
Utica Junior College
Utica, Mississippi 39175
*Gifted Education Areas*
Creative Writing
Grouping Practices
Student Identification

**Eva C. Davis**
Supervisor and Coordinator,
  Gifted
Clarksdale Separate School
  District
P. O. Box 1088

Clarksdale, Mississippi 38614
*Gifted Education Areas*
Program Development
Program Objectives
Student Identification

**Sharon A. Dugan**
Teacher, Gifted
Columbia High School
Broad Street
Columbia, Mississippi 39429
*Gifted Education Areas*
Independent Study
Student Identification

**Nancy A. Ehret**
Teacher, Gifted
Parks Elementary School
Terrace Road
Cleveland, Mississippi 38732
*Gifted Education Areas*
Classroom Organization
Divergent Thinking
Values Clarification

**Totsy W. Fuller**
Teacher, Gifted
Starkville Public Schools
303 McKee Street
Starkville, Mississippi 39759
*Gifted Education Areas*
Grouping Practices
Program Development
Teaching Methods

**Di Ann Lewis**
Director
North Mississippi
  Retardation Center
Highway 7 South
Oxford, Mississippi 38655
*Gifted Education Areas*
Program Development
Student Identification
Teaching Methods

**Kathern L. Lucas**
Teacher, Gifted
East School

Meadowbrook Road
Greenwood, Mississippi 38930
*Gifted Education Areas*
Student Identification

**Walter H. Moore**
Assistant Director of
  Instruction
Special Education Division
Mississippi State Department
  of Education
P. O. Box 771
Jackson, Mississippi 39205
*Gifted Education Areas*
Program Development

**Mary S. Morgan**
Teacher, Gifted
Lafayette County Schools
Route 5
Oxford, Mississippi 38655
*Gifted Education Areas*
Art
Program Development
Program Evaluation
Student Identification,
  Artistically Talented

**Tempe J. O'Nan**
Teacher, Gifted
Henderson Junior High School
Starkville, Mississippi 39759
*Gifted Education Areas*
Community Resources
Values Clarification

**Jean C. Prather**
Teacher, Gifted
Key Elementary School
699 McDowell Road
Jackson, Mississippi 39204
*Gifted Education Areas*
Program Development
Program Evaluation
Teaching Methods

**Judy J. Roy**
Teacher, Gifted
Gautier Elementary School

505 Magnolia Street
Gautier, Mississippi 39553
*Gifted Education Areas*
Program Development
Program Evaluation
Student Identification

**Mary E. Shelton**
Administrator, Federal Projects
Starkville Public Schools
Starkville, Mississippi 39759
*Gifted Education Areas*
Program Development
Student Identification

**Mary L. Terry**
Teacher, Gifted
Jackson Public Schools
156 Flag Chapel Road
Jackson, Mississippi 39213
*Gifted Education Areas*
Program Development
Program Evaluation
Student Identification

**Jo Rita VanDevender**
Director, Guidance and
   Special Programs
Lauderdale County School
   District
Court House Annex
Meridian, Mississippi 39301
*Gifted Education Areas*
Program Development
Program Evaluation
Student Identification

**Paul R. Van Zandt**
Teacher, Gifted
Thames Junior High School
Jamestown Road
Hattiesburg, Mississippi 39401
*Gifted Education Areas*
Grouping Practices
Student Identification
Teaching Methods

**Jo Anne R. Welch**
Director, Special Education

Brookhaven Public Schools
P. O. Box 540
Brookhaven, Mississippi 39601
*Gifted Education Areas*
Program Development
Program Evaluation
Teaching Methods

**Lee R. Walker**
Coordinator, Gifted
Hattiesburg Separate School
   District
846 Main Street
Hattiesburg, Mississippi 39401
*Gifted Education Areas*
Materials Design
Program Development
Teaching Methods

# MISSOURI

**Reuben Altman**
Professor
University of Missouri,
  Columbia
515 South Sixth Street
Columbia, Missouri 65201
*Gifted Education Areas*
Curriculum Development
Program Planning
Program Evaluation

**Julie A. Bradbury**
Director, Federal Programs
Kirkwood R-7 School District
1110 South Glenwood Lane
Kirkwood, Missouri 63122
*Gifted Education Areas*
Program Development
Program Objectives
Student Identification

**Elizabeth S. Campbell**
Counselor, Elementary
Consolidated Schools No. 4
724 Main Street
Grandview, Missouri 64030
*Gifted Education Areas*
Program Development
Teacher Training

**Marjory Farrell**
Director, Special Education
Kansas City, Missouri,
  School District
1211 McGee
Kansas City, Missouri 64106
*Gifted Education Areas*
Program Development
Program Objectives
Teaching Methods

**Gayle A. Hurst**
Central Office Administration
North Kansas City School
  District
2000 Northeast Forty-sixth Street
Kansas City, Missouri 64116

*Gifted Education Areas*
Program Development
Program Objectives
Teaching Methods

**Delma D. Johnson**
Administrator
Kansas City School District
1211 McGee
Kansas City, Missouri 64106
*Gifted Education Areas*
Program Development
Program Objectives
Student Identification

**Russell M. Johnson**
Teacher Educator
Southeast Missouri State
  University
College of Education
Cape Girardeau, Missouri 63701
*Gifted Education Areas*
Program Development
Teaching Methods
Teacher Training

**Shirley D. King**
Director, Gifted and
  Talented
Ferguson Reorganized School District
1248 North Florissant Road
Ferguson, Missouri 63135
*Gifted Education Areas*
Curriculum Development
Program Evaluation
Parent Involvement

**Ronald G. Lightle**
Coordinator, Gifted and
  Talented
Normandy School District
7855 Natural Bridge Road
St. Louis, Missouri 63121
*Gifted Education Areas*
Program Development
Program Evaluation
Teaching Methods

**Martha A. Sherman**
Instructor
Department of Nursing
Central Missouri State
  University
Warrensburg, Missouri 64093
*Gifted Education Areas*
Alternative Programs, Rural
  Areas
Grouping Practices
Student Identification

**Kathleen W. Voelz**
St. Louis Board of Education
5910 Clifton
St. Louis, Missouri 63109
*Gifted Education Areas*
Independent Study
Language Arts
Student Identification

# MONTANA

**Andrea U. Bartelt**
Coordinator, Gifted
Great Falls Public Schools
Skyline Center
3300 Third Street NE
Great Falls, Montana 59404
*Gifted Education Areas*
Program Development
Student Identification
Teaching Methods

**J. Patrick Brunker**
Principal
Colstrip Public Schools
P. O. Box 127
Colstrip, Montana 59323
*Gifted Education Areas*
Program Development
Program Evaluation
Program Objectives
Student Identification

**Elaine L. Capener**
Teacher and Coordinator,
  Gifted
Missoula School District
  No. 1
215 South Sixth West
Missoula, Montana 59801
*Gifted Education Areas*
Program Development
Program Objectives
Teaching Methods

**Donald B. Gundlach**
Principal
School District No. 1
716 South Cale
Miles City, Montana 59301
*Gifted Education Areas*
Program Development
Program Objectives
Student Identification

**Yvonne S. Hunnewell**
Board Member
School District No. 33,

Liberty County
Box 52
Chester, Montana 59522
*Gifted Education Areas*
Program Development
Program Evaluation
Theatre
Writing

**Fran F. McDermott**
Teacher, Gifted
Billings School District
  No. 2
2801 Iowa
Billings, Montana 59102
*Gifted Education Areas*
Curriculum Development
Program Planning

**Cristina M. Troxel**
Director, Curriculum
Missoula School District No. 1
215 South Sixth West
Missoula, Montana 59801
*Gifted Education Areas*
Program Evaluation
Program Objectives
Student Identification

## NEBRASKA

**Cynthia A. Andersen**
Consultant, Gifted
Educational Service Unit
No. 11
815 Fourth Avenue
P. O. Box 485
Holdrege, Nebraska 68949
*Gifted Education Areas*
Individually Presented
Instruction
Future Problem Solving

**Jody Batten**
Consultant, Gifted
Lincoln Public Schools
720 South Twenty-second
Lincoln, Nebraska 68510
*Gifted Education Areas*
Program Planning
Teaching Strategies

**Melodee A. Landis**
Consultant and Teacher,
Gifted
Nebraska State Department
of Education
301 Centennial Mall South
Lincoln, Nebraska 68509
*Gifted Education Areas*
Program Development
Student Identification
Teaching Strategies
Visual and Performing Arts

**Penny H. Rehberg**
Coordinator, Gifted and Talented
Millard Public Schools
13747 F Street
Omaha, Nebraska 68137
*Gifted Education Areas*
Program Development
Rural Gifted
Teaching Methods

**Jan M. Rogers**
Consultant, Rural Gifted
Educational Service Unit

No. 2
2320 North Colorado Avenue
Fremont, Nebraska 68025
*Gifted Education Areas*
Curriculum Design
Program Development
Program Objectives

**Sandra Watkins**
Consultant, Gifted and
Talented
Omaha Public Schools
3902 Davenport Street
Omaha, Nebraska 68131
*Gifted Education Areas*
Program Development
Student Leadership
Student Underachievers

**Frances C. Wilkinson**
Consultant, Gifted
Grand Island Public Schools
2013 North Oak Street
Grand Island, Nebraska 68801
*Gifted Education Areas*
Independent Study
Program Development
Program Evaluation

# NEVADA

**Julie B. Cooper**
Coordinating Teacher, Gifted
Clark County School District
Will Beckley Elementary
    School
3223 South Glenhurst
Las Vegas, Nevada 89109
*Gifted Education Areas*
Program Development
Program Objectives
Teaching Methods

**Judi K. Steele**
Director, Special Student
    Services
Clark County School District
2832 East Flamingo Road
Las Vegas, Nevada 89121
*Gifted Education Areas*
Program Development
Program Objectives
Teaching Methods

## NEW HAMPSHIRE

**Martha J. Cray-Andrews**
Teacher, Gifted
Hollis Elementary School
Hollis, New Hampshire 03049
*Gifted Education Areas*
Curriculum Development
Differentiated
  Instruction
Program Planning

**Ann H. Crow**
Director and Coordinator,
  Gifted
Enfield Elementary School
Box 366
Enfield, New Hampshire 03748
*Gifted Education Areas*
Program Development
Student Identification
Teaching Methods

**Barbara T. Eves**
Chairperson, Guidance
  Department
Dover Junior High School
Locust Street
Dover, New Hampshire 03820
*Gifted Education Areas*
Grouping Practices
Program Development
Student Identification

**Richard A. Gustafson**
Associate Dean
Keene State College
Main Street
Keene, New Hampshire 03431
*Gifted Education Areas*
Career Education
Program Development
Program Evaluation
Student Identification

**David P. Miller**
Principal
Enfield Elementary School
Box 366

Enfield, New Hampshire 03748
*Gifted Education Areas*
Program Development, Rural Gifted
Student Identification

**Cheryl H. Nolan**
Coordinator and Teacher,
  Gifted and Talented
Conway School District
Box 650
North Conway, New Hampshire 03860
*Gifted Education Areas*
Community Involvement
In-service Education
Program Development

**Elizabeth P. Storrs**
Teacher and Counselor,
  Gifted
Hanover Street School
193 Hanover Street
Lebanon, New Hampshire 03766
*Gifted Education Areas*
Program Development
Program Objectives
Teaching Methods

**Tara N. Stuart**
Associate Professor
Keene State College
Main Street
Keene, New Hampshire 03431
*Gifted Education Areas*
Drama
Teacher Training

**Virginia H. Trumbull**
Assistant Professor
Keene State College
Main Street
Keene, New Hampshire 03431
*Gifted Education Areas*
Student Identification
Teacher Training

**Jane S. Weissmann**
Director, Special Education
Tri-City Special Education
  Consortium

The Professional Building
2 Central Street
Franklin, New Hampshire 03235
*Gifted Education Areas*
In-service Education
Program Development
Student Identification

## NEW JERSEY

**James J. Alvino**
Assistant Director, Northeast
　Exchange
Educational Improvement
　Center, South
P. O. Box 209
Sewell, New Jersey 08080
*Gifted Education Areas*
Critical Thinking Skills
Instructional Media
Philosophy

**Susan A. Berkowitz**
Consultant, Gifted and
　Talented
Educational Improvement
　Center, Northwest
202 Johnson Road
Building No. 3
Morris Plains, New Jersey 07950
*Gifted Education Areas*
Program Development
Teaching Methods

**Gina Ginsberg**
Executive Director
Gifted Child Society, Inc.
59 Glen Gray Road
Oakland, New Jersey 07436
*Gifted Education Areas*
Community Resources
Parent Advocacy
Public Relations

**T. Patrick Hill**
Regional Coordinator, Gifted
New Jersey State Department
　of Education
Educational Improvement Center,
　Northeast
2 Babcock Place
West Orange, New Jersey 07052
*Gifted Education Areas*
Program Development
Program Objectives
Teaching Methods

**Marian Leibowitz**
Coordinator, Special Education
Educational Improvement
　Center
Route 1, Box 3684
Princeton, New Jersey 08540
*Gifted Education Areas*
Program Development
Student Identification
Student Underachievers

**E. Susanne Richert**
Director
Institute for Gifted and
　Talented Education
Educational Improvement
　Center, South
Route 4
Box 209
Sewell, New Jersey 08080
*Gifted Education Areas*
Program Development
Program Evaluation
Teacher Training

# NEW YORK

**Phyllis W. Aldrich**
Coordinator, Gifted
Saratoga-Warren BOCES
School No. 4
Spring Street
Saratoga Springs, New York 12866
*Gifted Education Areas*
Program Development
Student Identification

**Orrin H. Bowman**
Assistant Superintendent for
  Instruction
Monroe No. 2-Orleans BOCES
3599 Big Ridge Road
Spencerport, New York 14559
*Gifted Education Areas*
Program Development
Program Evaluation
Program Objectives

**Virginia Z. Ehrlich**
Director
Gifted Child Studies (Astor
  Program)
Teachers College
Columbia University
490 Hudson Street
Room 203
New York, New York 10014
*Gifted Education Areas*
Curriculum Developing
Program Planning

**Patricia K. Fulmer**
Coordinator, Gifted
Dutchess County Board of
  Cooperative Educational Services
R.D. No. 1
Salt Point Turnpike
Poughkeepsie, New York 12601
*Gifted Education Areas*
Alternative Programs
In-service Education
Science

**Judith T. Golden**
Director, Gifted Resource
  Center
New York State Education
  Department
3961 Hillman Avenue
New York City, New York 10463
*Gifted Education Areas*
Program Development
Student Identification
Teaching Materials
Teaching Methods

**Donald Kaplan**
Director, Gifted
School District 18
755 East 100th Street
Brooklyn, New York 11230
*Gifted Education Areas*
Curriculum Development
Program Evaluation
Teaching Methods

**Grace N. Lacy**
Supervisor, Gifted
New York City Board of
  Education
School Development Center
131 Livingston Street
Brooklyn, New York 11201
*Gifted Education Areas*
Program Development
Program Objectives
Social Studies
Student Identification

**Joy Liasson**
Educational Consultant
BOCES Sothern Westchester
14 Brook Lane
Scarsdale, New York 10583
*Gifted Education Areas*
Program Development
Program Objectives
Student Identification

**Regan A. McCarthy**
Coordinator, Gifted and

Talented
BOCES Cultural Arts Center
Ketchams Road
Syosset, New York 11791
*Gifted Education Areas*
Program Planning
Program Evaluation
Teacher Training

**Sol Meldon**
Coordinator, Gifted
Center for School Development
131 Livingston Street
Brooklyn, New York 11201
*Gifted Education Areas*
Program Development
Program Evaluation
Program Objectives

**Gladys A. Pack**
Coordinator, Gifted
Yonkers Board of Education
145 Palmer Road
Yonkers, New York 10701
*Gifted Education Areas*
Program Development
Program Objectives
Student Identification
Teaching Methods

**Richard W. Rich, Sr.**
Coordinator, Federal Funding
Horseheads Center School
  District
Board of Education
Horseheads, New York 14845
*Gifted Education Areas*
Program Development
Program Objectives
Student Identification

**R. Ann Ruvolo**
Supervisor of Gifted
Livingston-Steuben-Wyoming
  County BOCES
Lackawanna Avenue
Mount Morris, New York 14510
*Gifted Education Areas*

Program Development
Student Identification

**Cathy F. Siano**
Teacher and Coordinator,
  Gifted
Batavia City School District
39 Washington Street
Batavia, New York 14020
*Gifted Education Areas*
Program Objectives
Creative Writing
Teaching Methods

**Stanley Seidman**
Principal
Hunter College Elementary
  School
71 East Ninety-fourth Street
New York City, New York 10028
*Gifted Education Areas*
Program Development
Student Identification
Teaching Methods

**Elane D. Stoddard**
Director, Gifted
Schenectady City School
  District
108 Brandywine Avenue
Schenectady, New York 12307
*Gifted Education Areas*
Program Administration
Teaching Strategies
Visual and Performing Arts

**Robert B. Wagoner**
Principal
Evans Mills Elementary
  School
Main Street
Evans Mills, New York 13637
*Gifted Education Areas*
Program Development, Rural
Program Evaluation
Student Identification,
  Rural

**Ralph M. Watson**
Coordinator, Gifted and
   Talented
Onondaga-Madison BOCES
6820 Thompson Road
Syracuse, New York 13211
*Gifted Education Areas*
Curriculum Development
Program Planning
Science
Student Identification

**Judith S. Wooster**
Teacher and Consultant,
   Gifted
Union Free School District
   No. 1
432 Mill Street
Williamsville, New York 14221
*Gifted Education Areas*
Classroom Management
Instructional Materials
Language Arts
Social Studies

## NORTH CAROLINA

**Lyn Aubrecht**
Assistant Professor
Department of Psychology
Meredith College
Raleigh, North Carolina 27611
*Gifted Education Areas*
Parent and Professional
   Advocacy
Research
Teacher Training

**Patricia S. Ball**
Teacher, Gifted
Wake County Public Schools
1600 Fayetteville Street
Raleigh, North Carolina 27605
*Gifted Education Areas*
Critical Thinking Skills
Program Development
Teaching Methods

**Maria L. Barker**
Assistant Director
PAGE Saturday Morning Program
2400 McMillan Avenue
Lumberton, North Carolina 28358
*Gifted Education Areas*
Instructional Resources
Program Development, Early
   Childhood
Student Identification

**Elizabeth Broome**
Regional Coordinator,
   Exceptional Children
North Carolina State
   Department of Public
   Instruction, Regional
   Center
P. O. Box 549
Knightdale, North Carolina 27545
*Gifted Education Areas*
Program Development
Program Objectives
Teaching Methods

**C. Douglas Carter**
Assistant Superintendent
Winston-Salem/Forsyth
   County Schools
P. O. Box 2513
Winston-Salem, North Carolina 27104
*Gifted Education Areas*
Art
Program Development
Student Identification

**Theodore R. Drain**
Director
Division for Exceptional
   Children
North Carolina State
   Department of Public
   Instruction
Education Building
Raleigh, North Carolina 27611
*Gifted Education Areas*
Program Administration
Program Development

**Smith Goodrum**
Director, Gifted
Department of Education
Mars Hill College
Mars Hill, North Carolina 28754
*Gifted Education Areas*
Early College Admissions
Residential Programs
Teacher Training

**Henry L. Johnson**
Coordinator, Staff Development
Division for Exceptional
   Children
North Carolina State
   Department of Public
   Instruction
Education Building
Raleigh, North Carolina 27611
*Gifted Education Areas*
Program Development
Student Identification
Teaching Methods

**Julie Long**
College Instructor and
  Consultant
Department of Education
Mars Hill College
Mars Hill, North Carolina 28787
*Gifted Education Areas*
Program Development
Student Identification
Teaching Methods

**LeRoy B. Martin, Jr.**
Professor
North Carolina State
  University
Box 5445
Raleigh, North Carolina 27650
*Gifted Education Areas*
Community Advocacy
Program Development
Program Objectives

**Ruth S. Marshall**
Coordinator, Gifted and
  Talented
Wake County Public School System
Pool Building
1600 Fayetteville Street
Raleigh, North Carolina 27603
*Gifted Education Areas*
Program Development
Student Identification .
Teaching Strategies

**Joseph O. Milner**
Chairman
Department of Education
Wake Forest University
102 Tribble Hall
Winston-Salem, North Carolina 27109
*Gifted Education Areas*
Developmental Constructs
Language Arts
Residential Curriculum

**Fred T. Poplin**
Director, Gifted and
  Talented

Trinity High School
Trinity, North Carolina 27370
*Gifted Education Areas*
Curriculum Development
Summer Programs
Teaching Methods

**John T. Richards**
Chairperson
Special Education Department
East Carolina University
Speight Building
Greenville, North Carolina 27834
*Gifted Education Areas*
Program Development
Teacher Training

**Donald W. Russell**
Professor
School of Education
University of North Carolina
  at Greensboro
Greensboro, North Carolina 27412
*Gifted Education Areas*
Program Evaluation
Program Objectives
Student Identification

**Gail Smith**
Consultant, Gifted
Division for Exceptional
  Children
North Carolina State
  Department of Public
  Instruction
Education Building
Raleigh, North Carolina 27611
*Gifted Education Areas*
Program Development
Student Identification
Teaching Methods

**Betty J. Stovall**
Curriculum Specialist, Gifted
Charlotte-Mecklenburg Schools
701 East Second Street
Charlotte, North Carolina 28202
*Gifted Education Areas*

Program Development
Student Identification
Teaching Methods

# NORTH DAKOTA

**Bonita-Jo H. Berryman**
Resource Teacher, Gifted
Longfellow Elementary School
Sixteenth Street NW
Minot, North Dakota 58701
*Gifted Education Areas*
Learning Centers
Program Objectives
Resource Room Procedures
Teaching Methods

**Nancy L. Burkland**
Coordinator, Gifted and
Talented
Fargo Public Schools
1104 Second Avenue South
Fargo, North Dakota 58102
*Gifted Education Areas*
Program Development
Student Identification
Teaching Methods

**Rene G. Hersrud**
Teacher, Gifted
Mott Public School District
No. 6
Mott, North Dakota 58646
*Gifted Education Areas*
Creative Writing
Student Identification
Teaching Methods

**Donald L. Hoff**
Coordinator, Gifted
Velva Public School District
No. 1
Velva, North Dakota 58790
*Gifted Education Areas*
Program Development
Student Identification
Teaching Methods

**Lauren A. Marks**
Teacher, Gifted and Talented
Fargo Public Schools
1104 South Second Avenue
Fargo, North Dakota 58102

*Gifted Education Areas*
Art and Theater
Curriculum Development

**Deborah R. Wahus**
Teacher
Williston Public School
District No. 1
712 Thirteenth Avenue West
Williston, North Dakota 58801
*Gifted Education Areas*
Program Development
Teaching Methods

## OHIO

**Joanne F. Barrere**
Coordinator and Teacher,
  Gifted
Upper Arlington Public Schools
2900 Tremont Road
Columbus (Upper Arlington),
  Ohio 43221
*Gifted Education Areas*
In-service Education
Program Development
Teaching Methods

**John E. Beard**
Coordinator, Gifted and
  Talented
Trumbull County Board of
  Education
P. O. Box 1310
Warren, Ohio 44482
*Gifted Education Areas*
Program Development
Program Evaluation
Program Objectives

**Marlene B. Bireley**
Associate Dean
College of Education
Wright State University
322 Millett Hall
Dayton, Ohio 45435
*Gifted Education Areas*
Affective Activities
Program Development
Student Identification

**Robert D. Blanchard**
Supervisor, Enrichment Programs
Wayne County Board of
  Education
428 West Liberty Street
Wooster, Ohio 44691
*Gifted Education Areas*
Instructional Materials
Program Development
Program Objectives
Student Identification

**Naomi H. Cook**
Coordinator, Gifted
Steubenville City Schools
932 North Fifth Street
Steubenville, Ohio 43952
*Gifted Education Areas*
Program Development
Program Evaluation
Student Identification

**Carolyn D. Fleming**
Director, Enrichment Programs
Delaware City Schools
248 North Washington Street
Delaware, Ohio 43015
*Gifted Education Areas*
Community Resources
Program Development,
  Mini-courses

**Susan S. Friend**
Coordinator, Gifted and
  Talented
Madison County Schools
59 North Main Street
London, Ohio 43140
*Gifted Education Areas*
Curriculum Development
Program Planning
Student Identification

**Penny R. Guy**
Coordinator, Special Education
London City Schools
60 South Walnut Street
London, Ohio 43140
*Gifted Education Areas*
Program Administration
Program Development

**Janet C. Hartman**
Coordinator, Gifted and
  Talented
Lucas County Office of
  Education
3350 Collingwood Boulevard
Toledo, Ohio 43610
*Gifted Education Areas*

Creativity
Language Arts
Mathematics
Teaching Strategies

**Dennis E. Hern**
Director, Gifted and
 Talented
Warren County Schools
416 South East Street
Lebanon, Ohio 45036
*Gifted Education Areas*
Language Arts
Program Development
Program Evaluation
Student Identification

**Jeanne Hilson**
Supervisor, Gifted
Alum Crest Instructional
 Center
Columbus City Schools
2200 Winslow Drive
Columbus, Ohio 43207
*Gifted Education Areas*
Program Development
Teaching Methods

**Phillip Isaac**
Director, Pupil Services
Rocky River City Schools
21600 Center Ridge
Rocky River, Ohio 44116
*Gifted Education Areas*
Grouping Practices
Program Evaluation
Student Identification

**Charles N. Jordan**
Educational Consultant, Gifted
12900 Lake Avenue
Suite 609
Lakewood, Ohio 44107
*Gifted Education Areas*
Community Resources
Instructional Strategies
Program Development

**Dave C. Kowalka**
Coordinator, Gifted
Ashland City Schools
738 Claremont Avenue
Ashland, Ohio 44805
*Gifted Education Areas*
Creativity
Mathematics
Teaching Methods

**Evelyn B. Loucks**
Coordinator, Gifted
Special Education Regional
 Resource Center
Lake County Board of
 Education
8870 Mentor Avenue
Mentor, Ohio 44060
*Gifted Education Areas*
In-service Education
Learning Disabled, Gifted
Program Development

**Sara J. Lowe**
Coordinator, Gifted and
 Talented
Montgomery County Public Schools
451 West Third Street
Box 972
Dayton, Ohio 45422
*Gifted Education Areas*
In-service Education
Instructional Materials
Teaching Strategies

**Nanci D. Lucas**
Director, Gifted
Toledo Public Schools
Manhattan and Elm Streets
Toledo, Ohio 43608
*Gifted Education Areas*
Grouping Practices
Program Development

**Jane Navarre**
Educational Consultant
Bowling Green State University
445 South Grove Street

Bowling Green, Ohio 43402
*Gifted Education Areas*
Creativity
Program Development, Rural
Structure of the Intellect

**Beverly J. Ness**
Graduate Research Associate
Ohio State University
356 Arps Hall
1945 North High
Columbus, Ohio 43210
*Gifted Education Areas*
Program Development
Student Identification
Teacher Training

**Rita A. Price**
Teacher and Coordinator, Gifted
Erie County Board of Education
1200 Sycamore Line
Sandusky, Ohio 44870
*Gifted Education Areas*
Parent and Child Relations
Program Development
Teaching Strategies

**Peg Ray**
Coordinator, Gifted and
  Talented
Oregon City Schools
5665 Seaman Road
Oregon, Ohio 43616
*Gifted Education Areas*
Independent Study, Projects
Program Development

**Paris H. Roland**
Coordinator, Gifted and
  Talented
Southeastern Ohio Voluntary
  Education Cooperative
52 University Terrace
Athens, Ohio 45701
*Gifted Education Areas*
Community Resources
Language Arts
Program Development

**Patricia A. Schultz**
Supervisor, Gifted
Lawrence County Schools
608 Cemetery Lane
Coal Grove, Ohio 45638
*Gifted Education Areas*
Individually Prescribed
  Instruction
Program Development
Teaching Strategies

**Wilber D. Simmons**
Associate Professor and
  Coordinator
Gifted Education Programs
Kent State University
401 White Hall
Kent, Ohio 44242
*Gifted Education Areas*
Instructional Strategies
Program Administration
Program Development
Program Evaluation

**Raymond H. Swassing**
Associate Professor
Ohio State University
356 Arps Hall
1945 North High
Columbus, Ohio 43210
*Gifted Education Areas*
Program Development
Program Evaluation
Program Objectives
Research

**Franklin B. Walter**
Superintendent of Public
  Instruction
Ohio State Department of
  Education
State Office Building
Room 808
65 South Front Street
Columbus, Ohio 43215
*Gifted Education Areas*
Program Administration

## OKLAHOMA

**Mary L. Gossett**
Teacher, Gifted and Talented
McAlester High School
304 Saunier Way
McAlester, Oklahoma 74501
*Gifted Education Areas*
Creative Projects
Program Development
Teaching Methods

**Sharon A. Harris**
Teacher, Gifted
Mid-Del Public Schools
213 Elm
Midwest City, Oklahoma 73110
*Gifted Education Areas*
Mathematics
Teaching Methods

**Johnelle K. Jones**
Teacher and Coordinator,
    Gifted
Whittier Middle School
2000 West Brooks
Norman, Oklahoma 73069
*Gifted Education Areas*
Program Development
Student Identification
Teaching Methods

**L. Kathleen Kaufman**
Teacher and Coordinator,
    Gifted
Will Rogers School
1215 East Ninth
Edmond, Oklahoma 73034
*Gifted Education Areas*
Creative Thinking Skills
Program Development
Program Objectives

**Charles J. Migliorino**
Teacher, Gifted
Ardmore High School
2600 Harris
Ardmore, Oklahoma 73401
*Gifted Education Areas*

Program Objectives
Social Studies
Teaching Methods

**Diane L. Miller**
Teacher, Gifted
Weatherford Public Schools
811 West Huber
Weatherford, Oklahoma 73096
*Gifted Education Areas*
Program Development
Program Objectives

**Billye M. Van Schuyver**
Associate Professor
Oklahoma City University
2501 North Blackwelder
Oklahoma City, Oklahoma 73106
*Gifted Education Areas*
Program Development
Program Objectives
Student Identification
Teaching Methods

**Shirley M. Warner**
Director, Gifted and Talented
Putnam City School District
5501 Northwest Thirty-ninth
    Street
Oklahoma City, Oklahoma 73122
*Gifted Education Areas*
Multiple Talented
Program Development
Program Evaluation

## OREGON

**Martin J. Birnbaum**
Specialist, Gifted and Talented
Multnomah County Educational
   Service District
220 Southeast 102nd Avenue
Portland, Oregon 97216
*Gifted Education Areas*
Career Education
Community Advocacy
Program Planning

**Lloyd L. Lovell**
Professor
College of Education
University of Oregon
1761 Alder Street
Eugene, Oregon 97403
*Gifted Education Areas*
Creative Problem Solving
Program Development
Program Objectives

**Sue Ann Novotny**
Teacher and Consultant,
   Gifted
Portland Public Schools
Capitol Hill School
8401 Southwest Seventeenth
   Avenue
Portland, Oregon 97219
*Gifted Education Areas*
Case Studies
Program Objectives
Teaching Strategies

**Marsha C. Rhodes**
Specialist, Gifted and
   Talented
Beaverton Schools
P. O. Box 200
Beaverton, Oregon 97005
*Gifted Education Areas*
Community Resources
Enrichment Triad Model
Mentor Programs
Program Implementation

**George Shepard**
Professor
College of Education
University of Oregon
Eugene, Oregon 97403
*Gifted Education Areas*
Program Development
Student Identification
Student Underachievers

**Benda L. Vines**
Coordinator
Southern Oregon Gifted Program
Jackson County Educational
   Service District
101 North Grape
Medford, Oregon 97501
*Gifted Education Areas*
Creative Problem Solving
Program Development
Program Objectives
Teaching Methods

# PENNSYLVANIA

**T. Noretta Bingaman**
Advisor, Special Education
  (Gifted)
Pennsylvania State Department
  of Education
Box 911
Harrisburg, Pennsylvania 17126
*Gifted Education Areas*
Program Development
Program Evaluation
Program Objectives

**G. Bruce Gurcsik**
Supervisor, Gifted and
  Talented
ARIN Intermediate Unit
Box 175
Shelocta, Pennsylvania 15774
*Gifted Education Areas*
Instructional Strategies
Program Planning
Program Evaluation
Structure of the Intellect

**Randall L. Manning**
Supervisor, Gifted
Appalachia Intermediate
  Unit 08
Department for Exceptional Children
227 Bedford Street
Hollidaysburg, Pennsylvania 16648
*Gifted Education Areas*
Affective Education
Social Studies
Teaching Methods

**Shirley A. Pittman**
Coordinator, Library Services
McIntyre Elementary School
200 McIntyre Road
Pittsburgh, Pennsylvania 15237
*Gifted Education Areas*
Individually Prescribed
  Instruction
Media Selection

**Louise R. Roslund**
Teacher, Gifted
McKeesport Area School
  District
Eden Park Boulevard
McKeesport, Pennsylvania 15132
*Gifted Education Areas*
Environmental Education
Program Development
Teaching Methods

**Donald L. Schiele**
Supervisor, Gifted and
  Talented
Westmoreland Intermediate
  Unit
409 Coulter Avenue
Greensburg, Pennsylvania 15601
*Gifted Education Areas*
Differentiated Curricula
Parent Advocacy
Program Initiation

## RHODE ISLAND

**Terence L. Belcher**
Associate Professor
Department of Psychology
Rhode Island College
Providence, Rhode Island 02908
*Gifted Education Areas*
Program Evaluation
Psychological Factors
Student Identification

**Fay R. Bodner**
Special Assistant to the
  Commissioner/Special
  Populations
Rhode Island State Department
  of Education
199 Promenade Street
Providence, Rhode Island 02903
*Gifted Education Areas*
Program Development
Program Objectives
Student Identification

**Karen L. Carroll**
Administrator, ARB
Providence School Department
86 Fourth Street
Providence, Rhode Island 02906
*Gifted Education Areas*
Arts
Career Education
Student Identification

**John M. Crenson**
Professor
Rhode Island College
600 Mount Pleasant Avenue
Providence, Rhode Island 02908
*Gifted Education Areas*
Mathematics
Program Development
Program Objectives

**Richard G. Nelson**
Associate Professor
Department of Education
University of Rhode Island

705 Chafee Building
Kingston, Rhode Island 02881
*Gifted Education Areas*
Program Development
Program Evaluation
Student Identification

**Sidney P. Rollins**
Professor
Rhode Island College
600 Mount Pleasant Avenue
Providence, Rhode Island 02908
*Gifted Education Areas*
Program Development
Program Evaluation
Student Identification

**Richard E. Sullivan**
Professor
Department of Education
University of Rhode Island
Kingston, Rhode Island 02881
*Gifted Education Areas*
Grouping Practices
Program Objectives
Student Identification

**Catherine A. Valentino**
Director, Elementary Education
North Kingstown School
  Department
100 Fairway
North Kingstown, Rhode Island 02852
*Gifted Education Areas*
Creative Thinking Skills
Program Development, Early Childhood
Teaching Methods

# SOUTH CAROLINA

**Gary L. Awkerman**
Director, Planning and
  Management
Charleston County School
  District
The Center
Hutson and Meeting Streets
Charleston, South Carolina 29403
*Gifted Education Areas*
Creative Problem Solving
Program Development
Teaching Methods

**Martha D. Bishop**
Professor
Department of Education
Winthrop College
Rock Hill, South Carolina
  29730
*Gifted Education Areas*
Program Development
Student Identification
Teaching Methods

**Jane O. Bryan**
Coordinator, Gifted
Kershaw County School District
DuBose Court
Camden, South Carolina 29020
*Gifted Education Areas*
Program Development
Program Objectives
Teaching Methods

**Paul C. Fisher**
Director
The Governor's School of
  South Carolina
College of Charleston
Charleston, South Carolina 29401
*Gifted Education Areas*
Program Administration
Summer Programs

**William H. Foster**
Director of Instruction
Oconee County Schools

Box 5
West Union, South Carolina 29696
*Gifted Education Areas*
Program Administration
Program Development
Program Objectives

**Thomas W. Graham**
Board Member (retired)
Florence School District
  No. 1
P. O. Box 1268
Florence, South Carolina 29503
*Gifted Education Areas*
Program Development
Program Evaluation
Program Objectives
Science

**Sidney W. Hopkins**
Coordinator, Gifted and
  Talented
Richland County School
  District Two
6831 Brookfield Road
Columbia, South Carolina 29206
*Gifted Education Areas*
Program Development
Program Evaluation
Student Identification
Teaching Methods

**Bryan E. Lindsay**
Associate Professor
University of South Carolina
  at Spartanburg
Highway 176 at I-85
Spartanburg, South Carolina 29303
*Gifted Education Areas*
Creative Problem Solving
Futuristics
Humanities
Technology and Human Values

**James P. Mahaffey**
Associate Professor
Department of Education
Furman University

P. O. Box 28627
Greenville, South Carolina 29613
*Gifted Education Areas*
Program Development
Program Evaluation
Student Identification
Teaching Methods

**Maudianna W. Pruitt**
Teacher and Director, Gifted
Anderson School District Five
P. O. Drawer 439
Anderson, South Carolina 29622
*Gifted Education Areas*
Program Objectives
Program Planning
Student Identification

**Herbert B. Tyler**
Associate Superintendent
Richland County School
   District Two
6831 Brookfield Road
Columbia, South Carolina 29206
*Gifted Education Areas*
Curriculum Development
Program Objectives
Program Planning

**Winnie V. Williams**
Assistant Professor
Central Wesleyan College
Central, South Carolina 29630
*Gifted Education Areas*
Program Evaluation
Program Objectives
Student Identification

## SOUTH DAKOTA

**Floyd R. Hunking**
Coordinator, Gifted
Sioux Falls Public Schools
1600 South Cliff
Sioux Falls, South Dakota 57103
*Gifted Education Areas*
Mentor Programs
Student Counseling

**Taylor B. Merrick**
Director, Gifted and Talented
Shannon County Schools
Batesland, South Dakota 57716
*Gifted Education Areas*
Program Development
Student Identification
Visual Arts

**Bruce G. Milne**
Professor
School of Education
University of South Dakota
Vermillion, South Dakota 57069
*Gifted Education Areas*
Career Education
Curriculum Development

## TENNESSEE

**Ralph C. Bohannon**
Supervisor, Special Education
Greeneville City School
  System
P. O. Box 30
Greeneville, Tennessee 37743
*Gifted Education Areas*
Program Development
Program Evaluation
Program Objectives

**Irma S. McGuffey**
Head Teacher, Gifted
Special Services
Knoxville City Schools
101 East Fifth Avenue
Knoxville, Tennessee 37917
*Gifted Education Areas*
Program Objectives
Teaching Methods

**Wanda L. Moody**
Director, Special Services
Knoxville City Schools
101 East Fifth Avenue
Knoxville, Tennessee 37917
*Gifted Education Areas*
Program Development
Program Objectives
Teaching Methods

**Sallye T. Moore**
Coordinator, Special Education
Clarksville-Montgomery County
  School System
501 Franklin Street
Clarksville, Tennessee 37040
*Gifted Education Areas*
Program Development
Program Objectives
Teaching Methods

**Joanne R. Whitmore**
Professor
George Peabody College for
  Teachers
Vanderbilt University

Box 50
Nashville, Tennessee 37203
*Gifted Education Areas*
Emotional and Social
  Development
Program Development
Student Underachievers

# TEXAS

**Joe Austin**
Assistant Superintendent for
  Instruction
La Porte Independent School
  District
301 East Fairmont Parkway
La Porte, Texas 77571
*Gifted Education Areas*
Program Development
Program Evaluation
Program Objectives

**Terry A. Brandt**
Director, Staff Development
Harris County Department of
  Education
6208 Irvington Boulevard
Houston, Texas 77022
*Gifted Education Areas*
Program Development
Student Identification
Teaching Methods

**Scherry S. Chapman**
Supervisor, Federal Programs
Georgetown Independent
  School District
1201 Maple
Georgetown, Texas 78626
*Gifted Education Areas*
Program Development
Program Evaluation
Program Objectives

**G. Woodie Coleman**
Director, Gifted and Talented
Education Service Center,
  Region XVII
700 Texas Commerce Building
Lubbock, Texas 79401
*Gifted Education Areas*
Program Development
Program Implementation
Student Contracts

**June R. Cox**
Academic Director

Gifted Students Institute for
  Research and Development
611 Ryan Plaza Drive
Suite 1119
Arlington, Texas 76011
*Gifted Education Areas*
Community Based Programs
Community Advocacy
International Programs

**Allen E. dePagter**
Director, Gifted and Talented
Education Service Center,
  Region I
1900 West Schunior
Edinburg, Texas 78539
*Gifted Education Areas*
Alternative Programs
Bilingual Programs
Student Identification,
  Minority Disadvantaged

**Alice Duerksen**
Teacher, Gifted
Alamo Elementary School
Drawer B
Forst Stockton, Texas 79735
*Gifted Education Areas*
Grouping Practices
Language Arts
Reading
Teaching Methods

**Martha A. Ferrell**
Reading Coordinator
Irving Independent School
  District
901 O'Connor Road
Irving, Texas 75061
*Gifted Education Areas*
Program Development
Program Objectives
Teaching Methods

**Juan M. Flores**
Assistant Superintendent
Dallas Independent School
  District

3700 Ross Avenue
Dallas, Texas 75204
*Gifted Education Areas*
Program Development
Program Objectives
Student Identification

**Charlie Henderson**
Facilitator, National
    Diffusion Network
Education Service Center,
    Region IV
1750 Seamist
P. O. Box 863
Houston, Texas 77001
*Gifted Education Areas*
Program Development
Program Objectives
Student Identification

**Luke Lyons**
Analyst, Educational Program
Education Service Center,
    Region IV
1750 Seamist
P. O. Box 863
Houston, Texas 77001
*Gifted Education Areas*
Program Development
Program Evaluation
Program Objectives

**Sidney W. McCallister**
Assistant Superintendent for
    Instruction and Personnel
Fort Stockton Independent
    School District
P. O. Box 1628
Fort Stockton, Texas 79735
*Gifted Education Areas*
Program Development
Program Evaluation
Student Identification

**Judith L. Martin**
Consultant, Gifted and
    Talented
Education Service Center,

Region XX
1550 Northeast Loop 410
San Antonio, Texas 78209
*Gifted Education Areas*
Teacher Training
Teaching Methods

**Phillip L. Mitchell**
Director of Instruction
Fort Stockton Independent
    School District
P. O. Box 1628
Fort Stockton, Texas 79735
*Gifted Education Areas*
Program Development
Program Evaluation
Program Objectives
Student Identification

**William R. Nash**
Professor
Department of Educational
    Psychology
Texas A & M University
College Station, Texas 77843
*Gifted Education Areas*
Program Development
Student Identification
Teaching Methods

**Joe Parks**
Executive Director
Education Service Center,
    Region XIII
7703 North Lamar
Austin, Texas 78752
*Gifted Education Areas*
Program Development
Teaching Methods

**Thomas H. Scannicchio**
Assistant Superintendent for
    Instruction
Snyder Independent School District
2901 Thirty-seventh Street
Snyder, Texas 79549
*Gifted Education Areas*
Program Development

Staff Development
Student Identification

**Evelyn S. Sechler**
Curriculum Consultant
West Orange-Cove Independent
  School District
Box 1107
Orange, Texas 77630
*Gifted Education Areas*
Program Development
Program Objectives

**Maxine B. Walker**
Coordinator
Alice Independent School
  District
200 North Reynolds
Alice, Texas 78332
*Gifted Education Areas*
Program Development
Student Identification
Teaching Methods

**Patricia E. Wallace**
Assistant Superintendent,
  Curriculum and Instruction
Weslaco Independent School
  District
P. O. Box 266
Weslaco, Texas 78596
*Gifted Education Areas*
Needs Assessment
Program Objectives
Student Identification

**Warren T. White, Jr.**
Supervisor, Program Proposals
Fort Worth Independent School
  District
3210 West Lancaster
Fort Worth, Texas 76107
*Gifted Education Areas*
Staff Development
Student Identification
Theatre

**Donald G. Williams**
Consultant, Elementary

Birdville Independent School
  District
6125 East Belknap Street
Fort Worth, Texas 76117
*Gifted Education Areas*
Program Development
Program Objectives
Student Identification

## UTAH

**Allen E. Bauer**
Curriculum Director
Murray City School District
147 East 5065 South
Murray, Utah 84107
*Gifted Education Areas*
Program Objectives
Teaching Methods

**Ronald G. Cefalo**
Teacher, Gifted
North Ogden Junior High
575 East 2900 North
Ogden, Utah 84404
*Gifted Education Areas*
Program Development
Program Objectives
Science
Teaching Methods

**H. Wallace Goddard**
Director, Gifted and Talented
Vintah School District
635 West 200 South
Vernal, Utah 84078
*Gifted Education Areas*
Film Making

**Laurie E. Maak**
Director
Intermountain Center for
   Gifted Education
P. O. Box 7726
Salt Lake City, Utah 84107
*Gifted Education Areas*
Student Counseling
Program Administration
Student Identification

**JoAnn B. Seghini**
Curriculum Consultant
Jordan School District
9361 South 400 East
Sandy, Utah 84070
*Gifted Education Areas*
Grouping Practices
Program Development

Social Studies
Teaching Methods

**Norman L. Skanchy**
Director, Elementary Education
Ogden City School District
2444 Adams Avenue
Ogden, Utah 84401
*Gifted Education Areas*
Program Development
Program Objectives
Visual Arts

**Barbara A. Swicord**
Associate Director
Intermountain Center for
   Gifted Education
P. O. Box 7726
Salt Lake City, Utah 84107
*Gifted Education Areas*
Creative Problem Solving
Differentiated Curriculum
Futuristics
Teacher Training

**Calvin W. Taylor**
Professor
Department of Psychology
University of Utah
Building 404
Salt Lake City, Utah 84112
*Gifted Education Areas*
Program Evaluation
Student Identification
Teaching Methods

**Dallas R. Workman**
Director, Elementary
Curriculum
Davis County School District
45 East State Street
Farmington, Utah 84025
*Gifted Education Areas*
Program Development
Student Identification

## VERMONT

**Gary J. Confessore**
Dean of Academic Affairs
Johnson State College
Johnson, Vermont 05656
*Gifted Education Areas*
Community Resources
In-service Education
Program Development
Teacher Training

**Helene W. Lang**
Associate Professor
College of Education and
    Social Services
University of Vermont
427 Waterman Building
Burlington, Vermont 05405
*Gifted Education Areas*
Reading
Student Identification
Writing

**Mary M. Pierce**
Faculty Member
College of Education and
    Social Services
University of Vermont
532 Waterman Building
Burlington, Vermont 05401
*Gifted Education Areas*
Program Development
Program Objectives
Student Identification

**Barbara M. Sofferman**
Parent and Secretary
State Association for Gifted
    Education
Galvin Hill Road
Colchester, Vermont 05446
*Gifted Education Areas*
Legislation
Parent Advocacy

## VIRGINIA

**Herbert A. Alf**
Professor and Director
Optimal Development Program
University of the District
of Columbia
6461 Linway Terrace
McLean, Virginia 22101
*Gifted Education Areas*
Career Education
Environmental Education
Student Identification

**K. Edwin Brown**
Director, Gifted and
Talented
Virginia Beach City Public
Schools
P. O. Box 6038
Virginia Beach, Virginia 23456
*Gifted Education Areas*
Program Administration
Teaching Strategies
Unit Planning

**Una L. Coleman**
Coordinator, Gifted
Prince William County Schools
Box 389
Manassas, Virginia 22110
*Gifted Education Areas*
Community Resources
In-service Education
Program Development

**Jennie J. DeGenaro**
Elementary Supervisor,
Special Program
Henrico County Schools
P. O. Box 40
Highland Springs, Virginia 23075
*Gifted Education Areas*
Curriculum Development
Program Planning
Student Identification

**Nedra I. Harkavy**
Director, Gifted

Hampton City School System
1306 Thomas Street
Hampton, Virginia 23669
*Gifted Education Areas*
Program Objectives
Student Identification
Teaching Methods

**Jane S. Heard**
Specialist, Gifted
Chesterfield County Public
Schools
P. O. Box 40
Chesterfield, Virginia 23832
*Gifted Education Areas*
Parent Involvement
Student Identification
Teaching Methods

**Vincent F. Kashuda**
Coordinator, Gifted and
Talented
Fairfax County Public
Schools
9517 Main Street
Fairfax, Virginia 22031
*Gifted Education Areas*
Grouping Practices
Program Development
Program Objectives
Student Identification

**Jeffrey H. Orloff**
Coordinator, Gifted
Falls Church City Public
Schools
7124 Leesburg Pike
Falls Church, Virginia 22043
*Gifted Education Areas*
Community Advocacy
Grouping Practices
Program Development

**Kathleen R. Schoonmaker**
Administrator, Gifted
Central Norfolk Public
Schools
800 East City Hall Avenue

Norfolk, Virginia 23508
*Gifted Education Areas*
Instructional Methods
Program Administration
Program Development

298        *Gifted and Talented Education*

# WASHINGTON

**Robert E. Clairmont**
Coordinator
Mentally Gifted Minors
  Program
Department of Romance
  Languages
University of Washington
Seattle, Washington 98195
*Gifted Education Areas*
Program Objectives
Structure of the Intellect
Student Identification

**Ora L. Franklin**
Principal
Seattle School District
  No. 1
12515 Greenwood Avenue North
Seattle, Washington 98133
*Gifted Education Areas*
Communication Strategies
Staff Development

**Janice E. Fluter**
Teacher, Gifted
Tyee Junior High
13630 Allen Road
Bellevue, Washington 98006
*Gifted Education Areas*
Language Arts
Program Development
Social Studies
Teaching Methods

**Mildred E. Kersh**
Associate Professor
Department of Education
University of Washington
115 Miller Hall DQ-12
Seattle, Washington 98195
*Gifted Education Areas*
Curriculum Theory
Instructional Materials
Program Development

**Rex P. Martin**
Teacher, Gifted

Rose Hill Elementary School
8044 128th Avenue NE
Kirkland, Washington 98033
*Gifted Education Areas*
In-service Education
Foreign Languages
Language Arts
Teaching Methods

**Larry D. Pollock**
Teacher, Gifted
Benjamin Rush Elementary School
6101 152nd Avenue NE
Redmond, Washington 98052
*Gifted Education Areas*
Curriculum Development
Enrichment Models
Grouping Practices

**C. K. Rekdal**
Teacher and Consultant,
  Gifted
Bellevue School District
7558 Ravenna Avenue NE
Seattle, Washington 98115
*Gifted Education Areas*
Creativity Theory
Critical Thinking Skills
Curriculum Development
Student Identification

**Patricia K. Riffle**
Teacher, Gifted
Edmond School District
7200 191st SW
Lynnwood, Washington 98036
*Gifted Education Areas*
Parent Education
Program Development

**Louisa B. Thompson**
School Psychologist
Seattle Public Schools
815 Fourth Avenue North
Seattle, Washington 98109
*Gifted Education Areas*
Parent Counseling
Parent Education

Student Counseling
Student Identification

**Janet A. Zuber**
Teacher, Gifted
Somerset Elementary School
14100 Somerset Boulevard SE
Bellevue, Washington 98008
*Gifted Education Areas*
Curriculum Development
Differentiated Instruction
Program Objectives

## WEST VIRGINIA

**Allen Blumberg**
Program Director
Department of Special
    Education
West Virginia College of
    Graduate Studies
Institute, West Virginia 25112
*Gifted Education Areas*
Program Development
Program Evaluation
Teaching Methods

**Dorothy S. Drake**
Teacher, Gifted
Hardy County Schools
510 Ashby Street
Moorefield, West Virginia 26836
*Gifted Education Areas*
Critical Thinking Skills
Student Contracts
Teaching Methods

**Kay F. Johnston**
Coordinator, Gifted
Resa III
200 Elizabeth Street
Charleston, West Virginia 25311
*Gifted Education Areas*
Program Development

**George S. Krelis**
Director, Student Services
Ohio County Board of Education
2203 National Road
Wheeling, West Virginia 26003
*Gifted Education Areas*
Program Development
Student Identification

**Gail E. Looney**
Coordinator, Gifted and
    Talented
Ohio County Board of
    Education
2203 National Road
Wheeling, West Virginia 26003
*Gifted Education Areas*

Music
Program Development
Teaching Methods

**Gabriel A. Nardi**
Professor
Department of Special
    Education
West Virginia University
805 Allen Hall
Morgantown, West Virginia 26506
*Gifted Education Areas*
Program Development
Program Evaluation
Student Identification

**Edwina D. Pendarvis**
Assistant Professor
Marshall University
Room 109
Jenkins Hall
Huntington, West Virginia 25701
*Gifted Education Areas*
Program Evaluation
Teacher Training

**Virginia G. Simmons**
Teacher, Gifted
Kanawha County Schools
Exceptional Children, Unit II
200 Elizabeth Street
Charleston, West Virginia 25311
*Gifted Education Areas*
Curriculum Development
Model Programs
Test Instruments

**Connie T. Strickland**
Teacher and Facilitator,
    Gifted
Kanawha County Schools
Gifted Department
200 Elizabeth Street
Charleston, West Virginia 25311
*Gifted Education Areas*
Language Arts
Program Development
Teaching Methods

**Diane R. Szakonyi**
Coordinator, Gifted Program
Mercer County Schools
1420 Honaker Avenue
Princeton, West Virginia 24740
*Gifted Education Areas*
Curriculum Development
Program Objectives
Program Planning

## WISCONSIN

**Byron L. Barrington**
Professor
University of Wisconsin
  Center—Wausau
518 South Seventh Avenue
Wausau, Wisconsin 54401
*Gifted Education Areas*
Program Administration
Needs Assessment
Social and Emotional
  Needs

**Robert E. Clasen**
Professor
University of Wisconsin—
  Extension
235 Lowell Hall
Madison, Wisconsin 53706
*Gifted Education Areas*
Program Development
Program Evaluation
Teaching Methods

**Gary A. Davis**
Professor
Psychology Department
University of Wisconsin—
  Madison
1025 West Johnson Street
Madison, Wisconsin 53706
*Gifted Education Areas*
Student Identification

**Glenn A. Davison**
District Administrator
Joint School District No. 2
220 Kroncke Drive
Sun Prairie, Wisconsin 53590
*Gifted Education Areas*
Program Development
Simulation
Student Identification

**Ellen D. Fiedler**
Director, Gifted
Stevens Point Area Public
  Schools

Gifted and Talented Center
1519 Water Street
Stevens Point, Wisconsin 54481
*Gifted Education Areas*
Curriculum Development
Program Planning
Student Identification

**A. Gayle Grabish**
Coordinator, Project Fiesta
University of Wisconsin
South Hall
River Falls, Wisconsin 54022
*Gifted Education Areas*
Creative Arts
Program Development
Student Identification

**Fran P. Kimmey**
Private Consultant, Gifted
  and Talented
314 Maple Drive
Mt. Horeb, Wisconsin 53572
*Gifted Education Areas*
In-service Education
Program Development
Student Identification

**Barbara H. LeRose**
Director, Federal Projects
Racine Unified School
  District
2326 Mohr Avenue
Racine, Wisconsin 53405
*Gifted Education Areas*
Program Development
Program Objectives
Student Identification

**Jean W. McQueen**
Director, Title IV-C
Cooperative Educational
  Services Agency No. 7
801 Highway 10 West
Stevens Point, Wisconsin 54481
*Gifted Education Areas*
Career Education
Program Development, Rural
Student Identification

**William G. Melville**
Associate Professor
College of Education
The University of Wisconsin
Platteville, Wisconsin 53818
*Gifted Education Areas*
Grouping Practices
Program Development
Teaching Methods

**Philip A. Perrone**
Professor
School of Education
University of Wisconsin
Room 352
1000 Bascom Mall
Madison, Wisconsin 53706
*Gifted Education Areas*
Parent Counseling
Program Evaluation
Research

**Beecham R. Robinson**
Associate Professor
University of Wisconsin—
    Parkside
215 Greenquirt Hall
Kenosha, Wisconsin 53140
*Gifted Education Areas*
Drama
In-service Education
Language Arts
Teaching Methods

**Robert G. Rossmiller**
Professor
University of Wisconsin—
    Stevens Point
Room 458
COPS Building
Stevens Point, Wisconsin 54481
*Gifted Education Areas*
Program Development
Student Identification
Teaching Strategies

## WYOMING

**Margaret L. Albert**
Coordinator, Art
Laramie County School
    District No. 1
2810 House Avenue
Cheyenne, Wyoming 82001
*Gifted Education Areas*
Program Development
Student Identification
Visual Arts

**Owen Jones**
Principal
Crest Hill Elementary School
4445 South Poplar
Casper, Wyoming 82601
*Gifted Education Areas*
Program Development
Structure of the Intellect
Student Identification

**Susan L. True**
Chairman
State Gifted and Talented
    Advisory Council
P. O. Box 2360
Casper, Wyoming 82602
*Gifted Education Areas*
Parent Advocacy

# SECTION V
# RESOURCES IN GIFTED EDUCATION

In addition to the national leaders, state consultants, and local resource persons identified in earlier chapters, numerous other resources are available to educators and lay persons interested in developing and expanding programs and services for the gifted and the talented. Resources identified in this chapter include information services, funding sources, organizations, publications, alternative schools and programs, and teacher training institutions.

## PART A
## INFORMATION SERVICES

National and international information sources are available to persons interested in the gifted and talented. Additionally, consultants for gifted education in each state department of education can identify information sources in their respective states.

### National

National Clearinghouse for the Gifted and Talented
The Council for Exceptional Children
1920 Association Drive
Reston, Virginia 22091

National/State Leadership Training Institute on the Gifted and Talented
316 West Second Street, Suite 708
Los Angeles, California 90012

Office of Gifted and Talented
U. S. Office of Education
Washington, District of Columbia 20202

### International

World Council on Gifted and Talented Children
1 South Audlay Street
London, W1Y 5DQ, England

## PART B
## FUNDING SOURCES

Funding for gifted and talented education is available from a variety of public and private agencies at the local, state, and national levels. Important among these sources, but often overlooked, are federal agencies and private foundations.

### Federal Agencies

Proposals may be prepared and submitted for funding to a wide variety of federal agencies. The amount of money available and the program emphasis will vary for each fiscal year. Included among the federal agencies are:

Bureau for the Education of the Handicapped
U.S. Office of Education
Washington, District of Columbia 20202

Bureau of Occupational and Adult Education
U.S. Office of Education
Washington, District of Columbia 20208

National Endowment for the Arts
Washington, District of Columbia 20506

National Endowment for the Humanities
Washington, District of Columbia 20506

National Institute of Education
U.S. Department of Education
Washington, District of Columbia 20208

National Institute of Mental Health
Rockville, Maryland 20852

National Science Foundation
Washington, District of Columbia 20550

Office of Gifted and Talented

U.S. Office of Education
Washington, District of Columbia 20202

Office of Career Education
U.S. Office of Education
Washington, District of Columbia 20013

## Foundations

Private foundations have given financial support for a wide variety of activities in gifted education. Grants have provided funds for research, program development, graduate fellowships, newsletters, and conferences. Funding can be specific to a state, region, or available on a national basis. Recipients of foundation awards have been universities, state departments of education, and other agencies and organizations which support gifted education. Included among these foundations are:

The Vincent Astor Foundation
405 Park Avenue
New York, New York 10022

Cafritz Foundation
18205 K Street NW
Washington, District of Columbia 20006

Robert Sterling Clark Foundation
100 Wall Street
New York, New York 10005

Geraldine R. Dodge Foundation
163 Madison Avenue
Morristown, New Jersey 07960

Frick Educational Commission
1924 Frick Building
Pittsburgh, Pennsylvania 15219

Grant Foundation
130 East Fifty-ninth Street

New York City, New York 10022

International Paper Company Foundation
220 East Forty-second Street
New York, New York 10017

Noble Foundation
32 East Fifty-seventh Street
New York City, New York 10022

Northwest Area Foundation
W-975 First National Bank Building
St. Paul, Minnesota 55101

Jessie Smith Noyes Foundation
16 East Thirty-fourth Street
New York City, New York 10016

The Spencer Foundation
John Hancock Center
875 Michigan Avenue
Chicago, Illinois 60611

Levi Strauss Foundation
Two Embarcadero Center
San Francisco, California 94106

Z. Smith Reynolds Foundation, Incorporated
1225 Wachovia Building
Winston-Salem, North Carolina 27101

The Leonardo Trust
20 Daleham Gardens
London, NW3 5DA, England

## PART C
## ORGANIZATIONS

There are several national and international groups interested in promoting a better understanding of the gifted, talented, and creative. Members in some associations receive a journal and in some cases a newsletter as well.

### National

The American Association for the Gifted
15 Gramercy Park
New York, New York 10003

The Association for the Gifted
The Council for Exceptional Children
1920 Association Drive
Reston, Virginia 22091

The Council of State Directors of Programs for Gifted
Ms. Cornelia Tongue
Division of Exceptional Children
North Carolina State Department of Public Instruction
Raleigh, North Carolina 27602

Gifted Child Society, Incorporated
59 Glen Gray Road
Oakland, New Jersey 07436

Gifted Students Institute for Research and Development
611 Ryan Plaza Drive, Suite 1149
Arlington, Texas 76011

The National Association for Creative Children and Adults
8080 Spring Valley Drive
Cincinnati, Ohio 45236

National Association for Gifted Children
217 Gregory Drive
Hot Springs, Arkansas 71901

## International

American Mensa, Limited
1701 West Third Street
Brooklyn, New York 11223

National Association for Gifted Children
1 South Audley Street
London, WIY 5DQ, England

World Council for Gifted and Talented Children
1 South Audlay Street
London, W1Y 5DQ, England

## PART D
## PUBLICATIONS

Information on the psychology and education of the gifted and talented is available in printed form at the local, state, and national levels. Major sources of current information are professional journals and newsletters distributed nationally.

## Journals

Current information on all aspects of gifted education may be found in several professional journals. Information on research, identification of students, program development and evaluation, parenting, and creativity are some of the many topics included.

### National

**The Gifted Child Quarterly**
National Association for Gifted Children
217 Gregory Drive
Hot Springs, Arkansas 71901

**Gifted/Creative/Talented**
G/C/T Publishing Company
Box 66654
Mobile, Alabama 36606

**Roeper Review: A Journal for Gifted Child Education**
Roeper City and Country Day School
Bloomfield Hills, Michigan 48013

**The Journal of Creative Behavior**
Creative Education Foundation
State University of New York, College at Buffalo
1300 Elmwood Avenue
Buffalo, New York 14222

**North Carolina Association for the Gifted and Talented Quarterly Journal**
The North Carolina Association for the Gifted and Talented

Department of Special Education
Appalachian State University
Boone, North Carolina 28608

*The Creative Child and Adult Quarterly*
The National Association for Creative Children and Adults
8080 Spring Valley Drive
Cincinnati, Ohio 45236

*Journal for the Education of the Gifted*
The Association for the Gifted
1920 Association Drive
Reston, Virginia 22091

*International*

*Gifted and Talented Education*
8 Slavyanska Street
Sofia, Bulgaria

## Newsletters

Several newsletters concerning current events, issues, and directions in gifted and talented education are distributed nationally by various professional associations and institutions of higher learning. Included among these are:

*The Gifted Children Newsletter*
530 University Avenue
Palo Alto, California 94301

*Gifted/Talented Education*
Box 533
Branford, Connecticut 06405

*Intellectually Talented Youth Bulletin*
Study of Mathematically Precocious Youth
The Johns Hopkins University
Baltimore, Maryland 21218

***TAG Update***
The Association for the Gifted
The Council for Exceptional Children
1920 Association Drive
Reston, Virginia 22091

## PART E
## ALTERNATIVE SCHOOLS AND PROGRAMS

In the interest of meeting the unique educational requirements of a diverse gifted and talented student population, a variety of important alternative schools and programs have been established. Included among these alternatives are federal model projects, fine and performing arts programs, Governor's honors programs, Saturday programs, and summer programs.

### Model Projects

Five model projects have been funded through the Office of Gifted and Talented. Information concerning these projects may be obtained by contacting the project director.

*Model Project for Implementing*
*a Program for Gifted and Talented*
*in Rural Schools*
> Margaret Humphrey
> Shasta County Superintendent of Schools
> 1644 Magnolia Avenue
> Redding, California 96001

*Identification of High Potential*
*in Culturally Diverse Students*
*through Integrative Experiences*
*in Theatre Arts and Independent*
*Study*
> Mary Hunter Wolf
> Center for Theatre Techniques in Education, Incorporated
> 1850 Elm Street
> Stratford, Connecticut 06497

*Rural Preschool Program for*
*Gifted and Talented and for*
*Gifted and Talented*
*Handicapped*
> Gail Hanninen

Panhandle Child Development Association, Incorporated
418 Coeur d'Alene Avenue
Coeur d'Alene, Idaho 83814

**Model Project for the Creatively**
**Gifted and Talented in Science**
Vincent G. Galasso
New York City Board of Education
Bronx High School of Science
75 West 205th Street
New York, New York 10468

**Model Preschool Program for**
**Gifted Children**
Halbert Robinson
Child Development Research Group
University of Washington
Guthrie Annex II
Seattle, Washington 98195

## Fine and Performing Arts Programs

Several high schools are designed to serve talented youth who are outstanding in the fine and performing arts. Criteria for selection, course offerings, and scheduling are specific to each school. Included among the schools are:

Alabama School of Fine Arts
280 North Eighteenth Street
Birmingham, Alabama 35203

Arts Magnet School
2501 Flora Street
Dallas, Texas 75201

Educational Center for the Talented in the Arts
55 Audubon Street
New Haven, Connecticut 06511

Florida School of the Arts
St. Johns River Community Academy
5001 St. Johns Avenue
Palatka, Florida 32077

High School for the Performing Arts
3512 Austin Street
Houston, Texas 77004

New Orleans Center for Creative Arts
6048 Perrier Street
New Orleans, Louisiana 70118

North Carolina School for the Arts
P. O. Box 12189
Winston-Salem, North Carolina 27107

School of the Arts
Thirty-fifth and R Streets NW
Washington, District of Columbia 20007

## Governor's Honors Programs

Designed for students at the high school level, governor's honors programs provide a wide variety of academic experiences. In addition, students greatly benefit from interaction with other gifted pupils in a residential setting. Admission to a program in a particular state is limited to students residing within that state. These programs include:

Governor's Honors Program
Georgia State Department of Education
156 Trinity Avenue SW
Atlanta, Georgia 30303

Governor's Program for Gifted Children
McNeese State University
Lake Charles, Louisiana 70609

The Governor's Schools of North Carolina
North Carolina State Department of Public Instruction

Governor's School West
Drawer H, Salem Station
Winston-Salem, North
   Carolina 27108

Governor's School East
St. Andrews Presbyterian
   College
Laurinburg, North
   Carolina 28352

Governor's School for the Arts
Bucknell University
P. O. Box 213
Lewisburg, Pennsylvania 17837

The Governor's School
College of Charleston
Charleston, South Carolina 29401

Governor's School for the Gifted
P. O. Box 6-Q
Richmond, Virginia 23216

### Saturday Programs

A wide range of courses is provided to gifted students through Saturday programs. Administrative arrangements for conducting programs vary from one sponsoring agency to another. Included among these programs are the following:

Catskills Saturday Seminars
State University of New York, College at Oneonta
Oneonta, New York 13820

College of Kids
147 North Franklin Street
Wilkes-Barre, Pennsylvania 18711

Gifted Child Foundation
University of South Florida
FAO 150
Tampa, Florida 33620

U.S.A. Saturday Gifted Child Program
Department of Special Education
College of Education
University of South Alabama
Mobile, Alabama 36688

Saturday Gifted Studies Program
Center for Gifted Studies
University of Southern Mississippi
Hattiesburg, Mississippi 39401

Saturday School Extended Services for the Gifted
Department of Special Education
College of Education
Georgia State University
Atlanta, Georgia 30303

The Saturday Workshop
Gifted Child Society, Incorporated
Ridgewood, New Jersey 07451

Talcott Mountain Science Center
Montevideo Road
Avon, Connecticut 06001

### Summer Programs

Many states have some type of summer program, either residential or nonresidential, for gifted students. Summer programs can expand interests and abilities of these students. Residential programs available to gifted students from across the nation are conducted by various institutions. Examples of these programs are:

Twin Lakes Camp Program for the Gifted
Twin Lakes Camp
1429 Southwest Fifteenth Street
Miami, Florida 33145

Summer Gifted Studies Program
Center for Gifted Studies
University of Southern Mississippi
Hattiesburg, Mississippi 39401

Summer Enrichment for Gifted Children
Appalachian State University
Boone, North Carolina 28608

Scholastics and Arts Programs
Mars Hill College
Mars Hill, North Carolina 28754

G/T Summer Enrichment Program
Sacred Heart College
Belmont, North Carolina 28012

The Cullowhee Experience
Summer Programs for Gifted Students
216 Killian Building
Western Carolina University
Cullowhee, North Carolina 28723

Gifted Students Institute for Research and Development
611 Ryan Plaza Drive, Suite 1149
Arlington, Texas 76011

## PART F
## TEACHER TRAINING INSTITUTIONS

Almost every state has one or more institutions of higher education which offer undergraduate and graduate level course work for teachers and others interested in the gifted and talented. Included among these are:

**ALABAMA**

Alabama Agricultural and Mechanical University—Graduate
Normal, Alabama 35762

Auburn University—Graduate
Auburn, Alabama 36830

University of Alabama—Graduate
University, Alabama 35486

University of Alabama in Birmingham—Graduate
Birmingham, Alabama 35294

University of South Alabama—Undergraduate and Graduate
Mobile, Alabama 36688

**ALASKA**

University of Alaska—Undergraduate
Fairbanks, Alaska 99701

**ARKANSAS**

University of Arkansas at Little Rock—Graduate
Little Rock, Arkansas 72204

**CALIFORNIA**

California State University, Dominguez Hills—Undergraduate
and Graduate
Carson, California 90747

California State University, Fresno—Undergraduate and
Graduate
Fresno, California 93740

California State University, Fullerton—Undergraduate and
Graduate
Fullerton, California 92634

California State University, Long Beach—Undergraduate and
Graduate
Long Beach, California 90840

California State University, Los Angeles—Undergraduate
and Graduate
Los Angeles, California 90032

California State University, Northridge—Undergraduate
and Graduate
Northridge, California 91330

Chapman College—Graduate
Orange, California 92666

San Diego State University—Graduate
San Diego, California 92182

San Jose State University—Graduate
San Jose, California 95192

University of California—Undergraduate
Davis, California 95616

University of the Pacific—Undergraduate and Graduate
Stockton, California 95204

University of San Francisco—Graduate
San Francisco, California 94117

University of Santa Clara—Graduate
Santa Clara, California 95053

**COLORADO**

University of Colorado at Colorado Springs—Undergraduate
Colorado Springs, Colorado 80907

University of Denver—Undergraduate and Graduate
Denver, Colorado 80210

University of Northern Colorado—Undergraduate and Graduate
Greeley, Colorado 80631

**CONNECTICUT**

Central Connecticut State College—Graduate
New Britain, Connecticut 06050

St. Joseph College—Graduate
West Hartford, Connecticut 06117

Southern Connecticut State College—Undergraduate and
    Graduate
New Haven, Connecticut 06515

Trinity College—Graduate
Hartford, Connecticut 06106

University of Bridgeport—Graduate
Bridgeport, Connecticut 06602

University of Connecticut—Graduate
Storrs, Connecticut 06268

Western Connecticut State College—Undergraduate
Danbury, Connecticut 06810

**DELAWARE**

University of Delaware—Graduate
Newark, Delaware 19711

## DISTRICT OF COLUMBIA

Trinity College—Undergraduate
Washington, District of Columbia 20017

University of the District of Columbia—Undergraduate and
  Graduate
Washington, District of Columbia 20009

## FLORIDA

Florida Atlantic University—Graduate
Boca Raton, Florida 33431

Florida State University—Graduate
Tallahassee, Florida 32306

University of Florida—Graduate
Gainesville, Florida 32611

University of South Florida—Graduate
Tampa, Florida 33620

## GEORGIA

Columbus College—Graduate
Columbus, Georgia 31907

Georgia College—Graduate
Milledgeville, Georgia 31061

Georgia Southern College—Graduate
Statesboro, Georgia 30458

Georgia State University—Graduate
Atlanta, Georgia 30303

University of Georgia—Graduate
Athens, Georgia 30601

Valdosta State University—Graduate
Valdosta, Georgia 31601

## HAWAII

University of Hawaii—Graduate
Honolulu, Hawaii 96822

University of Hawaii at Hilo—Undergraduate
Hilo, Hawaii 96720

## IDAHO

Boise State University—Graduate
Boise, Idaho 83725

College of Idaho—Undergraduate
Caldwell, Idaho 83605

Idaho State University—Graduate
Pocatello, Idaho 83209

Lewis-Clark State College—Graduate
Lewiston, Idaho 83501

University of Idaho—Graduate
Moscow, Idaho 83843

## ILLINOIS

Chicago State University—Graduate
Chicago, Illinois 60628

National College of Education—Undergraduate
Evanston, Illinois 60201

Northern Illinois University—Graduate
DeKalb, Illinois 60115

Southern Illinois University—Carbondale—Graduate
Carbondale, Illinois 62901

University of Illinois at Urbana-Champaign—Graduate
Urbana, Illinois 61801

## INDIANA

Ball State University—Graduate
Muncie, Indiana 47306

Butler University—Graduate
Indianapolis, Indiana 46207

Indiana State University—Graduate
Terre Haute, Indiana 47809

Purdue University—Graduate
Lafayette, Indiana 47907

## IOWA

Buena Vista College—Graduate
Storm Lake, Iowa 50588

Clarke College—Graduate
Dubuque, Iowa 52001

Drake University—Graduate
Des Moines, Iowa 50311

Iowa State University of Science and Technology—Graduate
Ames, Iowa 50010

Marycrest College—Graduate
Davenport, Iowa 52804

Morningside College—Graduate
Sioux City, Iowa 51106

University of Iowa—Graduate
Iowa City, Iowa 52242

University of Northern Iowa—Graduate
Cedar Falls, Iowa 50613

**KANSAS**

Emporia State University—Graduate
Emporia, Kansas 66801

Kansas State University—Graduate
Manhattan, Kansas 66506

The University of Kansas—Graduate
Lawrence, Kansas 66045

**KENTUCKY**

Eastern Kentucky University—Graduate
Richmond, Kentucky 40475

Morehead State University—Graduate
Morehead, Kentucky 40351

Murray State University—Graduate
Murray, Kentucky 42071

**LOUISIANA**

Louisiana State University and Agricultural and Mechanical
   College—Graduate
Baton Rouge, Louisiana 70803

McNeese State University—Graduate
Lake Charles, Louisiana 70609

Northwestern State University of Louisiana—Graduate
Natchitoches, Louisiana 71457

University of Southwestern Louisiana—Graduate
Lafayette, Louisiana 70501

**MAINE**

University of Maine at Orono—Undergraduate
Orono, Maine 04473

University of Southern Maine—Undergraduate
Portland, Maine 04100

University of Maine at Presque Isle—Undergraduate
Presque Isle, Maine 04769

**MARYLAND**

The Johns Hopkins University—Graduate
Baltimore, Maryland 21218

Towson State University—Undergraduate and Graduate
Towson, Maryland 21204

University of Maryland at Baltimore—Graduate
Baltimore, Maryland 21201

**MASSACHUSETTS**

Lesley College—Undergraduate
Cambridge, Massachusetts 02138

Northeastern University—Undergraduate
Boston, Massachusetts 02115

**MICHIGAN**

Central Michigan University—Graduate
Mount Pleasant, Michigan 48859

Eastern Michigan University—Graduate
Ypsilanti, Michigan 48197

Michigan State University—Graduate
East Lansing, Michigan 48824

University of Michigan—Graduate
Ann Arbor, Michigan 48109

Western Michigan University—Graduate
Kalamazoo, Michigan 49001

## MINNESOTA

Bemidji State University—Undergraduate
Bemidji, Minnesota 56601

Mankato State University—Undergraduate and Graduate
Mankato, Minnesota 56001

Moorhead State University—Undergraduate and Graduate
Moorhead, Minnesota 56560

Saint Cloud State University—Undergraduate and Graduate
St. Cloud, Minnesota 56301

University of Minnesota—Undergraduate and Graduate
Minneapolis, Minnesota 55455

University of Minnesota-Duluth—Undergraduate and Graduate
Duluth, Minnesota 55812

Winona State University—Undergraduate and Graduate
Winona, Minnesota 55987

## MISSISSIPPI

Delta State University—Graduate
Cleveland, Mississippi 38732

Jackson State University—Graduate
Jackson, Mississippi 39217

Mississippi State University—Graduate
Mississippi State, Mississippi 39762

University of Southern Mississippi—Undergraduate and
   Graduate
Hattiesburg, Mississippi 39401

University of Mississippi—Graduate
University, Mississippi 38677

## MISSOURI

Southeast Missouri State University—Undergraduate and
Graduate
Cape Girardeau, Missouri 63701

University of Missouri—Undergraduate and Graduate
Columbia, Missouri 65201

## NEBRASKA

Creighton University—Undergraduate
Omaha, Nebraska 68178

Kearney State College—Undergraduate
Kearney, Nebraska 68847

University of Nebraska-Lincoln—Undergraduate and Graduate
Lincoln, Nebraska 68588

University of Nebraska at Omaha—Undergraduate and Graduate
Omaha, Nebraska 68101

## NEW HAMPSHIRE

Keene State College—Graduate
Keene, New Hampshire 03431

## NEW JERSEY

Glassboro State College—Undergraduate and Graduate
Glassboro, New Jersey 08028

Jersey City State College—Graduate
Jersey City, New Jersey 07305

Kean College of New Jersey—Undergraduate and Graduate
Union, New Jersey 07083

Monmouth College—Undergraduate and Graduate
Long Branch, New Jersey 07764

Montclair State College—Undergraduate
Montclair, New Jersey 07043

Rutgers University—Graduate
Brunswick, New Jersey 08903

Trenton State College—Undergraduate and Graduate
Trenton, New Jersey 08625

The William Peterson College—Graduate
Wayne, New Jersey 07470

**NEW MEXICO**

The University of New Mexico—Graduate
Albuquerque, New Mexico 87131

**NEW YORK**

Manhattanville College—Graduate
Purchase, New York 10577

State University of New York, College at Brockport—Graduate
Brockport, New York 14420

State University of New York, College at Buffalo—Graduate
Buffalo, New York 14222

State University of New York at Albany—Graduate
Albany, New York 12222

Columbia University, Teachers College—Graduate
New York City, New York 10027

**NORTH CAROLINA**

Appalachian State University—Graduate
Boone, North Carolina 28608

Atlantic Christian College—Undergraduate and Graduate
Wilson, North Carolina 27893

Bennett College—Undergraduate and Graduate
Greensboro, North Carolina 27420

Duke University—Undergraduate and Graduate
Durham, North Carolina 27706

East Carolina University—Undergraduate and Graduate
Greenville, North Carolina 27834

Greensboro College—Undergraduate and Graduate
Greensboro, North Carolina 27420

Guilford College—Undergraduate and Graduate
Greensboro, North Carolina 27410

Lenoir-Rhyne College—Undergraduate and Graduate
Hickory, North Carolina 28601

North Carolina State University at Raleigh—Graduate
Raleigh, North Carolina 27607

St. Andrews Presbyterian College—Undergraduate and Graduate
Laurinburg, North Carolina 28352

University of North Carolina at Chapel Hill—Undergraduate
    and Graduate
Chapel Hill, North Carolina 27514

University of North Carolina at Charlotte—Undergraduate
    and Graduate
Charlotte, North Carolina 28223

Western Carolina University—Undergraduate and Graduate
Cullowhee, North Carolina 28723

**NORTH DAKOTA**

University of North Dakota—Undergraduate
Grand Forks, North Dakota 58202

Minot State College—Undergraduate
Minot, North Dakota 58701

**OHIO**

Kent State University—Undergraduate and Graduate
Kent, Ohio 44242

Ohio State University—Undergraduate and Graduate
Columbus, Ohio 43210

Wright State University—Undergraduate and Graduate
Dayton, Ohio 45435

**OREGON**

University of Oregon—Graduate
Eugene, Oregon 97403

**PENNSYLVANIA**

Beaver College—Graduate
Glenside, Pennsylvania 19038

Clarion State College—Graduate
Clarion, Pennsylvania 16214

Pennsylvania State University—Graduate
University Park, Pennsylvania 16802

Shippensburg State College—Graduate
Shippensburg, Pennsylvania 17257

University of Pennsylvania—Graduate
Philadelphia, Pennsylvania 19104

University of Pittsburgh—Graduate
Pittsburgh, Pennsylvania 15260

## RHODE ISLAND

University of Rhode Island—Graduate
Kingston, Rhode Island 02881

## SOUTH CAROLINA

Clemson University—Graduate
Clemson, South Carolina 29631

Francis Marion College—Graduate
Florence, South Carolina 29501

Furman University—Graduate
Greenville, South Carolina 29613

University of South Carolina—Graduate
Columbia, South Carolina 29208

Winthrop College—Graduate
Rock Hill, South Carolina 29733

## SOUTH DAKOTA

Black Hills State College—Undergraduate and Graduate
Spearfish, South Dakota 57783

University of South Dakota—Undergraduate and Graduate
Vermillion, South Dakota 57069

## TENNESSEE

George Peabody College for Teachers—Graduate
Nashville, Tennessee 37203

Memphis State University—Graduate
Memphis, Tennessee 38152

University of Tennessee at Chattanooga—Graduate
Chattanooga, Tennessee 37403

University of Tennessee at Knoxville—Graduate
Knoxville, Tennessee 37916

## TEXAS

Baylor University—Graduate
Waco, Texas 76706

Midwestern State University—Graduate
Wichita Falls, Texas 76308

Texas A & M University—Graduate
College Station, Texas 77843

Texas Tech University—Graduate
Lubbock, Texas 79409

Texas Woman's University—Graduate
Denton, Texas 76204

University of Texas at Austin—Graduate
Austin, Texas 78712

University of Texas at Dallas—Graduate
Dallas, Texas 75080

## UTAH

University of Utah—Undergraduate
Salt Lake City, Utah 84112

## VERMONT

Castleton State College—Graduate
Castleton, Vermont 05735

## VIRGINIA

College of William and Mary in Virginia—Undergraduate
Williamsburg, Virginia 23185

University of Virginia—Undergraduate and Graduate
Charlottesville, Virginia 22903

**WASHINGTON**

Central Washington University—Undergraduate and Graduate
Ellensburg, Washington 98926

Eastern Washington University—Undergraduate
Cheney, Washington 99004

Seattle University—Undergraduate
Seattle, Washington 98122

University of Puget Sound—Undergraduate
Tacoma, Washington 98416

University of Washington—Undergraduate
Seattle, Washington 98195

Washington State University—Undergraduate
Pullman, Washington 99163

Western Washington University—Undergraduate
Bellingham, Washington 98225

**WEST VIRGINIA**

Marshall University—Graduate
Huntington, West Virginia 25701

West Virgina College of Graduate Studies—Graduate
Institute, West Virginia 25112

**WISCONSIN**

University of Wisconsin-Madison—Graduate
Madison, Wisconsin 53706

University of Wisconsin-Milwaukee—Graduate
Milwaukee, Wisconsin 53201

University of Wisconsin—Oshkosh—Graduate
Oshkosh, Wisconsin 54901

University of Wisconsin—Stevens Point—Graduate
Stevens Point, Wisconsin 54481

University of Wisconsin—Whitewater—Graduate
Whitewater, Wisconsin 53190

**WYOMING**

University of Wyoming—Graduate
Laramie, Wyoming 82071

# SELECTED REFERENCES

Abraham, Willard et al.: *Gifts, Talents, and the Very Young: Early Childhood Education for Gifted/Talented.* Ventura, National/State Leadership Training Institute on the Gifted and the Talented, Office of the Ventura County Superintendent of Schools, 1977.

Baldwin, Alexinia Y., Gear, Gayle H., and Lucito, Leonard: *Educational Planning for the Gifted: Overcoming Cultural, Geographic, and Socioeconomic Impediments.* Reston, The Council for Exceptional Children, 1978.

Barbe, Walter B., and Renzulli, Joseph S.: *Psychology and Education of the Gifted.* 2nd ed. New York, Halsted Press, 1975.

Boston, Bruce O. (Ed.): *Gifted and Talented: Developing Elementary and Secondary School Programs.* Reston, The Council for Exceptional Children, 1975.

Boston, Bruce O. (Ed.): *Resource Manual of Information on Gifted Education.* Reston, The Council for Exceptional Children, 1975.

Clark, Barbara: *Growing Up Gifted.* Columbus, Charles Merrill, 1979.

Crow, Lester Donald, and Crow, Alice (Eds.): *Educating the Academically Able.* New York, McKay, 1963.

Cutts, Norma E., and Moseley, Nicholas: *Teaching the Bright and Gifted.* Englewood Cliffs, Prentice-Hall, 1957.

DeHann, Robert Frank, and Havinghurst, Robert J.: *Educating Gifted Children.* Chicago, University of Chicago Press, 1961.

Dennis, Wayne, and Dennis, Margaret W. (Eds.): *The Intellectually Gifted: An Overview.* New York, Grune and Stratton, 1976.

Epstein, Carol B.: *The Gifted and Talented: Programs that Work.* Arlington, National School Public Relations Association, 1979.

Fleigler, Louis A.: *Curriculum Planning for the Gifted.* Englewood Cliffs, Prentice-Hall, 1961.

Fortna, Richard O., and Boston, Bruce O.: *Testing the Gifted Child: An Interpretation in Lay Language.* Reston, The Council for Exceptional Children, 1976.

Freehill, Maurice F. : *Gifted Children: Their Psychology and Education.* New York, Macmillan, 1961.

French, Joseph L. (Ed.): *Educating the Gifted: A Book of Readings.* New York, Holt, Rinehart & Winston, 1964.

Gallagher, James J.: *Teaching the Gifted Child.* Boston, Allyn and Bacon, 1975.

Gallagher, James J., and Weiss, Patricia: *The Education of Gifted and Talented Students: A History and Prospectus.* Washington, Council for Basic Education, 1979.

Gold, Milton J.: *Education of the Intellectually Gifted.* Columbus, Charles Merrill, 1965.

Gowan, John, Khatena, Joseph, and Torrance, E. Paul (Eds.): *Educating the Ablest: A Book of Readings.* Itasca, F. E. Peacock, 1979.

Hildreth, Gertrude H.: *Introduction to the Gifted.* New York, McGraw-Hill, 1966.

Hoyt, Kenneth B., and Hebeler, Jean R. (Eds.): *Career Education for Gifted and Talented Students.* Salt Lake City, Olympus, 1974.

Kaplan, Sandra N.: *Providing Programs for the Gifted and Talented: A Handbook.* Ventura, National/State Leadership Training Institute on the Gifted and Talented, Office of the Ventura County Superintendent of Schools, 1975.

Keating, Daniel P. (Ed.): *Intellectual Talent: Research and Development.* Baltimore, Johns Hopkins Press, 1976.

Keating, Daniel P., and Stanley, Julian C.: *From Eighth Grade to Selected College in One Jump: Case Studies in Radical Acceleration.* Baltimore, Johns Hopkins Press, 1972.

Kough, Jack: *Practical Programs for the Gifted.* Chicago, Science Research Associates, 1960.

Krueger, Mark, and Newman, Elizabeth (Eds.): *Perspectives on Gifted and Talented: Arts and Humanities.* Reston, The Council for Exceptional Children, 1974.

Lawless, Ruth F.: *A Guide for Educating a Gifted Child in Your Classroom.* Buffalo, Disseminators of Knowledge, 1976.

Lawless, Ruth F.: *Program for Gifted, Creative, Talented Children.* Buffalo, Disseminators of Knowledge, 1977.

Laycock, Frank: *Gifted Children.* Glenview, Scott, Foresman & Co., 1979.

Maker, C. June: *Providing Programs for the Gifted Handicapped.* Reston, The Council for Exceptional Children, 1977.

Maker, C. June: *Training Teachers for the Gifted and Talented: A Comparison of Models.* Reston, The Council for Exceptional Children, 1975.

Marland, Sidney P.: *Education of the Gifted and Talented: Report to the Subcommittee on Education, Committee on Labor, and Public Welfare, United States Senate.* Washington, United States Government Printing Office, 1972.

Martinson, Ruth A. et al.: *Curriculum Enrichment for the Gifted in the Primary Grades.* Englewood Cliffs, Prentice-Hall, 1968.

Martinson, Ruth A.: *A Guide Toward Better Teaching for the Gifted.* Ventura, National/State Leadership Training Institute on the Gifted and the Talented, Office of the Ventura County Superintendent of Schools, 1976.

Martinson, Ruth A.: *The Identification of the Gifted and Talented.* Ventura, National/State Leadership Training Institute on the Gifted and the Talented, Office of the Ventura County Superintendent of Schools, 1973.

Miley, James F. et al.: *Promising Practices: Teaching the Disadvantaged Gifted.* Ventura, National/State Leadership Training Institute on the Gifted and the Talented, Office of the Ventura County Superintendent of Schools, 1975.

Olivero, James L., and Sato, Irving S.: *PAB Conference Report and Follow-up.* Ventura, National/State Leadership Training Institute on the Gifted and the Talented, Office of the Ventura County Superintendent of Schools, 1974.

Passow, A. Harry (Ed.): *The Gifted and Talented: Their Education and Development.* Chicago, National Society for the Study of Education Yearbook, 1979.

Renzulli, Joseph S.: *The Enrichment Triad Model: A Guide for Developing Defensible Programs for the Gifted and Talented.* Mansfield Center, Creative Learning Press, 1977.

Renzulli, Joseph S.: *A Guidebook for Evaluating Programs for the Gifted and Talented.* Ventura, National/State Leadership Training Institute on the Gifted and the Talented, Office of the Ventura County Superintendent of Schools, 1975.

Renzulli, Joseph S., and Smith, Linda H.: *A Guidebook for Developing Individualized Educational Programs for Gifted and Talented Students.* Mansfield Center, Creative Learning Press, 1979.

Reynolds, Maynard C. (Ed.): *Early School Admission for Mentally Advanced Children.* Reston, The Council for Exceptional Children, 1962.

Rice, Joseph P.: *The Gifted: Developing Total Talent.* Springfield, Charles C Thomas, Publisher, 1970.

Rivlin, Harry N.: *Advantage: Disadvantaged Gifted.* Ventura, National/State Leadership Training Institute on the Gifted and Talented, Office of the Ventura County Superintendent of Schools, 1978.

Sanderlin, Owenita: *Teaching Gifted Children.* New York, A. S. Barnes, 1973.

Sato, Irving S., Birnbaum, Martin, and LoCicero, June E.: *Developing a Written Plan for the Education of Gifted and Talented Students.* Ventura, National/State Leadership Training Institute on the Gifted and Talented, Office of the Ventura County Superintendent of Schools, 1974.

Stanley, Julian C., George, William C., and Solano, Cecillia H.: *Educational Programs and Intellectual Prodigies.* Baltimore, Johns Hopkins Press, 1978.

Sumption, Merle R., and Luecking, Evelyn M.: *Education of the Gifted.* New York, Ronald Press, 1960.

Syphers, Dorothy F.: *Gifted and Talented Children: Practical Programming for Teachers and Principals.* Reston, The Council for Exceptional Children, 1972.

Tempest, N.R.: *Teaching Clever Children: 7-11.* Boston, Routledge and Kegan Paul, 1974.

Thomas, George I., and Crescimbeni, Joseph: *Guiding the Gifted Child.* New York, Random House, 1966.

Torrance, E. Paul: *Discovery and Nurturance of Giftedness in the Culturally Different.* Reston, The Council for Exceptional Children, 1977.

Torrance, E. Paul: *Gifted Children in the Classroom.* New York, Macmillan, 1966.

Ward, Virgil: *Educating the Gifted, an Axiomatic Approach.* Columbus, Charles Merrill, 1961.

Witty, Paul A. (Ed.): *The Gifted Child.* Boston, D. C. Heath, 1951.

Wolfe, Dael (Ed.): *The Discovery of Talent.* Cambridge, Harvard University Press, 1969.

Wooster, Judith S.: *What to do for the Gifted Few.* Buffalo, Disseminators of Knowledge, 1978.